OPALESCENT

by

Judith Alapi Higgins

and

Thomas E Higgins

Tear of the Clouds BOOKS

Dedication

This book is dedicated to our families who settled in the Adirondacks and the locals who welcomed them and who introduced us to the beauties of the High Peaks.

Illustrations

The Pencil illustrations in this book were drawn by the authors and Nate Higgins, their son.

Nate drew the illustrations at the beginnings of Chapters 1, 3, 5, 10, 13 and 22.

Judith drew the illustrations on the cover and at the beginnings of Chapters .2, 8, 9, 15, 16, 17, 18, 19, 20, 21. 23, 24, and 25.

Thomas drew the Tear of the Clouds Books Logo, illustrations at the beginnings of Chapters 4, 6, 7, 11, 12, 14, and the signs used in Chapters 2, 5 and 13.

Chapter 1

"I need to see you, Michael," came the crisp, light voice from the answering machine. "I need those numbers for Wednesday's paper. When can we meet?" There was unveiled urgency in the words.

The machine clicked off. Michael stared at it pensively in the semidarkness. The dark shapes of trees outside the window blocked the remaining light, the hedges beyond formed a colorless barricade that stretched down the hill. To one side stood the cord of wood he had recently finished chopping, the even pieces stacked tightly in neat rows. Chopping wood was a chore he relished as something that kept his muscles fit, and for the clean satisfaction he found in physical exertion. His eyes strained to follow to the brook, but the familiar terrain became a blur in the settling night. He heard the first croak of a bullfrog, and small, rustling noises outside; tiny wild creatures finding their nests for the night, or perhaps awakening to forage or hunt.

Sometimes when the noises came from under the porch or among the boards of the house, he knew that he and Becky were sharing their home with uninvited guests. He would smile, happy to feel part of the wilderness, to know that the walls of the house didn't isolate him from the woodland creatures. He never killed the crickets he found jumping on the rug, nor the spiders that spun their webs in rarely used closets. Last year when Becky found a nest of six baby mice in the pocket of her jacket, he would not kill them. They were helpless, hairless and pink, and he moved them to a shoe box under the porch. She had laughed at him, and a few days later he noticed that they were gone.

Undecided, he scrutinized the answering machine that was just a formless object on the desk. He listened for Becky moving around upstairs but it was quiet; she had gone to bed. Michael had known the message would be there, and had been avoiding it all day, just as he had avoided Maggie for the past several days. And now here it was, forcing him to make the decision that could be postponed no longer.

2

Michael Ryan moved to the old easy chair in the corner of his study and stared at the bookshelves along the wall. He stroked the worn corduroy upholstery that nearly matched his brown corduroy pants, and sank into its sagging depths. He rolled down the cuffs of his wool overshirt as the chair enveloped him. Once again he thought of replacing it, and once again he dismissed the idea. He couldn't bring himself to throw it out. The chair had been with him since his college days, and it had been old then. He sat in it studying for exams--chemistry, calculus, and microbiology. The last he almost flunked but had managed to pass with the help of an all-night cram session. Before a hockey game, when anticipation and excitement made his blood race, he had relaxed in it, meditating, conserving his strength. It was his favorite place to think or read, to regain his inner balance.

He closed his eyes and lay his dark head back, waiting for calm to replace his inner tension. But tonight peace eluded him. Her voice would not go away, would not let him forget the problem. He rubbed his temples, forcing his mind to clear, the questions to stop nagging at him. Instead, he heard Maggie's voice echoing in his mind. He saw her face--intense gray eyes questioning him. I need to see you Michael. I need to see you too, Maggie, but not until I know what to tell you, not until I'm sure. Not yet.

Restless, he rose from the chair and opened the door of the ancient cast iron stove. The black stove stood on three short legs, its smooth, rounded belly easing to a flat top. From the center a flue extended upwards, disappearing into the ceiling. Its doors were textured with a pattern that reminded him of tiny bird tracks in the snow and they opened with a latch that was often too hot to touch. A narrow grating across the front kept the fire from spilling out. Beside the stove stood a bucket and shovel for the ashes.

From a hand-woven basket he selected a few pieces of kindling and tossed them atop the smoldering log. He poked at the dying fire, aimlessly trying to revive it, then picked up the bellows and gently blew air on the coals. Here in the mountains the summer nights were cool and it was pleasant to sit by a fire in the evenings. He was reminded of campfires shared years ago with Jake and Maggie. It was a different life then, before college, hockey and marriage to Becky ended their alliance. There had been good times since then, but none like those. He sighed.

With a sudden noise the burnt logs crumbled and Rusty raised his head from the hearthrug where he had been sleeping. The golden retriever gave a warning growl, then looked up to his master for reassurance. Michael knelt and fondled his soft, amber coat and silky ears. With a contented grunt the dog rolled onto his side, demanding more. Michael smiled, and for a moment his serious, troubled face relaxed. With Rusty things were always so simple, the way Michael's life had been years ago.

"How does one decide something like this?" he murmured. At the sound of his voice the dog perked up his ears. For a while both dog and master stared into the smoldering fire, lost in their separate worlds. Then, Michael began to pace the room, his right hand ruffling his thick hair until it reflected the disorder of his thoughts.

I can't keep avoiding a decision, he thought. Life here is going to change, whether I take part in it or not. My family, friends and neighbors are bound to be hurt by whatever happens. It's up to me to minimize the hurt, but I don't want the responsibility. All I wanted when I returned home from the city was the peace and beauty of the mountains I missed so much. The city's problems were apparent to everyone; I found them and helped cure them. The mountains hid their problems well, but not well enough. I found one, but can I cure it?

He stopped before the bookshelves he had built, feeling the smoothness of the white pine with his hand. He had selected the wood carefully, spent hours measuring, sawing, and nailing the shelves. The nails had been countersunk and covered with wood filler, the boards sanded and finished to

4

reveal their natural pattern. They matched the paneling in the room, and blended pleasingly with the warm colors of the Indian rug. He had designed the house years ago, when he and Becky were still living in their New York apartment. After they returned to the Adirondacks and found the perfect site, he spent all his spare time building their home, working with the respect he felt for the wood itself.

National Geographics lined the shelves, along with chemistry and engineering journals. On an adjacent wall hung his credentials: two diplomas, a B.S. in Civil Engineering from Newgate College, and an M.S. in Environmental Engineering from Columbia; membership certificates from the American Society of Civil Engineers and the Water Pollution Control Federation; his State of New York Engineering License, with the code of ethics. Absently he traced the letters spelling his name in calligraphy.

His eyes rested on the words: "If in the performance of his duties, the professional engineer discovers that the safety, health, property or welfare of the public are endangered, he shall inform his employer or client and notify the appropriate authorities." Those words had seemed so clear then, but the code contained no guidance for situations where protecting the safety and health of the public meant endangering their property and welfare.

On a high shelf stood his prize possession, a duplicate of the NCAA Hockey Championship Trophy. He held it in his hands and caressed the small gilded figure with the hockey stick, then returned it carefully to its place. Next to it was the photo of his hockey team on the ice, Michael's leg in a temporary splint, raised on the shoulders of his teammates, holding the National Championship Trophy high in his right hand. They were laughing and shouting, triumphant, loving their sport and the camaraderie, certain of the future. He sighed, spoke half out loud: "But for that broken leg I could be playing hockey now. I could be playing my life away." He laughed wistfully as he looked at his hockey skates hanging on a peg.

They were old and worn, the leather scuffed, but he couldn't put them away. He fingered the broken hockey stick, cracked down the middle, sharp splinters at the exposed edges. He wondered if his bone had looked like that, never to be perfect again. It was almost as good as before, except that he couldn't play professional hockey. There was a weakness in the leg, a loss of control.

His heart pounded when he remembered that game, his last. He was at Newgate on a hockey scholarship and captain of the team in his junior year, its spark plug. He had taken the team farther than they had ever gone before. They were playing for the National Championship, playing against powerful Minnesota. They were not given much chance of winning by the New York papers but they played with confidence. He felt in perfect form, skimming the ice, practically dancing on it. He was good; he knew it. He had proven himself on the ice, and would be playing professionally in another year.

It was a close, defensive game, a scoreless tie with two minutes left to play. Minnesota had the puck and their offensive players were flying toward the Newgate goal. Suddenly, Michael's teammate stole the puck. The crowd roared. Jimmy slipped a pass between two defenders, the puck reaching Michael just as he crossed the blue line. It was a breakaway, with nothing between him and the net but the goalie. He was alone, pushing the puck down the ice, the cheers of the crowd in his ears, ice-dust flying in diamond sparkles from his skates.

It was the same feeling of exhilaration he remembered as a child flying over the frozen ponds, or sliding down the toboggan run, his breath suspended in a sudden rush of adrenaline. He was nearing the goal, edging over, putting everything he had on a low shot to the right of the goalie when the stick came from out of nowhere. A player hooked him from behind, swiftly, awkwardly. The stick caught his skate pulling Michael off his feet. With a wrenching sound his leg twisted, buckled beneath him and cracked against the rigid surface. Sliding along the ice into the wall he saw the goalie's face, heard the roar of the crowd as the pounding in his head turned to blackness. When he came to, the doctor was putting his leg in a splint, and a stretcher was waiting to take him to the hospital.

He knew that he had made the goal; he knew that they would win, but he wouldn't leave until the game was over. The team carried him aloft in victory. Jimmy gave him the winning puck, the one that stood before the team picture on his shelf. Even then, Michael suspected that his hockey career was over. Fortunately it was the end of the season and the championship was theirs. He was the hero that year, loving it, unwilling to admit his fear. In the summer he hiked and did all the things he was accustomed to doing, and nearly convinced himself that all was well. But when his skating didn't return to form, he knew that he would never play professional hockey.

Even older memories lay on the shelves nearby: an award for his science fair project on Giardia, an intestinal parasite, in Adirondack lakes and streams, an early sign of the interests that would lead to his change in careers; scholarship awards to two universities; pictures of himself, tall, well-built and very young, smiling with untried confidence.

Becky smiled up at him in her cheerleader's uniform, her golden coloring complemented by the sky blue of the outfit. He had his arm around her, proudly possessive of the prettiest girl in the class. They made the perfect couple, everyone said, she with her beauty and social position, he, the handsome and intelligent athlete. They never questioned that they were meant for each other, never really had any reason to. Even throughout college, when they were separated, there were no serious doubts. The infrequency of their meetings made them all the more exciting, fanning their passion for each other.

A ten pound bass was mounted on the wall; a faded photograph tucked behind one corner showed Jake smiling at Maggie and Michael, two grinning eleven year olds, proud of their catch. It was a rare shot, the three of them together. Jake didn't usually bother with photographs; he felt that they didn't do justice to the experience. This time they had taken Becky along too, and she had preferred taking pictures to fishing. After that it was just he, Jake and Maggie on fishing trips, with no one to take pictures.

He sat down on the pine stool near the window and stared into fast-falling darkness. The hours and days spent with Jake were the best times of his youth--fishing, hiking, and learning from him, absorbing the knowledge that emanated from him, learning from his every action. Jake, who never cared for the town, nor the people in it. "Old man Hughes" they called him with contempt, ridiculing his ways, his isolation and independence. He lived in an old cabin outside of town, alone with his daughter, rarely meeting people, rarely needing them. Only as a guide did people treat him with true respect. There were few Adirondack guides left, and none better than Jake Hughes. People said he was part Indian, that's why he knew so much about the woods. Seeing Maggie with her red hair and freckles, it was hard to believe that she had any Indian blood in her.

Jake didn't like many people, but Michael was an exception. By the time he was ten years old, Michael knew he was always welcome at the Hughes cabin. Soon he was following Jake around in the woods, setting traps, gathering plants, fishing, hiking. He was usually included in Jake and Maggie's plans, without discussion. Eagerly he learned to fish from Jake as they sat by remote lakes in the twilight, reeking of Old Woodsman's repellent while mosquitoes swarmed around their heads. Michael watched as Jake's catch increased, while his line hardly had a nibble. "I guess I'm just not lucky like you, Jake," he sighed. "Luck's got nothing to do with it," the older man replied. "Watch, and maybe you'll learn something." He squatted by the bucket of worms that Michael dug the night before and took out a couple from the wriggling mass, rubbing them around in his hands. "Fish don't like our smell, so I learned to fool 'em. Cover your smell with worms, and see how many bites you get." Michael did, and soon after that caught the ten pound bass.

He smiled as he fingered his Forty-sixer patch. He was proud of climbing the forty-six highest peaks of the Adirondacks. It was difficult to earn the patch, but at fourteen Michael was determined. On one of their hikes, Michael asked Jake if he was a Forty-sixer. Jake took his time replying. "I don't rightly know," he said, "but I do know that I climbed some of them forty-six times." He laughed at the puzzled boy, then sat down on a log. "My father taught me something when I was your age. The mountains are there to enjoy, not to collect like a trophy. Some peaks are worth climbing over and over. You never get tired of them. They become old friends what never bore you; they always have something new to teach. Then there are others that just ain't worth climbing. It's a personal kinda thing."

Jake stopped to fill his pipe as Michael watched him, puzzled. He lit the pipe, then continued: "My father's favorite peak was Adams. I kinda favor it myself. He used to say you could see the town from there, just a small speck surrounded by wilderness. You could see Marcy to the east, and the Opalescent sparkling below. It helped him see things the right way." Michael listened to him, perplexed. He still wanted to conquer the peaks, and eventually he did, but it wasn't as important anymore. It was nearly dark in the room now, and as he turned to switch on the lamp next to his chair, he stumbled over something on the floor. In the subdued light he recognized his hiking boots. He picked one up and held it in his hand thoughtfully. I need time. Time to think, time without demands, time to sort this thing out alone.

The ring of the telephone broke into his thoughts. Rusty raised his face questioningly to his master, who remained at the far end of the room. On the fourth ring the answering machine clicked and soon he heard the familiar voice. "Michael, I've been trying to reach you for days. We have to talk. I'll be over at ten tomorrow." She hung up and he stared at the phone, troubled. How like Maggie to be so terse and businesslike. And how like her to be honest and straightforward too. But he couldn't see her yet. He needed time. He looked at the boot in his hand and strode to the cupboard under the stairway. He began to pull out camping gear, everything he might need for a week in the woods. He could fit everything in one large backpack, with the tent tied on top and the bedroll below. He had done it often enough. As he packed, words escaped from him: "Oh Maggie, you don't know what you're getting yourself into."

Chapter 2

Michael awoke before six. The cool morning air brought a trace of dampness with it through the open window and made him draw the quilt closer around his shoulders. Rusty stirred at the foot of the bed and came around to nuzzle his hand. He lay still for a moment thinking, planning his day. He ran through his list of equipment and supplies, a list committed to memory long ago, and checked off each item. Stove, fuel, waterproof matches, flashlight, knife, hatchet, rope, poncho, sleeping bag, canteen, mess kit, coffee, freeze dried food, trail mix, Old Woodsman's, toiletries, a roll of toilet paper, a first aid kit and iodine water purification tablets had all been packed. He wouldn't need much, but what he took was essential. To forget something could mean the difference between comfort and misery. He must remember to find his maps and a book, and some money, in case of an emergency.

Quietly, trying not to wake Becky, he slipped from the bed and began to dress. Jeans, sweater, wool socks, and his well-worn hiking boots. Hat, jacket, and a change of clothes would be packed in the outside pouch of his pack. He stood by the bed looking at Becky sleeping, at her small pouting mouth and delicate chin, the wispy blond hair framing her round face. She's hardly changed since we were in high school, he thought. Sometimes I wish I hadn't, either. He turned to leave, not wanting to disturb her, not really wanting to talk. But somehow she felt him nearby.

"Michael?"

He stopped but did not turn to face her. "Go back to sleep, Becky."

"Where are you going?" she asked sleepily.

"I'm going up around Marcy for a few days." He paused. Then, "I have to go."

Now fully awake, she sat up in bed, shivering in her light cotton nightgown. "Why?"

"I just have to Becky. I need time to think."

She looked at him closely, her large blue eyes searching his face. "It's about that problem you think you found, isn't it?"

"Yes, it is. I want to be sure I'm doing the right thing." He felt slightly irritated with himself for avoiding her gaze, and with her for her questions.

"The right thing! Isn't it obvious what the right thing is?" she asked, her voice rising.

"No, it isn't. I wish it were. It's not as simple as you think."

"Yes, it is. It's a matter of loyalty to family, of love!" She swung out of bed and stood in the center of the braided rug, barefoot, shivering.

"This affects more than your family, Becky. I wish you would see that."

She stood before him and placed her hand on his arm. Her voice became low, urgent. "Oh, Michael, I see that. You'd be hurting my father, the family name, the business, but you would also be harming all the people in town who depend on the Company for their living. Besides, you aren't even sure there's a real danger. Think what you'd be doing to the whole town!"

"I am thinking! What do you think I've been doing all summer? Believe me, I know all the implications. But I have a responsibility to protect the people's health," he said with conviction.

"Responsibility!" she jeered, stepping back, "and don't you have any responsibility to me? Or to our future? My grandfather and great-grandfather built this town. There wouldn't be a town without the Company. Are you going to destroy all that?"

"Not unless I have to. Remember, the Company's been just as important to my family as to yours; they're going to be affected as well by whatever happens."

"Well, there's your answer right there," she said, throwing up her arms. "Even if you don't care about my family, maybe you care enough about your own to keep your mouth shut."

"Of course I care about our families," he cried, exasperated, "but it's not as simple as that!"

"It's as simple as you choose to make it. I'm warning you, Michael, you ruin my father and we're finished!"

She looked at him with real hatred in her eyes. For a moment they were locked in a wordless battle, mute with hostility. He searched her face, looking for a trace of the softness that had captivated him years ago, then turned and walked out.

Rusty rose expectantly, and followed as Michael raced down the stairs. He found his master in the study collecting his gear. After a few minutes of watching the frenzied activity, the dog sat down in the doorway with a questioning yip. As Michael noticed him for the first time, the tension in his face dissolved into a smile. Kneeling, he stroked the dog's soft coat as Rusty nuzzled his hand. "Yes, old boy, we're going for a walk, a long one. That should make you happy." He laughed as Rusty perked up his ears at the welcome words and danced toward the door. Michael called him back. "Wait, let's get something to eat first. We have a long hike ahead of us."

Michael leaned his pack against the kitchen door before pouring himself some coffee. He sat at the pine kitchen table by the window facing the woods. He loved to start his day there, usually alone except for Rusty, watching birds feeding at the birdhouse they had hung in a tall old pine, the morning coming to life before him. Further down the hill, the brook glimmered, reflecting the brilliance of the rising sun.

He loved the winter there, too, the blue-black pine branches so weighed down with snow that every year he feared they would break, and the cardinals and blue jays that showed like Christmas ornaments against the whiteness. He sat there in the mornings before the sun was fully up and looked for signs of life in the snow, tiny tracks criss-crossing an otherwise unbroken field, a squirrel running head first down the trunk of a tree stealing bird seed from the feeder, a snowshoe hare disappearing across the frozen brook.

The early sun warmed his face. Light scattered through the stained glass sun catcher and lit up the objects on the window sill: Becky's pot of chives with their tiny purple flowers, the macramé hanging she had made for their first apartment, the basket of leaves, branches of berries and ferns they had collected and dried. They were happy after they returned to the Adirondacks, excited to be back, to be building a home, making plans for their future. Their roots were here. At first, it was like returning to their youth, to the time of their early infatuation. He shook his head and stared off into the distance.

I love it here, he thought. I came back because I knew I belonged here. But it's not the way I remembered. I never knew what was really going on before. He wrapped his fingers around the earth colored mug with the silhouettes of pine trees etched around it in dark green, then took a well-folded newspaper article from his pocket and laid it on the table, smoothing out the creases. It was from the Langston Gazette, dated the week before. Slowly, thoughtfully he reread it.

OPALESCENT POISONED BY ACID RAIN

by Maggie Hughes

Air pollution from Pittsburgh and Cleveland may be threatening the purity of the Adirondacks. Acid rain has turned our mountain lakes and streams into barren wastes, and is killing the few remaining stands of virgin pine. All this threatens our way of life. Will tourists come when there are no trout and the trees are barren?

Yet an even more insidious danger has been uncovered recently. Studies have shown that the acid waters can draw

15

toxic metals from lake beds, contaminating our once pure mountain streams.

Of special interest to us is a study being done by Langston High School senior Steve Harper, who found that the Opalescent River above its confluence with the Hudson contains high concentrations of lead. The Opalescent is the source of Langston's drinking water.

The town's water treatment plant was not designed to remove toxic metals, according to Bob Walters, the town supervisor. The plant takes the water from the Opalescent and passes it through a sand filter, then chlorine is added to kill bacteria, and finally it is piped to our homes.

If acid rain continues to leach the toxic lead out of the soil, how long before our drinking water becomes dangerously contaminated? When that happens, how will we prevent lead poisoning from affecting every person in Langston?

It seems that our future, our very health, is being determined by what is happening in Midwestern cities. We who live in the Adirondacks love the mountains and treasure the quality of our clean air and water. Our challenge for the future is to ensure that these things will not be spoiled by careless, indifferent people living in polluted cities hundreds of miles away.

Only hesitating a moment, he scribbled a note on the back of an envelope. Maggie, (it read) I'm going up Marcy for a few days. We'll talk when I get back. In the meantime, tell Jake not to drink the water from his well--it's important! I'll explain when I get back.

He looked up to see Becky in the doorway. She held a blue robe around her, the one that complemented the freshness of her coloring. She looked worried, no longer angry. She twisted the cord of the robe around her finger, and he wanted to reach out to her.

16

"Michael, I'm afraid. What's going to happen to us?" She came and stood beside his chair. He reached up and stroked her golden hair.

"We'll be all right, honey. Just try to understand me."

She pulled away. "But why can't you understand that I love my father and that I couldn't live with you if you hurt him? How could you be that ungrateful? Without Daddy's help we couldn't afford this house!"

He stepped back. The tenderness, the openness he felt toward her a moment ago was gone. "Is that what you're worried about? Losing the house? Your personal comfort? If that's more important to you than people's health, there's nothing more I can say."

He stamped out of the kitchen, Rusty close behind him. As the door slammed he heard her call after him: "I care about my family and if you don't, then we really don't have much of a future together."

Rusty trotted ahead, plumed tail waving, nose to the ground, sniffing the dewy grass and moist earth. Michael swung the pack onto his shoulders and hooked the army canteen into his belt before following Rusty along the drive to the main road. His house was set back among the trees, and he paused to look at it before turning onto the road. It was a contemporary home built of light wood and native stones that blended so beautifully with the trees and granite mountains of the Adirondacks, as if it had grown there naturally.

Michael had designed the house, and Becky's father helped build it after they decided to leave the city and come home. Michael supervised the construction, making sure the house was finished the way they wanted, with spacious windows overlooking the brook and mountains, and massive beams across the cathedral ceiling of the family room. He worked on it himself, wanting to see it grow under his hands, to feel it as an extension of himself. He wanted Becky to help too, but she only laughed and watched from a comfortable distance, and bandaged his fingers whenever his zeal exceeded his skill.

He looked back at the house and was touched by the harmony and beauty of it all, their home in the woods, and the surrounding mountains. Did he have a right to jeopardize all that, to disrupt the lives of so many people, especially those closest to him? He hesitated, and nearly retraced his steps. Then his thoughts turned to Maggie and old Jake Hughes and all that they represented, strength and independence, living on the edge of town in the ancient cabin that had been theirs for five generations. He thought of the things Jake had taught him over the years, and of what he was becoming now, old and feeble. Jake was being betrayed, perhaps even by him. "I can't let this go on Rusty," he spoke to the dog sitting at his feet. "But, what am I going to do about Becky?"

Yellow Birch Trail wound through woods for half a mile before connecting to the main road leading into town. As Michael sighted the smokestacks of the paint factory, he frowned. He didn't want to meet anyone, but the quickest way to the Opalescent River Trail was through town. From the sun's elevation he estimated it to be seven o'clock, then remembering his watch, he read six forty-five. It was still early and with luck he should be able to reach the trail without seeing anyone. With Rusty at his side, Michael emerged from the trees at the outskirts of town. The weathered sign proclaimed:

As he approached the complex of factory buildings, the trees progressively thinned, until only a few birch and mountain ash encircled the premises. He skirted the tall fence, stopping opposite the sign that read: Opalescent Paints, Established 1919 by Randolph Lang & Sons. Michael watched as the graveyard shift poured out of the factory. Taking care not to be noticed, he continued into town.

He passed O'Leary's Outdoor Store with its prominent display of fishing tackle, wool plaid shirts, and a Coleman canoe. As a kid he used to make money digging worms and selling them to Mr. O'Leary. He glanced up at the Langston Gazette offices situated over the store, to the window that he knew was Maggie's. He half expected to see her curly red hair, but there was no sign of her and he hurried on. He walked quickly past Ed's barbershop, the Rexall drug, and Betty's cafe, all closed until nine.

At the high school he stopped for a drink from his canteen while Rusty watered the flowerbeds. The old building was crumbling, badly in need of major renovation or replacement. Michael had talked to Tom Lang about it, and Tom had smiled, patting him on the back, telling him not to worry. Later he learned that Tom had made a sizable contribution toward construction of a new school. Michael shook his head and walked on. Tom Lang was sometimes hard to understand.

This end of town was more wooded and hilly. Several motels were set among the pines. The Swiss Chalet, with its swimming pool and deck, advertised a magnificent view of the mountains. Paleface Lodge was a favorite skiing resort, but most of the hotels were full all summer as well as during the skiing season. In the 1930's, The Sparkling Mineral Baths and Hotel had attracted socialites from New York City during the summer months. The mineral springs were famed as cures for many things, from colic to rheumatism. Some swore by them and returned regularly; others came back for the sports and scenery. In contrast to the warm, gently effervescent mineral water of the spa, the Opalescent River flowed cold and clear. Leaving the road, Michael followed the river northeast into the mountains.

Around a bend in the river, the abandoned sawmill came into view. Michael removed his pack and found a stick for Rusty. Knowing the game, the dog danced around his master, eager to begin. The stick broke the surface of the water an instant before the plunging dog. Only his black nose and wet face were visible as he swam silently toward it. Half-turning, he closed his mouth around the stick and carried it to shore. Dropping it at Michael's feet he shook his dripping coat. Michael jumped back reflexively. "Won't you ever learn not to shake yourself on me, Rusty?" he laughed.

Little of the original mill remained, but the site was known by most natives as the origin of Langston. The old building had been rebuilt by Becky's grandfather, Ernest Lang. The renovated sawmill was a barn-like structure, dominated by a large waterwheel extending from its side. In the days of its operation, water from the dammed pond turned the waterwheel and powered the saw. The waterwheel had been renovated by Tom Lang twenty years ago, although he didn't repair the dam. Now the giant saw was still, the waterwheel merely a decoration, a nostalgic tribute to the past. The dam was long gone, the river had returned to its natural path, and the trees damaged by the flooding millpond had gradually been replaced by second growth.

The site was a favorite tourist attraction. Near the entrance a bronze plaque proclaimed: "On this spot, Stuart Lang built a sawmill in 1832. He was born in County Cork, Ireland, immigrated to the United States, and founded the town of Langston around this mill." Parents and grandparents told their children that "but for the old sawmill there wouldn't be a Langston." And but for "Old Mr. Lang," as everyone referred to him, there wouldn't have been a sawmill.

Stuart Lang arrived on Ellis Island in 1820, a hopeful young man of twenty-one, green and inexperienced but ambitious. During the first year he moved from job to job in New York, looking for the great opportunity he knew was waiting for him. His chance came when he went to work for George Corrigan, a wealthy businessman who was looking for new ventures to invest in. Stuart hadn't worked for him long when Corrigan began to notice his drive, his unflagging energy, and his original way of attacking problems. Corrigan began testing Stuart's loyalty and honesty in small, secret ways. Once satisfied, Corrigan called Stuart into his office with a proposition.

"Do you like working for me, Stuart?" Corrigan asked him.

Stuart hesitated. "Yes, sir, I like it well enough."

"But?"

"Well, I don't mean to sound ungrateful, Mr. Corrigan. You've been very kind to me and the job is all right as far as it goes, but it's not something I'd want to do for the rest of my life.

I mean, I'm looking for something more, something to call my own, though I don't really know what that might be right now. I want to be my own boss, and if I ever have the opportunity, I'll take it."

Corrigan smiled. "I'm glad you're so honest with me, Stuart. I noticed that you've been a little restless lately. What would you say if I offered you that opportunity?"

"Sir?" Stuart looked at his employer, uncomprehending but alert.

"Do you know anything about lumbering, Stuart?"

"Not much, Sir, but I learn fast."

"Good. I'm buying timber land in the North Country and starting a lumbering operation soon." He unfurled a map showing the wilderness area of northern New York. "From what I hear, there's still plenty of red spruce and even some white pine left. We can float the logs down the Opalescent River and build a sawmill somewhere around here," he said, pointing to the map. "And I think you're the man I want to be running the operation. You'll be on your own, and it'll be up to you what you make of it. I'll make you part owner--how about ten percent? What do you say?"

Stuart answered without thinking, without having to. "Yes! It's what I've been waiting for." He knew he would succeed. And if he didn't know much about lumbering, did anyone before they started? He would learn and learn well.

Chapter 3

Michael and Rusty left the sawmill and continued their hike on the Opalescent Trail. The trail followed the river, sometimes diverging slightly, sometimes hugging the bank, but never straying far from it. They were walking through open meadow now, in late August yellow with goldenrod, interspersed with delicate Queen Anne's Lace. He could hear the hum of bees in the still air as they worked over the blossoms, in a hurry to store nectar before the first frost. Mostly birch and aspens grew along the water, with an occasional beech or maple. Where the river formed small, still pools, wild asters grew along the bank among tall reeds and grasses. Rusty found a bullfrog sunning itself on the bank with half-closed eyes, and chased it with wild leaps until the frog disappeared in the reeds.

When they reached a dirt road Rusty ran ahead, diverting from their original path. Michael hesitated, looked toward the river, then turned to follow the dog. Behind him, just up the river was a growth of spruce and balsam, and beyond that stood the Hughes cabin.

"All right Rusty, we'll go this way for a little while. I don't want to run into Maggie just yet."

They followed deserted railroad tracks for a quarter of a mile to the patch of wild raspberries that grew in the sandy soil. Michael stopped to gather the berries that were at their juiciest right now, with a flavor and aroma that he could only describe as ripened sunshine. Startled by the whirring wings of a cedar waxwing, Rusty charged into the bushes after the bird. His feathery undercoat caught in the brambles, he strained to free himself. Laughing, Michael untangled the dog's silky hair. "I'll bet you won't tangle with raspberries again," he said to the whining dog.

The dirt road turned in the direction of the old mine-site. It wasn't a pleasant route, but Michael wanted to avoid Maggie and Jake today. The mineshaft was filled with an accumulation of many years' waste, mostly from the paint factory. As teenagers they had frequented the place on summer evenings, several piling into a car to watch black bears feasting on the town's garbage. Michael stopped to look at it, following Rusty's explorations with his gaze. The dog was busily digging in the dirt that covered the waste, then lay down to chew on his prize, a length of soggy cardboard tubing. Michael's tone was sharp as he called to the dog, "No Rusty, no! Come!" and hurried him away from the mine-site.

They cut through the meadow in a northeasterly direction, then headed west again to rejoin the river north of the Hughes cabin. Michael looked back at the cabin from the bend at East River Falls. A thin line of smoke rose from the chimney and he heard the sound of wood being chopped.

Jake, he thought. But no, it wasn't likely. He hasn't been well enough to exert himself lately, hasn't been able to do much at all. It must be Maggie then, taking over more of the chores, although she hasn't been looking too well herself. The chopping stopped and she emerged from the woodpile carrying a bucket. Michael pulled back into the shadows, holding onto Rusty's collar. Rusty looked up at him expectantly. The dog was fond of Maggie and Jake, ready to run to them. Maggie set the bucket down by the well and began pumping water. Anxiety surged through Michael as the bucket filled. I shouldn't let them drink the water, he thought. I should warn them now! He hesitated. No, it's not time yet. They'll be all right for a few days, he reassured himself. Then he turned away and continued northeast along the Opalescent.

Maggie Hughes wiped her hands on the worn khaki trousers she wore for heavy chores around the house. She set the bucket down while she surveyed the morning from the rickety front porch. The wood she had chopped would be enough for a few days, since it was summer and they only needed it for cooking. She would bring in another bucket of water before leaving for town. The kitchen garden needed weeding; the weeds had grown taller than the tomato plants, and she could barely find the squash vines that trailed along the ground among them. Only the sunflowers did well on their own, their flat yellow heads nodding under the weight of the ripening

25

seeds. But she just didn't have time to do everything. It was not like Jake to let things go, and she was worried about him. Her face clouded and she looked off toward the mountains, brushing the hair out of her eyes with the back of a narrow wrist.

She carried the water into the kitchen and added wood to the stove. A pot of stew was simmering slowly on the stove; it would last him a couple of days, perhaps longer if his appetite didn't improve. She walked through the storage room, past Jake's tools and traps, their fishing tackle and his guns, and two pairs of snowshoes hanging from the rafters.

Jake was sitting on a stool in the front room, the parlor as they jokingly called it. His back towards her, he was working by the light of the large front window. He was wearing the red buffalo plaid shirt that she had given him for his birthday, baggy trousers of indeterminate color and suspenders. She stopped to watch him, bent over the gun he was cleaning, absorbed in his task. His hair was white but wavy and full, the back of his neck tanned and creased from a lifetime of exposure to the Adirondack seasons. She touched his shoulder lightly as she went past, and sat down across from him on the creaking sofa. It was covered by an Indian blanket that had been in their family for generations.

The old man looked up at her touch. His clear blue eyes contrasted with the aging, leathery face. Now the eyes went soft, and the creases arranged themselves into a smile.

"Maggie! You were up early this morning. What you been doing with yourself?"

"Oh, I just chopped some wood for the stove, Dad, and started a kettle of stew for you. There are a couple of buckets of water in the kitchen, too."

The smile left Jake's face. "You shouldn't be doing all that heavy work, child. I could've done it later. I can still take care of myself." He pulled himself up, and the old glimmer of pride showed in his eyes.

26

"I know, Dad." Careful, Maggie, careful, she thought. You know he's touchy about his independence. "But I'm going to be in town for a couple of days and wanted to make you some stew. You know how you love my stew," she said, smiling.

"I'm sorry darling, I didn't mean to be ungrateful. But I don't want you to be spending your time taking care of me. I do love your stew, it's just that I ain't been very hungry with these belly cramps."

She sat forward, concerned, noting his paleness and the slight tremor in his hand as he rubbed the cleaning cloth over the gun barrel. "You haven't been feeling any better, have you Dad? I wish you'd see a doctor!"

He waved the suggestion aside. "I know you want I should do this, but it's nothing, Maggie. Just the years sneaking up on me," he smiled wryly.

She sighed, then rose from her seat. "What will you do while I'm gone?"

"I'm gonna finish cleaning my gun, then I'm gonna straighten out the fishing tackle. It's 'bout time to go after catfish again. How about next Saturday we go fishing over to Bullhead Lake?"

Maggie nodded, then went to change into a shirtdress for work.

Backing her Jeep around the woodpile, she pulled out onto the dirt logging road that connected with the main road to Langston. There were no other cabins along this road, so for a while she had the road to herself. She spent the bumpy ride worrying about her father's health. He wasn't getting any better, if anything, worse. First there were the headaches and his lack of appetite, so unusual for him, then the stomach upsets, and now constant fatigue and weakness. He just didn't have energy for anything anymore. It was so unlike Jake, a man who had spent his life in the mountains, fishing, hunting and trapping.

Men from the city relied on him to guide them through the wilderness, carrying their supplies in a pack equal to his weight and portaging his guideboat between lakes. She thought about her heritage, about how the first Hughes had come to the Adirondacks, fell in love with the Opalescent River and never left. She thought she knew how he must have felt, and was glad that fate had brought him here.

When the first Jacob Hughes arrived in the North Country, he found the wilderness immensely attractive. He had left Ireland in 1820, after a series of crop failures convinced him that no future lay in farming. He was still young, unmarried and working on his father's farm when the thought of another blighted crop forced him to escape. He had seen his mother die in poverty and hunger, and his brothers grow old from their pointless struggle. He turned his back on farming, and sought a life that would be different and far removed from the one he was leaving.

The stories he heard of America were about rich cities and fertile farmlands, but these did not interest him. Then one day he heard a man talk about a land of mountains and streams, of wild forests that few men had seen save for the Indians, and an abundance of game and fish that was there for the taking. The stranger told him of the settlers who provided amply for their families by hunting, fishing and trapping. Jacob's eyes brightened as he listened. His needs were few; his past had taught him to be satisfied with the little he could wring from Ireland's rocky soil. He wanted to live in this new land where he could take what he needed without struggling. He knew that this was the place he was seeking, a place to call his own.

When he arrived in the North Country he breathed deeply of the pine scented air and surveyed the land around him. There were mountains in every direction, not wild craggy ones, but older, more rounded, friendlier ones. These mountains were but the roots of the ancient Adirondacks. They had been worn down by countless years of weathering, had withstood the assaults of rain, snow and wind, and the repeated onslaught of glaciers miles thick.

In his search for a place to settle that first year, Jacob explored a number of small lakes with clear, icy water. He fished for bass and trout, and trapped muskrat and mink along their shores. Climbing the high peaks and tramping through the forests of giant white pine and spruce, he experienced a sense of freedom he had never known in tilling the ungenerous soil of his native land.

His wanderings took him to Lake Champlain where he walked along the beaches, wondering at the oyster shells mixed with its sands. The lake was inviting with its rocky shoreline and level plains, but it was not what he was looking for. The forests along the great lake had been badly thinned. Most of the white pine in the area had been cut for ships' masts and spars, and floated to Montreal to be shipped to France for the royal navy. The British also took their share, and after the white pine was gone, they harvested the red spruce. Jacob wanted something wilder, less disturbed by man.

Jacob explored the Au Sable and Saranac Rivers, and by late summer he had moved south to a lovely little river that captivated him. Its clear waters sparkled green, gold and blue from the iridescent rocks that were to give it its name, the Opalescent. That first scarlet maple branch in late August warned of the coming fall. He was camped near Lake Sanford, and awoke stiff and cold from sleeping in the open. He started thinking about the winter. He knew he would need the shelter of a cabin soon. Judging from the cool nights and the icy mountain streams, the tops of the high peaks that always seemed shrouded in clouds, the winter would be long and difficult. He was far from the nearest settlement and probably would be snowed in much of the winter. He would have to learn to rely on himself. With the confidence of youth, he began to build a cabin and make preparations for his approaching isolation.

Fall was well advanced when Jacob finished building his log cabin in a clearing along a bend in the Opalescent River. He stacked his woodpile high and scanned the northern sky anxiously each morning, hoping that the first snow would hold off a little longer. He had to get supplies before the weather turned. He knew that a small tribe of Iroquois was camped north of Sanford Lake, along the Hudson. They were friendly and traded with him during the summer. He hoped to trade for blankets and dried fruits and corn. In return he would give them bullets and tobacco and maybe a little whiskey. He would have to do it soon, for snow clouds were gathering over Mt. Marcy.

By the time he reached the Indian camp snow was swirling around his face in light flurries. The Indian children greeted him with curiosity, following him through the settlement and touching his clothing. The men affected indifference; he learned that they masked their feelings well. Yet he also knew they were interested in his tobacco and bullets. By the time the trading was done and he had packed his new blankets and two baskets of dried food, the wind had turned into a gale that was straining against the entrance flap of the longhouse. The old chief studied the thick gray clouds that had settled over the forest and spoke to Jacob. "Snow bad. You stay," he said to the reluctant young man.

Three days passed before Jacob could leave the camp. They smoked many pipes together and finished the whiskey Jacob had brought, while the first snowstorm of the season spent its premature fury outside. During his stay he learned a number of things, enough to suspect how poorly he was prepared to winter alone in the wilderness. The Indians liked his enthusiasm and independence, and his desire to learn their methods of survival. When he left the old chief gave him a pair of snowshoes and some advice: "Come back in summer, then we talk more. Man is weak. Spirits strong." Here he made a sweeping motion with his arm that encompassed the mountains, forests and sky, and the new covering of snow. "Respect spirits and survive."

Jacob survived that first winter, though he didn't like to talk about it later. The winter seemed endless, and he grew to hate the very sight of snow. But not even at the worst times did he wish himself back on the farm. His cabin was drafty and cold, and his clothes inadequate protection from the blizzards that often piled snow high against the hides he used to cover the windows. He was awkward on snowshoes and inexperienced in winter hunting. He would often return empty handed after a day in the woods. His food supply was exhausted when the first green shoots broke through the snow.

But worse than these discomforts was the overwhelming loneliness. For days the only sounds he heard were the moaning of the wind and the sputter of the fire in the drafty fireplace. His feelings surprised and frightened him, for hadn't he been just as alone during most of the summer? But it wasn't the same; though he may have been without people during most of the summer, signs of life were all around him. Leaves and plants were moving and growing, and tiny creatures rustled in the underbrush. Even the flowing of the river was a live current, its gentle sound comforting and friendly.

Now the forest seemed empty, the skeletons of snow covered trees difficult to separate from the heavy clouds above. The small creatures of summer slept beneath the insulating layer of snow or burrowed through it silently. Even the river hibernated under its smooth, icy cover. He missed the crickets that had kept him company on starless nights, and the woodpecker that woke him with its staccato tapping.

Sometimes the isolation of his cramped cabin overwhelmed him, and he would rush out into the muffled world, his snowshoes marking his path with clumsy tracks. He would follow the finely etched trail of some bird or animal on the snow, searching for proof of life around him. Afterward he would return to the cabin, mind and body exhausted, to sleep and wait for spring.

The ice on Lake Sanford had turned dark and dirty and was beginning to show long cracks when Jacob headed for the Indian camp again. Spring was finally here with its heavy rains, damp earthy smells, and the sound of running water everywhere. In the woods the blacks and whites of winter were giving way to the fresh greens of moss clumps on rocks and lichens on the brown trunks of old trees. Snowdrops pushed their heads through dried leaves and swelling maple and birch buds showed lavender and rose on the still naked branches.

He found the Indian camp in an upheaval. The tribe was making ready to leave their settlement, assembling earthenware pots and baskets in piles, ready for moving. Children ran about excitedly underfoot, generally slowing the preparations. Jacob caught one of them as he ran by, and asked him what the tribe was doing. The little boy said something in Iroquois, but Jacob could only understand the word for "forest." When Jacob found the old chief, he nodded at Jacob, satisfied. "Good. You come in time. Now you see. We make Indian Sugar."

Jacob followed the tribe deep into the snow-covered forest, until they reached a large stand of sugar maples. Here they made camp, and after their evening meal the chief sat Jacob next to him by the fire. "We stay here, maybe two moons," he said. Making sugar much work, but long ago not so." He puffed on his pipe and began to relate an old Iroquois legend as the children gathered around him. He spoke in his own language, and Jacob strained to understand the unfamiliar words.

He told of a time, long ago, when the maple sap ran thick and rich straight from the tree. But the god Ne-naw-Bo-zhoo feared that because it was so easy to harvest, it would not be valued. He diluted the sap, put a curse on it. Now the Indians must collect forty tubs of sap and boil it down just to make one tub of syrup. The sweetness must be coaxed from the maple, and the Indians prize the syrup for all their hard work.

Over the next few weeks Jacob learned just how much work sugaring was, work involving every member of the tribe. First, the Indians made vertical slashes in the trunks of maples then drove flat reeds into the wounds. The sap ran down over the base of these reeds into birch or elm bark sap tubs. The tubs held one or two gallons of sap, and some families owned more than a thousand tubs.

Jacob watched the older squaws making new tubs out of peeled pieces of soft, pliable bark, stitching the corners together with thin fibers of spruce and sealing the edges with pine resin. Other members of the tribe boiled the sap in large hollowed-out logs until it thickened. Jacob took his turn pulling red-hot stones from the fire and dropping them into the boiling sap.

Some of the sap was concentrated by freezing overnight. In the morning a squaw chopped away the ice and collected the thickened syrup. This made the most desirable, purest syrup.

Most of the syrup was processed into maple sugar, since syrup containers were scarce. Jacob learned to stir the hot liquid rapidly with a wooden paddle until it cooled and crystallized. Finally, the warm sugar was poured into white birch bark boxes.

What Jacob enjoyed most about sugaring was the Maple Thanksgiving, when the Indians gave thanks to the Creator for allowing the sap to return each spring. One of the old squaws told him that the maple was the "goddess" of trees, a special gift from the Creator.

During the festivities, Jacob saw many of the uses the Indians had for maple syrup. Squaws cooked maple sugar in bear fat, producing a sauce for dipping roast venison. Not liking salt, the Indians added maple sugar to stews to reduce gaminess, and sprinkled it over boiled fish. Puddings were made by cooking corn meal and maple sugar with meat, dried beans, squash, dried cherries and chestnuts. At the feast, the braves drank fermented sap. Some of the fermented sap was allowed to turn into vinegar. With this they made a sweet and sour sauce, which was delicious with boiled venison.

They made Buffalo Dance Pudding, intended to cure diseases, for special ceremonies. Squaw corn was pounded into a meal, boiled into a pudding and sweetened with maple sugar. When Jacob caught a cold, the Indians urged him to drink sap straight from the tree as a tonic. Jacob was reluctant to leave the sugar camp.

Jacob visited the Iroquois camp frequently that summer. He grew to respect the knowledge that sustained their way of life. He knew that he would have to learn their ways to survive subsequent winters in the Adirondacks. The Indians taught him many things: how to fish for trout in the swift mountain streams, trap beavers, track the white tail deer and read animal signs. He learned to preserve and soften the hides of deer and made a pair of leggings for himself. He learned which plants could be used for food or medicine.

But there was another reason for his frequent visits, the chief's granddaughter, Oseetah. As summer turned to fall he began to think about spending another isolated winter, and was overcome with dread. Oseetah was quiet and gentle, and she seemed to like him. She loved the river and he often found her sitting by the waterfall weaving baskets. She showed him how to weave a simple pattern, and in return he taught her some English. When he asked for her in marriage, the old chief thought carefully before answering. He considered the young man who had grown so much in wisdom and knowledge that year. "You can take her, if she wants. But you must make a promise. Oseetah loves this land and water. Never take her away. Never take her children away."

Jacob promised. In the fall, he took his bride back to the cabin and they made preparations for the winter. With her help he sealed the holes in the drafty cabin and preserved food for the winter. Her companionship made the winter pass more quickly, almost comfortably. The following fall their son was born, and their second child, a girl, followed a year later.

During the next few years, the only white men they saw were occasional trappers, except during the rare trips they made to the settlements south along the Hudson to trade. Most of their human contact was with her people whom they visited with their two children during the warmer seasons. Jacob was content with his life and wanted his children raised as Indians. He felt he had found what he was looking for, where he belonged.

Six years after Jacob's first winter in the cabin, on a late spring day, Oseetah took their two young children to play near the falls where she loved to weave her baskets. A squirrel came up to her cautiously looking for food, and she fed it a few nuts from her basket. Patrick made canoes from sticks and strips of birchbark and Dawn placed them in the river, laughing as the swift current carried them downstream. Oseetah watched as the swollen spring waters tossed the fragile canoes over submerged rocks, threatening to swamp them.

She sat for a while, lost in thought, her hands pausing over her work. She loved the river in all its moods: in spring full and powerful with freshly melted snow rushing to the distant sea; peaceful and lazy in the summer when nature slowed her pace; or sleeping silently beneath the ice in winter. She hoped that her children would learn to love the river, too, and never stray far from its shores.

A log came crashing over the falls, startling Oseetah out of her reverie. Was this the first sign of a flash flood high in the mountains? She jumped to her feet, upsetting her basket. She looked for the children, but they had vanished. She ran along the shore, calling their names through the deafening roar as more logs plunged into the pool below the falls.

Terrified, she ran to the last place she had seen the children, but only found a few pieces of shredded birch bark. The river was soon a clogged mass of limbless trees pounding against the bank below. They were crushing her children, she thought, shaking. She fell to her knees, sobbing.

She didn't know how long she stayed kneeling on the damp ground, her mind blank with grief, when she felt something pulling on her skirt. She looked up, and with a cry embraced her children. The children had grown tired of their game and wandered into the forest, searching for pinecones.

Oseetah held them close, and together they watched the river carry its frightful burden downstream.

Gradually she calmed, and her fear was replaced by perplexity. This couldn't have been caused by a flash flood. The trees had all been stripped of their branches, like the logs in their cabin. But what fool would cut down trees only to throw them into the river? She must ask Jacob about it.

That night, after Jacob returned from hunting, she asked him what it meant. Jacob, too, had seen the logs and was disturbed. While hunting in the mountains he heard the dissonant chopping of axes in the clear, bright air. Curious, he approached the sound and saw giant white pines crash down from where they had stood for scores of years. Their stripped trunks were clogging the river, heading downstream past their cabin.

Jacob followed the logs along the river and found a new sawmill with a settlement growing up around it. A dam had been built on the free-flowing river, forming a millpond, on which floated hundreds of logs, waiting to be cut into lumber in the new mill. The land around the millpond had been cleared, majestic trees cut down to build the dam, leaving their amputated stumps behind.

That summer surveyors came from Riverview, as the small settlement around the sawmill was called, and set up their instruments near Jacob's cabin. Oseetah and the children watched them uneasily from the doorway. Jacob, angry but uncertain, strode over to them. The men looked up at him, surprised.

"And who might you be?" one of the men asked.

"I was about to ask you the same thing," Jacob retorted. "This is my house, and I don't like strangers nosing around it."

The men stopped their work and looked him over. They were dressed in city clothes, ill suited for working in the mountains. "This may be your house, friend, but it sure isn't your land. And unless you can think of a way to move your house off it, it won't be your house much longer, either," they laughed, returning to their instruments.

Jacob caught the man who had spoken by the arm. "Just what do you mean by that? And what are you doing with these, these things?" he said, gesturing at the unfamiliar equipment.

"We're surveying the land for Mr. Corrigan. He owns most of the land around here, and your house is on his property."

Stunned, Jacob stepped back. "Where do I find this Mr. Corrigan?"

"You'll have to talk to Mr. Lang down at the sawmill. He's in charge of things around here."

Chapter 4

Stuart Lang was eager to prove himself in his new job. Within two weeks of accepting Corrigan's offer, he was sailing up the Hudson. At Albany he was met by Corrigan's men who accompanied him on his journey north. On horseback they rode along the banks of the Hudson, then continued into the Adirondack high peaks region.

Mr. Corrigan had bought a huge piece of the wilderness, roughly 100,000 acres, for a mere 15 cents an acre. Stuart sighed, thinking of the opportunities this created for others, and for himself. He was in a hurry to start the operation, though the land had not been completely surveyed yet. He knew that the logging camp would have to be in the mountains to harvest the white pine and red spruce, and near a river that could be used for floating the logs to a sawmill.

Stuart climbed to the top of the nearest mountain and surveyed the wide valley that lay before him, virgin timber covering its floor and stretching to the mountains on three sides. At its center the Opalescent ran swift and clear, the perfect artery for carrying the logs in the spring. To the south, near a lake, where the river widened and flowed into the Hudson would be the ideal spot for a sawmill. Further upstream, past a waterfall, he laid out the logging camp, leaving the handful of men he had brought along to build a log shelter.

Stuart returned to the city to recruit men for the logging camp. If they cut a fair number of trees before winter, he reasoned, they could drag the logs out over the snow and have the first spring floods float them down the river to the sawmill.

Stuart was an entrepreneur, but he also had empathy, especially for Irish immigrants. And it was chiefly immigrants that he recruited for his logging operations. He was inexperienced at logging, and smart enough to know that his success depended upon hiring an experienced foreman. After a brief search he found Jeremy Dodd, a man who had spent many years logging in the Champlain Valley.

To fill out their crew, Stuart and Jeremy looked for men who had been farmers in the old country, men who could coax life from reluctant soil. Stuart sought out men who wanted roots in the new land, men who would give anything for land of their own. He offered each man a plot of land near the sawmill to farm in the spring, summer and early fall. In exchange, after the harvest was gathered, the men were to leave their farms and families and work as loggers during the idle winter months.

Stuart was fair and honest with the men. He warned them that the work would be difficult, for the mountains yielded their harvest reluctantly, and the land was rocky and ungenerous. But a living could be made, and if they worked hard the land would be theirs within fifteen years.

Stuart also hired men to build and work in the sawmill he had envisioned. Among the men he interviewed was an Irish Immigrant named Liam Ryan who was better educated than most immigrants and had experience running a sawmill. He put Ryan in charge of building the sawmill while he spent the fall and winter overseeing the logging.

Soon the sharp sound of axes cleaved the tranquil mountain air as the men cleared land for the sawmill. Small animals scampered from their homes frightened as giant trees crashed to the ground. Some of the logs were used to build a dam for the millpond; others formed the frame of the large sawmill. A wooden flume was built to carry water from the millpond to the waterwheel. Soon a giant circular saw was installed, and the men were cutting boards to enclose the sawmill and build their homes.

Despite the hard work and the fifteen-year wait, nine of the ten men who signed on that first year stayed to earn their own land. Perhaps it was because they trusted Stuart, recognized in him a man from their own ranks. He helped build their cabins before they left for the logging camp, and advanced their families money for winter supplies. When there was trouble, the wives knew they could rely on him in the absence of their men. Stuart was satisfied knowing that he was providing homes and a living for people whose roots were his own.

While some men stayed to finish the sawmill, others moved north to clear land for the logging camp. Logs from the felled trees were used to build a shanty for shelter, a stable, and a supply hut. Stuart was farsighted; he built the shanty much bigger than necessary for ten men. Fifty bunkbeds lined the walls. In the center of the room a huge cambuse fire burned constantly. The fire was the center of life for the camp. The two main meals were cooked over it. In the evening they sat around its comforting blaze on rough-hewn benches, silently eating their supper of beans, fatback pork, bread and cheese on tin plates, with hunting knives. They kept their hats on against the freezing air that came down through the chimney, smoked pipes and warmed themselves with boiling tea. They dried their boots and heavy wool socks by the fire, reluctant to leave its warmth for the cold, comfortless bunks.

Stuart spent most of that first winter in the camp, learning about logging, about his men. He collected stories about logging in the frigid North Country, especially about inexperienced or unlucky men who caused accidents. Back in the city he loved to tell them to incredulous friends who were hard put to believe him, except that he had a reputation for honesty.

Once, Stuart noticed one of the new men standing on top of a snowdrift, when someone shouted "Timber!" The fellow, perhaps dazzled by the whiteness around him, moved in the wrong direction, directly in the path of the falling tree. Stuart watched as the tree floated down toward the panic-stricken man, its branches waving their green needles in the morning brightness. In an instant he was gone. Only the tree remained, visible through a flurry of powdered snow. The men rushed to the spot where the young man was last seen and began digging frantically in the snow beneath the trunk. The victim was not near the surface, as they had expected. They found him at the bottom of the drift, unconscious but still breathing, saved by the depth of soft snow that cushioned the force of the blow.

Stuart learned that his foreman was responsible for far more than just directing the operation. One of the loggers slipped and drove the blade of his ax through his boot, nearly severing a toe. Jeremy Dodd rushed to the screaming man, shoved a plug of chewing tobacco into the wound to prevent infection, then bound the man's foot tightly with his shirt to stop the bleeding. Back at the shanty Jeremy sewed the cut up with a needle and thread, earning Stuart's respect as a man able to handle emergencies.

After the loggers felled the trees, skidders moved the logs over the snow with a horse drawn sled called a go-devil. Often the logs were barked, to make them slide more easily over the snow. The skidders piled their logs on skidways where the road to the river started. Once the logs were loaded onto a sled, the teamsters took over. A team of horses was able to pull forty logs or more at a time over the icy roads. On steep parts of the road hay or sand was spread to slow the sleigh down, but even then sometimes the sleigh went too fast and crashed into the horses in front, breaking their legs or killing them. On one pile-up the big bay mare Hanna had her harness ripped right off her body and was pitched into a snowbank. She got up, shook herself, snorting with snow in her ears and nostrils, but unhurt. The teamsters were superstitious men. After that, they all asked for Hanna when they drove out on the icy logging roads.

The winter cutting was good, and by spring the first harvest of logs was floating down the Opalescent to the sawmill, disturbing the lives of Oseetah and Jacob Hughes.

Stuart Lang sat in his office in the sawmill balancing the books of the lumbering operation. The figures looked good and if the price of lumber held up, a profit would be made even in this first season. Satisfied, he looked out the window at the bright summer day, past the turning waterwheel that supplied power to the sawmill. The sounds of rushing water and the buzzing of the big saw were a comforting background noise that he no longer noticed. He preferred to keep an office right on the premises, at the hub of the waterwheel.

Along the river, below the mill, the men were completing their cabins. They were developing into a small community that Stuart hoped would grow as the operation expanded. The women had planted kitchen gardens, and some were busily weeding between the first sprouts of early potatoes and string beans. Some of the cabins were surrounded by flowers and lilac bushes, adding color to the budding settlement. Several boys were fishing below the dam with worms wriggling at the end of homemade fishing lines. The banks of the river were covered with wild raspberry and blueberry bushes, their flowers promising an abundant harvest.

Stuart was pleased when he surveyed the happy activity around him. He felt partly responsible for their happiness, for finding them a place of their own in this new and bewildering land. After all, he too, had been an Irish immigrant, something he would never forget despite his improved position.

Across the river from his window, the spring snowmelt had caused the river to overflow its banks, forming a marsh. Stuart watched two small boys catching frogs, using a fishing pole and a bit of red cloth for bait, when Liam Ryan knocked on the door. He stood in the doorway looking worried.

"There's a man here who insists on seeing you, Stuart. His name is Jacob Hughes."

"Hughes? Doesn't sound familiar. Who is he?"

"He's the man the surveyor told us about. He lives in the cabin just up the river with an Indian woman. Seems pretty riled about something."

"Well, send him in. And Liam, you might as well stay too."

Stuart looked with surprise at the tall man who strode into the room without glancing left or right. He had a dark beard that

44

hadn't been cut in several years, and his hair was tied back, twisted around with leather thongs much as the Indians wore theirs. He wore a buckskin shirt and trousers, and moccasins on his feet. A long knife in a soft leather sheath hung at his waist. His clothes and his walk were Indian, but the intense blue eyes in the tanned face betrayed his Irish origin.

"Are you Stuart Lang?" he asked without ceremony, staring directly at Stuart.

"I am. And what can I do for you?"

"I'm Jacob Hughes. And I've come to ask you to stop ruining this beautiful land."

"Oh? And just how am I doing that?"

"You're stripping the trees from the mountains, leaving slopes bare, without protection from the rains. You're frightening the deer and the bear away. And you're choking the river with dead trees. Soon the fish and beaver will be gone too." Jacob's voice became louder, but he made a visible effort to control himself.

Stuart studied this enigma of an Irishman who lived with an Indian woman, who dressed and probably thought more like one of them than his own kinsmen. He was making ridiculous demands, yet there was something about his bluntness, his intensity, which made Stuart listen.

"And what do you propose I do different?" he asked.

"Stop cutting the trees down before it's too late!" Jacob spoke with fervor, thrusting his dark face close to Stuart's over the desk.

Stuart looked away thoughtfully for a minute then slowly answered, "I can't do that, Hughes. Logging this land has given jobs and homes to many people, people like you and me, people who had nothing in the old country. Look outside and see how prosperous they are. They hardly resemble the people

45

we left back home, starving, living hopeless lives in County Cork or Dublin."

Jacob looked out the window at the children running in the grass, at the housewives hanging their wash in the sun, the farmers tilling their fields in the distance. He remembered his own family, their poverty and desperation. Then he looked across the river toward the mountains he had grown to love and his resolve returned.

"You can't log this land. It belongs to the Indians. They've been living on it for thousands of years. They gave me a small piece of it with the promise that I wouldn't spoil it."

Stuart shook his head. "The Indians no longer own this land. This land, all of this land as far as you can see belongs to Mr. George Corrigan. He bought it, and has a deed from the state to prove it."

"What kind of a man is this Corrigan? How can he buy the Indians' land from the state? He can't take my land away, not without a fight! Where can I find this Mr. Corrigan?"

Stuart looked at Liam before responding. "Mr. Corrigan lives in New York. I represent him here. I'll speak to him, tell him what you said. In the meantime don't worry about leaving. We have no immediate plans for working the area around your cabin."

"You just tell him to come up here and see the mess he's making of his land. Maybe that'll change his mind," Jacob said, striding out the door.

Liam and Stuart were silent. They stared after Jacob as he left the office and headed up the river trail toward his house. His sincerity and conviction made the two men uncomfortable.

"He must be mad, expecting us to stop logging just because he likes the mountains the way they are," Stuart said with forced conviction. "People like him won't accept progress. God put these trees here for our use, to put roofs over the heads of His children. Does Hughes really expect us to sacrifice all that just so he and a few savages can have their own private game preserve? What do you think of this Jacob Hughes? I've never seen anyone like him, wearing Indian clothes like a savage, have you Liam?"

Liam studied Stuart silently before answering. "No, I haven't. I've heard the men talk about him, though. They say he spent the last five years up here alone with the Indians and that he's learned a lot from them. They say he knows these woods better than any other white man, can track a deer in pouring rain, and can handle one of those Indian canoes like he was born to it. It'd be a shame to chase a man like that off. He might be useful someday."

Stuart looked up with interest. "Liam, find out what more you can about him. I just might have a use for this man. I'm going to New York in a couple of weeks to see Mr. Corrigan. He's invited some of his friends to go hunting up here this summer, and he asked me to find them a guide, someone who knows the area well. Until now, I hadn't thought of anyone. The Indians seem to be the only ones who really know the wilderness, but I wouldn't trust them, even if they were interested. If I can get him to agree, Hughes might be the guide I'm looking for."

At first Jacob did not want any part of taking more white men into the mountains, but Oseetah said, "They will come anyway. It is better that you take them, you who know and love our forests. There is less chance that they will disturb things with you as their guide. Besides, if they learn to love the mountains the way we do, they may stop destroying them."

When Mr. Corrigan and his two friends arrived for their adventure dressed in slick leather shoes and stiff-necked shirts, Jacob led them directly to the new general store. He outfitted them in flannel shirts, rough wool trousers, and heavy leather boots. At first they were reluctant to dress in workmen's clothes, but after a few days hiking in the mountains and cold nights

47

sleeping in the open, Corrigan and his friends were thankful for their new clothes and learned to value Jacob's advice.

Jacob led them up the rocky slopes of the high peaks. In a clearing next to a stream he pitched camp and built a three-sided shelter he called a lean-to. The frame of saplings was covered over with pine boughs, the needles providing protection from the inevitable late afternoon summer showers. He covered the rocky floor of the lean-to with several inches of brown pine needles, making a soft mattress for their bedrolls. The shelter was open on the side facing the stream.

On the clearing in front of the lean-to Jacob prepared a rough fireplace, using rocks he found near the camp. One of the men brought some rocks from the stream before Jacob stopped him. He explained that the rock had soaked up water and would explode if placed near the fire. With his axe, Jacob flattened the top of a log, forming a bench for sitting by the fire in the evening. Finally, he dug a hole among the bushes for a privy. With camp completed, he sat down and lit his pipe.

The first night they had a stew that Jacob cooked with dried meat and potatoes from his pack, and greens that he picked along the trail. He showed the men how to find good firewood. He had them collect the dead lower branches of pine trees that could easily be broken off by hand. It was called squaw wood because it was so easy to collect, and the Indian squaws were the ones who usually gathered it.

The next day Jacob was out early, tracking a deer. He hurried the men through a cold breakfast of powdered Indian corn, maple sugar, and water. They took hollow quail's eggs filled with maple syrup, preserved fruits and jerky along with them on the hunt. For four hours they followed the trail of a three point buck that stayed just out of rifle range, until Corrigan, who proved to be a good shot, felled him with his first bullet. It was late afternoon when they returned to camp. Jacob spitted a large piece of the venison and cooked it over the open fire.

Animated by the excitement of the day, the men sat around the fire, talking. The sky was clear, filled with more stars, closer and brighter than Corrigan and his friends had ever seen before. With a little prompting, Jacob told them some of the stories he had learned from the Indians, the same ones Oseetah told their children around the evening fire.

"The Indians are a superstitious people," Jacob began. "They believe that everything around them, the trees, the clouds, even the rocks, have spirits. These spirits control our lives. Their medicine men, or sachems, were able to talk to the spirits, gain their favor, and were very important members of their tribes. Often a sachem was more important than the chief himself. Their legends say that some of the sachems were evil, and the Great Spirit locked them in hollow trees just like the one that's standing at the entrance to camp." Here Jacob lowered his voice and gestured toward an old fir with bent and crooked branches. "In their struggles to escape they thrust their arms through the closing bark and they remain as withered trunks and branches to this very day." Jacob stopped to refill his pipe as the fire sputtered in the suddenly eerie quiet. The men glanced furtively at the gnarled fir as it creaked in a gust of wind. Jacob continued:

"A long time ago, one of these sachems, Oquarah, escaped the Great Spirit's trap and became the medicine man of the Saranac Indians, my wife's people. At the time there was a rivalry between two young braves in the tribe named Eagle and Wolf, as to who could get the most scalps in battle. The tribe was divided in admiration of these daring and powerful warriors. Oquarah was jealous of the attention lavished on the two youths, attention he felt should have been his as the tribe's counselor.

"One day the two warriors set off together to hunt moose. The following day Wolf returned alone. He explained that during the hunt they had separated, and that despite much searching he had been unable to find his friend. Wolf thought that Eagle

49

must have returned ahead of him, but he was not at the camp. At that, the jealous Oquarah rose.

"I hear a forked tongue," he cried. "Wolf was jealous of Eagle, and his fangs have pierced Eagle's heart."

"Wolf doesn't lie," answered the young man.

"Then where is Eagle?"

"I have told you. I could not find him," Wolf replied.

"The old sachem raised his tomahawk to strike. The wife of Wolf threw herself before her husband, receiving the fatal blow. The sachem fell an instant later, with Wolf's knife in his heart.

"There was instant turmoil, and the tribe divided into two factions. Wolf took half the people down the river to new hunting grounds, and whenever the warring factions met, much blood was spilled.

"Years later, a brave of the upper tribe saw a canoe advancing from the north. An old man stepped from it: it was Eagle. After leaving Wolf he had fallen into a cleft in the rock, and was rescued by hunters from a Canadian tribe. He had married a northern squaw but returned to die with his own people. The warriors and sachems of both branches of the Saranacs were summoned to a council, where they swore peace in Eagle's presence and he was able to die content."

Jacob stood to put more wood on the fire. The flames threw sparks like thousands of fireflies into the night sky. The men stretched, their muscles stiff from the day's hunt. One got up and poured more coffee into their cups. Jacob walked to the edge of the woods and was swallowed up by the shadow of the gnarled fir. They all breathed easier as they heard the reassuring sound of Jacob relieving himself of the earlier coffee. The familiar sound reminded them of their own discomfort, and after Jacob returned the others followed his example. However, the men stayed within the reassuring circle of light from the fire, carefully avoiding the old fir.

The week went by quickly. The men took turns supplying meat for the evening meal. One day they didn't hunt at all, choosing instead to climb the mountain the Indians called Tahawus, or sky-splitter. The men stayed at the top a long time in the rarefied air, feeling the wind blowing across the bare rock, making their eyes water as they looked across at the other high peaks. Lake Champlain was visible forty miles to the east. The cabins around the sawmill were small dots in the distance. Compared to the land that was his, stretching for miles around him, Corrigan suddenly felt very small. The men were quiet when they returned to camp, feeling insignificant next to the vastness of the wilderness. Corrigan looked back from a bend in the trail. He had bought this land as an investment. But after spending a week in the wilderness, it was much more than just a sound investment.

Chapter 5

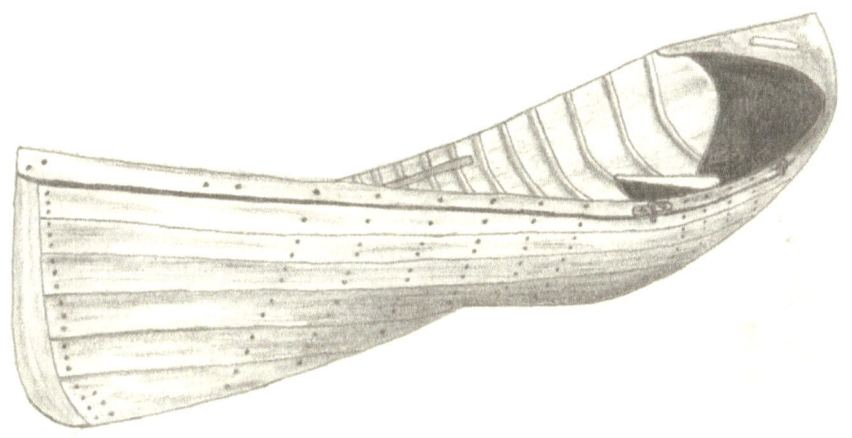

After returning to the settlement, Corrigan decided to stay for a few days to discuss business with Stuart. But there was more than business on his mind when he entered Lang's office in the sawmill.

Stuart stood up to greet his employer. "I'm glad you're here, Mr. Corrigan. I just finished updating the books, and it looks like we'll be making a profit even with the start up costs this first year," he said enthusiastically.

His triumph was met with uncharacteristic indifference. "You've done a great job, Stuart," Corrigan said, barely glancing at the books. "But there is something else I'd like to discuss before we sit down with the books."

As Stuart regarded the older man curiously, he saw that Corrigan looked younger. His step was lighter and he had color in his face. But most of all, his eyes looked alive; they fairly danced in his face.

Corrigan sat down in a chair opposite Stuart. "You know I bought this land as an investment. The price was right, and I knew that we could make a profit from it. From what you've shown me, I won't be disappointed." He leaned back in his chair as Stuart waited for him to continue.

"But now that I've spent a week in the woods with someone who taught me to understand the land, I can no longer consider it as just a business proposition. It's become much more personal." He paused, embarrassed, and cleared his throat.

"I know what you mean, sir; the land means a lot to me, too," Stuart said. His words seemed to put the older man at ease.

"I want to come back again, and bring my friends up here, too. There's a lot more that I can learn from this Jacob Hughes. I want you to offer him a contract to be my guide, and I'll want him to be available for my friends, too. Would you arrange it?"

"I'll certainly try, sir. But Hughes may be a problem."

Corrigan looked at him questioningly. "Oh? What kind of a problem?"

"Hughes isn't too anxious to have men overrunning the woods. He may not like the idea."

"We'll just have to make it worth his while. Is he still around?"

Stuart nodded.

"Then call him in, and let's talk to him right now."

Stuart left the room, returning with Jacob five minutes later.

"Sit down, Hughes," Corrigan began. "There's something I'd like to ask you."

Jacob remained standing. "Thank you, but I prefer to stand."

Corrigan glanced at Stuart. "We have a proposition for you," Stuart said. "Mr. Corrigan was impressed by your woodsmanship. He's offering you a contract to be his guide in the future."

Jacob's shifted his gaze from Stuart to Corrigan. "What are the terms?"

"You could remain on the land indefinitely. And I'll pay you five dollars a day, plus expenses. A hundred dollars a year, guaranteed."

Stuart caught his breath. That was as much as he paid the loggers for a season.

Jacob hesitated, then shook his head. "That's a generous offer. But I can't do it."

Stuart gaped at him. "Why ever not?"

"Your logging is destroying the wilderness, and I won't be a part of that. In a few years there won't be anything left for me to guide you to."

Corrigan looked at him thoughtfully, searching for a compromise. He realized that to offer more money would be an insult to Jacob. Then, "Stuart, what could we do to reduce the impact of logging?"

"Let me get Liam Ryan in here and have him bring some maps for us to look over. He usually has some good ideas."

Stuart summarized the problem for him as Liam walked over to the large map on the wall with the Corrigan purchase outlined in blue.

Liam stared at the map thoughtfully, then turned to his friend. "I have a suggestion for you Stuart, and for Mr. Corrigan," he said, nodding to his superior, "that may satisfy everyone."

"The Corrigan holdings are huge. There are plenty of areas outside the mountainous region that can be profitably logged, yielding a good return on your investment on the whole property. But some parts are too remote and inaccessible, there is no good access for carrying out the logs, and the slope is too steep." Liam pointed at the high peaks region on the map. "We were going to save this area for last, and even then it's doubtful that we could log it profitably."

Corrigan listened, intrigued. In another moment he was ahead of Liam. "Why don't we designate the area we can't use anyway, to be kept wild and free? Can either of you see any problems with that?"

The two men shook their heads. "Can't think of any," Stuart answered. In fact, he liked the idea. This way, Mr. Corrigan could bring his friends to the mountains, and Hughes would probably agree to guide them if they guaranteed to save some of his wilderness. And there would be enough land remaining to support the growing community that depended on him.

Jacob listened to the interchange quietly. Inwardly he was elated, but on the outside he remained calm, his face unreadable.

Corrigan turned to Jacob. "What do you say, Hughes? You and your family can stay on the land where your cabin stands. I'll turn the high peaks region into a preserve, and you can be its caretaker. I'll pay you the salary I mentioned if you agree to guide me and my friends. Have we got a deal?"

Slowly, Jacob nodded, as Corrigan beamed. The two men shook hands, the handshake the only contract needed between men who respected each other.

Jacob was satisfied. He had his wilderness, the land he called forever wild, and a paying job when he wanted it.

Jacob took some of his clients on fishing trips along the rivers and lakes of the lower regions of the Adirondacks. At first he tried using a birch bark canoe, which he learned to paddle silently from the Indians. But Jacob had to depend on having someone with experience in canoeing to paddle up front. The first rapids he took with two of Corrigan's friends, the man up front panicked, and swamped the canoe. Jacob knew he needed something better.

Jacob needed a boat that could carry several men and their gear, yet would be light enough for him to portage between lakes. He would keep the basic canoe form but widened it at the middle like a rowboat. This way he could control it from the middle seat, seating his passengers at the two ends. He started by collecting strong, naturally crooked above ground roots of trees and formed them into a frame on a flat, elliptical bottom. Over this frame he shaped thin planks of pine, carefully beveling their edges so that they overlapped.

The planks were fastened to the ribs with brass screws and the joints were nailed inside and out with copper tacks. Jacob then waterproofed the boat and added oars for pulling heavy loads across the water. The finished craft was 15 feet long and just over 100 pounds. It had a yoke in the middle so he could carry in on his shoulders, and was pointed on both ends so it would pass between the trees on the narrow trails. The boat was sturdy and seaworthy, a quality necessary in a place where storms whipped up without warning on the mountain lakes.

Jacob became known for his ability to read the signs of the forest. He showed the men he guided how to identify deer signs: "buck rubs," saplings with the bark rubbed off at knee height made by bucks in rut; the ragged, clipped branch tips of trees and shrubs where deer had browsed; the dark brown kidney bean like droppings that marked their trail. He taught them the meaning of different tree markings: the healed scars on a beech made by a bear's claws where the animal climbed the tree to harvest beechnuts; an enormous "nest" that a bear had built of broken beech branches in a crook high off the ground; toothmarks of a porcupine girdling a tree; the conical stumps left by beavers, and how to identify an architect by its nest. Jacob taught the men many things, arousing their curiosity so that they would return the following year.

Within five years Stuart Lang was showing handsome profits for George Corrigan from the logging and lumbering operations. In 1833, when Stuart was thirty-three years old, George Corrigan gave him a twenty-five percent share in the Company's profits, part of which he used to buy land for himself near the sawmill, and to build a small house. The relationship between the two men grew over the years. They discussed their plans for the Company, and Stuart learned much about the running of a large and complicated business. When Stuart finally married, Mr. Corrigan called him into his office.

"Will you have a drink with me Stuart, so we may toast your lovely new bride?"

"Thank you sir, I will indeed."

"You know I've been very pleased with the work you've done for me, Stuart, very pleased indeed." The old man looked at Stuart affectionately, handing him a whiskey. "But more than that, I've been very gratified by the friendship between us."

"It's been a pleasure to work for you Sir, and an honor to have you consider me your friend. You gave me my chance in life, and I swore I'd never disappoint you."

The old man waved the words aside. "You're one of the few men in this life who hasn't been a disappointment."

The two sat in silence a few moments, sipping their drinks. Then Corrigan set his drink on the heavy oak desk, and looked directly at Stuart.

"I want to tell you something Stuart, because I don't know if I'll have another chance to say it. You know I have no son, no heir to leave my holdings to when the time comes. I have no close relative whom I can trust to take good care of my land in the North Country. When I first bought the land, it was just another investment, but now, after my treks with Hughes, it means a lot more." He paused, studying Stuart, then continued.

"I think you can understand that. You've been like a son to me, and I've decided to leave the lumber company and its surrounding lands to you in my will. Use the land for the good of the people in our new town, but also keep and protect the wilderness area."

The old man sat back, relishing the effect of his words on the younger one. Stuart nearly dropped his glass. He placed it carefully on the desk and sat speechless for a long moment.

"Sir, I don't know what to say. `Thanks' would hardly do it."

"Say nothing my boy, just continue to be my friend and take care of our land."

"You can count on me, sir."

Stuart and his bride moved into their new house downriver from the sawmill. Soon their house was the center of a small but busy town. Three years later George Corrigan died, and the Langs came into their inheritance. It became Stuart's habit to step out onto his balcony before dinner, and survey the town. His children learned to take pride in what their father had built, and to appreciate how the town depended on the forest and the products of the sawmill. The Langs eventually built a school and a church, but the change that made Stuart proudest was the sign he personally placed by the road at the outskirts of town. It read:

Michael walked along the trail leisurely, but at a steady pace. He stopped to note some of the improvements made during the past few years by the Department of Environmental Conservation summer rangers. Over the years the Adirondack Park had become very popular. The Northway provided direct access from Albany and New York City. People built summer homes and came up on weekends to enjoy the mountains.

The old trail was worn and muddy from constant heavy use, increasing erosion and dirtying the streams. The trail had been rerouted, allowing the old trail to recover. Already vegetation was regaining its hold where heavy boots had smashed the delicate undergrowth. Corduroys, short parallel logs, were placed across the path to walk on, preventing further harm. Longer split logs formed primitive walkways over large mucky and marshy areas.

A small, brownish salamander crawled slowly over one of the logs, and Rusty stopped to nose the creature tentatively. A few Indian Pipe grew out of rotted wood along the side of the path, their waxy whiteness calling to mind their popular name, "ghost plant," by which he had known them. Amanita grew everywhere, the brilliant red buttons of new fungi brightening the forest floor while yesterday's toadstools stood with opened umbrella heads.

Michael came around a bend in the river when he saw them, the graceful doe and fawn, still as statues, immobilized with tension, every sense keenly alert. The doe was waiting to cross the brook, waiting to guide her fawn across the deceptively gentle stream that hid treacherous rocks and slimy moss underfoot, threatening danger. They stood among a sparse thicket of trees on the bank, the fawn more visible with its spots that had not faded yet. It was perfectly tuned to its mother, awaiting her signal, trusting its life to her judgment. Michael and Rusty were upwind of the deer so the dog didn't catch their scent, and in their immobility he didn't recognize them. Michael looked back at them as he passed. The doe's head turned to follow his trail.

Deer are an integral part of the Adirondacks. Michael often encountered them on his hikes, yet the unexpected sight of one was enough to make him catch his breath. He admired and respected the gentle creatures, but also prided himself on his skill in tracking and hunting them. Some of his friends in

New York who called themselves environmentalists were baffled by this apparent contradiction in him.

In the fall, when the leaves were at their most brilliant and the cold nights left them covered with a layer of sparkling frost, the deer sensed a change. With the first gunshots of the hunting season the bucks left their harems and moved to the more remote regions. O'Leary's Sporting Goods Store did a brisk business in guns and ammunition, and in bright red hunting jackets and caps. Sport hunters meant good business, and Adirondack merchants looked forward to the start of hunting season. To many Adirondack natives, hunting meant harvesting meat for their families. "Sports" wore fancy red shirts and carried shiny new rifles. They filled up the wayside motels for a few days each fall. Natives dressed in well worn overalls and buffalo plaid shirts, and carried weathered rifles that had been dulled by much use and frequent cleaning and oiling. But the hunting fever affected both.

Days before the first shot rang through the woods the natives congregated in the local taverns, drinking beer or whiskey around the rough pine tables. They told tales of previous hunts and exchanged tips about the current habits of the whitetail while the dusty heads of deer and moose stared down at them with vacant, glassy eyes.

Michael felt some of the same excitement as he remembered his first deer hunt. He was fourteen. Jake had introduced him to the ways of deer, their habits, favorite feeding grounds, and much more. In the weeks before hunting season, when the deer were in fresh meat, he and Jake made several treks into the forest. They followed deer paths that connected clearings containing their favorite foods with the more sheltered areas in which they bedded down. The main runway was the widest and the most beaten down, with smaller ones working off it, cutting through the more open areas. In a place where the undergrowth had turned wet and muddy the sharp imprint of narrow hooves was clearly outlined.

Jake picked up some deer droppings and squeezed them between his thumb and forefinger to test for freshness. The still moist droppings told him that the deer had passed recently. When they passed by a shallow pond Michael asked Jake why he didn't test the droppings nearby. "Don't need to," the old guide replied. "Deer only feed in shallow waters when the deer fly are out and the plants are growing. It's a bad thing, too. We lose a lot of deer to the liver fluke that way," he added. "In winter you might find them here again. They like to yard up in the swamps when it's cold."

When they came to a clearing Jake checked the trees. He was looking for witch hobble, birch, or maple, the deer's favorite food. The bark had been stripped from many of the trees, showing recent visits by deer. They stopped by a tree at the edge of a clearing where a buck had rubbed the bark off with his antlers. Beneath the tree the ground had been scraped. Jake took a handful of dirt from the scrape and smelled it. "Where there's scrapes like this, that's where you want to hunt," he told Michael. "You know the buck's in rut and not cautious like the rest of the year. A scrape that's freshly pawed out and smells of piss, is the best sign you can find."

While they tracked the deer Jake talked to Michael about hunting, how they needed to thin the deer herd. "When there's a good year with plenty of food and mild winters, the deer multiply. But the critters don't know when to stop. Soon there's too many of them. Come a bad winter, there ain't enough food and most starve to death. We help keep the balance by hunting," he explained. "Back in '50, before you were born, there was a huge blowdown. Most of the trees this side of Marcy got torn up. There was no more shade to keep the small trees from growing. These small trees were fine food and cover for whitetail. Pretty soon the herd grew and started to use up the food. We had a hard winter and the herd was nearly wiped out. So we gotta help keep the balance by hunting before there's too many deer again."

They walked on in silence for a while before Jake continued. "There's some who think otherwise about this. They say much of the land in the Park is gonna turn into a forest of old and aging trees. There wouldn't be enough undergrowth, food, or cover for the deer. Some people want to start lumbering again, cutting down old trees so as the new ones can grow and provide for the deer. But I'd never want to see that happen. I reckon an antlerless season'd be far better."

When the season opened, they were ready. Jake liked to be at his chosen spot before sunrise the first day of hunting season since the bucks moved to less accessible, more remote places after the first day of shooting. The does and fawns stayed behind, sensing that they were protected. The only time Jake postponed a trip was during a full moon. Michael thought at first that he was superstitious, but Jake only laughed. "No," he said, "it's real simple why I don't hunt when the moon's full. If there's enough light, the deer feed at night. Then, during the day they stay hid, and it's much harder to find them."

Michael began to learn the meaning of solitude and self-reliance during that early hunt with Jake as they crept shivering through the damp, awakening forest. Jake never hurried, never grew impatient, not even after crouching below the dripping branches of a thicket for what seemed like hours, the steady autumn rain drizzling relentlessly through the thinning branches overhead. In fact, Jake preferred a damp day for hunting, when moisture softened the fallen leaves. On clear days the leaves sounded like dry cereal beneath their feet.

They went out before dawn, reaching the spot they had marked earlier along a main runway. A gray fog enfolded the landscape in blurring lines. There they waited, making themselves as comfortable as possible among the soggy leaves on the uneven ground. Michael thought about Jake's words that morning. "Hunting is really scouting, then sitting and waiting and letting the deer come to you. You want to take a relaxed animal, not one that's frightened and running. A calm deer is much more tender; its muscles are relaxed, not tight and hard.

But if you can't sit still for a long time, then you might as well not hunt. Because you can count on it, as soon as you need to move your fanny from some sharp rock, a deer will be moving into sight and hear you rustling around. And there goes your chance."

Michael learned to sit still, curbing his impatience, rediscovering senses that had been deadened by lack of use. In the semidarkness of early dawn shapes were vague, obscured, and sight wasn't of much use. Instead he learned to rely on his hearing and sense of smell for cues, to identify the awakening life around him. The familiar call of a bird filled the forest. A mouse scurried through the undergrowth near his feet. The snap of a twig alerted him to the presence of a larger animal, possibly a deer. The damp smells of moldering leaves and undergrowth and the strong odor of pine filled his nostrils. Jake rubbed himself with pine resin when hunting in pine country and acorn juice when they hunted among oaks, to cover his scent. A few years later, following a night of rain when the trees were dripping with heavy accumulated drops, Michael even smelled a buck before he saw it. At first he could neither see nor hear the animal, only knew his presence by the thick, wet smell of his coat. It reminded him of Old Calamity, Jake's dog, after a swim.

Gradually, as the morning brightened, sight became more useful. At first the shapeless mass of tree trunks and rocks became defined, then the rounded heads of toadstools and the green fringe of ferns could be identified. As colors emerged, the berries of the white baneberry reached out from their background of grayish bracken, like so many doll's eyes on pinkish stalks.

Jake quietly scanned the clearing, alert for slight movements, looking for something that didn't quite match the cover. A gleam of white might be the neck patch of a deer or the flick of a nervous tail. Brown hair glistening in the sun is different than the brown of trees, and brown legs in a thicket are not shaped like saplings. Then, at a distance in low light, Jake pointed out the gray forms of deer. Michael noted the blocky outline of a buck, followed by the V-like forms of three does. The buck walked boldly, while his does took dainty, mincing steps.

Michael remembered freezing, remaining perfectly still and lowering his gaze, to keep from alerting the deer. Jake had warned him to avoid letting the deer see his eyes. "Never look a deer in the eye if you can help it," he had told Michael. "There is something about a man's eye that spooks them. It helps them recognize you as a man, as dangerous." Jake knew what he was doing, and without fail he would get his deer.

Michael watched as the buck approached the clearing, leading his does, just as Jake had predicted. Michael counted the buck's points, forgetting completely about his rifle. It had six points on its magnificent antlers. A nudge from Jake reminded him to prepare for the first shot. Jake had taught him well; his shoulder was still sore from shooting those boxes of 30-06 ammo at cans near the old mine. Michael was using Jake's old 30-06 bolt action Springfield. He had wanted to borrow his dad's semiautomatic, but Jake would only allow him one shot. If he didn't get the buck the first time, he wouldn't have a second chance.

Michael lined up the sights of the rifle just behind the buck's shoulder and slowly squeezed the trigger. Nothing happened. Then he remembered to take the safety off. The buck perked his ears up at the metallic click but remained still, not sure what to do. Michael realigned his sights on the stationary buck. He took a breath, let it halfway out, and squeezed the trigger. With an explosion the rifle slammed into his shoulder. The barrel jumped up, taking with it his view of the deer. When he brought the rifle down again, the deer were gone.

Disappointed, he turned to Jake, but the older man was smiling at him. Jake led him over to the spot where Michael last saw the buck. It lay on its side, its neck twisted at an unnatural angle, its eyes veiled, unseeing like the glass eyes of trophies.

An expanding patch of red on its white chest colored the leaves beneath him. Holding his rifle on the buck, Jake kicked a pinecone at it. Satisfied that it didn't move, he took out his folding buck knife and straddled the deer. With a quick motion he slit its throat. Then the real work began.

They dragged the buck by its antlers to a shady spot under a tree. Jake made a slit behind the tendons of its hind legs and threaded a rope through the openings. Throwing the other end of the rope over a branch, they hoisted the deer up until it hung upside down. That way its guts wouldn't fall out while Jake was working on it.

Out came Jake's knife again. While Michael held the deer steady, Jake cut a circle around its anus. Slipping the first two fingers of his left hand under the skin, he guided the knife down toward the deer's belly, slitting the skin, carefully avoiding the inner organs. Reaching into the abdominal cavity, he cautiously pulled out the deer's bladder and intestines. A punctured bladder or intestine would mean spoiled meat.

"You had a good shot, Michael. The bullet severed a major artery, passed through the lungs and out without shattering. Not much of the meat will be spoiled," Jake said, placing the heart and liver in a plastic bag.

The boy nodded, swelling with pride under the unaccustomed praise. New, overwhelming emotions made him dumb, as he watched his mentor avidly.

Jake cut the skin from around the ankles and pulled it down over the carcass as if he were removing a pair of gloves. He avoided the musk glands on the deer's legs, careful not to puncture them or contaminate the blade of his knife.

"You know, that's the `gamey' taste most people think of when they taste venison. You get a little on your knife, and it'll spoil the whole carcass," he explained.

Michael watched, fascinated, after overcoming his initial aversion, as the beautiful animal was reduced to its parts.

Jake took out a hacksaw and split the carcass in half. Soon the deer was in quarters, neatly wrapped in cheesecloth. He kept the head to prove it was a buck, and saved hair from its tail for fishing lures. He strapped the meat to pack frames, and they carried their heavy loads back to Jake's cabin.

Each fall Jake and Michael hunted together, and each season Michael learned more from the older man. If there was more than one buck within sight, Jake always dropped the lesser of the two. When Michael, in his adolescent pride, objected, Jake explained: "It's not important that we take the prettier buck. We're only going to butcher and eat him. And I don't collect heads to hang on my wall. It's more important that we leave the better, stronger buck to live and mate and improve the herd." He even put a lick out for the deer every year, salt in exchange for what he took.

Hunting with Jake was one of those experiences Michael remembered privately as marking his passage into manhood. The excitement of learning secrets that belonged to men only, of practicing patience, cunning, self-restraint, relying on his own abilities and resources--these were all things that lifted the boy out of the dependence of childhood and filled him with the promised strengths of imminent manhood. He never told anyone how he felt, partly because he was embarrassed and ashamed by the intensity of his feelings, partly because he was unable to put them into words, but mostly because he felt instinctively that Jake was the only one who would truly understand, and with him there was no need for words.

Chapter 6

Maggie parked in front of O'Leary's Outdoor Store and ran up the side steps that led to the newspaper office. The sign on the door was weathered and at least twenty years old. It read Langston Gazette, Editor Emmett Wilkins. As she walked quickly to her desk she could tell at a glance that Emmett was already there, although not in the room. The lights were on, and the news articles and human-interest stories she had straightened before leaving the previous night were again in disarray. Emmett's desk was cluttered with newspaper clippings, and crumpled typing paper littered the floor around the wastebasket. His ancient, worn cardigan hung precariously on the back of his chair, making her smile at the memory of their first meeting.

It was twelve years ago, and he was wearing the same cardigan, though it had been new then. She was sixteen and going through a painful time. She hadn't fit in at school, and was uncomfortable with herself. The other girls were caught up in themselves, in their own adolescent preoccupations. Their clothes and hair, sophisticated beyond their years, were meant to impress the boys, and each other. It made Maggie uncomfortable, not really wanting to be like the others, yet wanting to belong. She felt tall and gangly compared to the other girls, and embarrassed when Becky talked her into wearing some of her clothes instead of the sweaters and corduroys she found most comfortable. She knew she could never be like them, and in her private moments of honesty knew she didn't really care.

The boys had always treated her as a pal, someone they had grown up next to and played ball with. So after a time she stopped trying to be someone else and returned to being Maggie, who would just as soon accompany Jake on a fishing trip as go to a Saturday night dance. But it wasn't easy being different at that age, and knowing she couldn't be one thing, she needed to prove herself at something else.

It was then that she became interested in writing. Her teachers encouraged her, and soon she was editor of the school

70

paper. She knew she was good at it, and she threw herself into the job. Writing filled an emptiness, relieved her doubts about herself. Then one day she stumbled onto a story that was beyond the scope of the school paper. It had to do with the school administration, with money that had been designated for an enrichment program, only the program didn't get the money. Excited by her findings, she took them to the Gazette.

At first Emmett Wilkins listened to her indulgently, inwardly smiling at her accusations. But he began to pay more attention as she supplied him with facts that implicated the assistant principal. He scrutinized her sharply, this intense young woman, Jake's daughter, and he recognized a quality in her that he knew in himself. She was stubborn and dogged in her determination to follow a story to its end, and she had the unbounded enthusiasm of the very young, something he could no longer claim. He saw in her the makings of a writer, though of course she would need a lot of direction.

"Listen to me carefully, Maggie. What you have told me is important, but we can't print it until we have more proof. If you can get me proof we will go ahead with the story. Until then, don't talk to anybody about this," he warned her.

She got the proof and a lot more that she didn't expect. The story appeared, and the school was in an uproar. Maggie lost her job on the school paper and was nearly suspended from school until the matter was cleared up. When she next came to see Emmett, she was confused and angry.

"I'm very impressed with what you're doing, Maggie," he said to her with new respect.

"Well, the school sure isn't! I said nothing but the truth, Mr. Wilkins, and look where it got me! Why are they doing this to me?"

He spoke with compassion as he put his arm around her shoulders: "I know you went through a lot for this story, Maggie, and it's been hard. But maybe it was for a reason. Being a

71

reporter isn't easy. There are always risks when you go after an important story. Now you know what it's like. But you also know you can do it. Question is, do you want to?"

She looked at him, troubled. "Sure I want to do it, but how can I? They won't let me work on the school paper anymore."

"How would you like to work on a real newspaper? You have two more summers before you go to college, don't you? I'd like you to start working for me during the school year and full time next summer. Then, if things work out, well, we'll see."

Finally, there was a hearing at the school. The assistant principal was fired and Maggie was vindicated. By then, however, she didn't want to go back to working on the school paper; she was a reporter for a real newspaper.

Maggie stared at the newspaper on her desk for a moment, lost in thought. Emmett emerged from the back room with his usual bustling energy and hurried towards her. He wiped ink from his fingers with a rag as he pointed at the paper spread before her.

"Have you read it yet, Maggie? The New York Times picked up your article on acid rain. This could turn into something big -- you'd better follow it up."

She smiled at him as she clipped the article and folded it into her pocket. "I'm going right now, Emmett. I'll see if I can get something more out of that high school boy."

Emmett rubbed his chin thoughtfully, leaving a blue-black mark. "What about Michael Ryan? Have you been able to pin him down on anything yet?"

Maggie shook her head impatiently. "No. I've been trying to get hold of him for days! He's always out and he hasn't returned my calls. If I didn't know him better, I'd think he was avoiding me."

She had a vague feeling of unease as she drove toward Myrtle Lane, where the Harpers lived. There was something wrong, something that wasn't obvious, her intuition told her. There was more to this story than it appeared on the surface. But what? And why didn't Michael answer her calls? It wasn't like him. They had been friends for so long, since they were small, playing children's games together. It had always been the two of them, Michael and Maggie, playing ball, exploring the woods for birds' nests and wild berries, fishing with Jake during those long, memorable summers. When they grew older, they went camping in the mountains. At first Jake went with them and taught them woodcraft and survival, and later they went by themselves when he judged them to be ready. But when Michael became involved with Becky the two spent more time by themselves. He and Maggie remained friends through college, though things were not the same. After he married Becky, Maggie didn't see him much, at least until this past year. The past few months had been so good, almost like when they were kids. That's why it was so hard to believe that he could be avoiding her.

Steve Harper was sitting on the porch swing and looked less than pleased to see Maggie when she came up the walk.

"Hi," he mumbled, avoiding her eyes.

"Hello, Steve. Can I talk to you for a minute?"

"Yeah, I guess so. What about?" he said looking at his feet.

"I think you know what it's about," she said trying to find the right words. "It's about the story we printed in the paper last week. The one that talked about that science project you and Mr. Ryan were doing on acid rain," she said sitting next to him in the swing.

His discomfort mystified her, especially since he had been so eager to talk to her before. She continued.

73

"Can you tell me anything more about your studies? Do you have any new numbers for me?"

He glanced at her quickly. "No. I don't know anything else," then got up and walked over to the porch railing, his back turned to her.

"What do you mean?," she pressed him. "Have you stopped working on the project?"

The boy turned to look at her before he replied. "Look, you'll have to ask Mr. Ryan about it. I really don't want to get into it."

"Has Mr. Ryan told you not to talk to me?"

The boy shifted uncomfortably. "Look, why don't you just talk to him yourself and let him tell you what's going on?"

She watched the boy's tense profile for a moment, considered her chances of breaking through the unexpected hostility. "I will. Do you know where Mr. Ryan is today?"

"How should I know? He said something about taking some samples from another location. Look, I've got to go." With that he was gone, the screen door slamming after him.

She hurried back to the Jeep, only one thought on her mind. There was definitely more to this story than just acid rain, and she was going to find Michael and make him tell her what it was.

Back at the office Maggie tried calling Michael once more, without success. She decided to wait certain that he would return her call. But she couldn't shake that vague feeling that had plagued her all day, and by midafternoon the waiting was making her distracted. She covered her typewriter, jumped into her Jeep, and headed for Yellow Birch Trail.

When Becky opened the door, Maggie could see that she had been sulking. Even after a decade, Becky was still the same. Whenever things didn't go her way, Becky would lock herself in her room and pout. She would lie on her bed hugging one of the large plush animals that she collected, looking forlorn, her china blue eyes voicing an appeal more clearly than words. Maggie remembered and silently warned herself. Becky always got her way when they were girls, and Maggie had to resist her.

Becky curled up on the couch and hugged a pillow close to herself. Maggie looked at the small body outlined in her light summer shift, and was filled with admiration. She had been very attached to Becky when they were sixteen. Becky was all the things everyone at school admired all the things Maggie couldn't be. Even now, she couldn't help noting the contrast between them: Becky--soft, feminine, appealing; herself--tall, angular, direct. Back then Maggie had been happy just to be around her, flattered that Becky considered them to be best friends. She had been flattered until Becky took Michael away, wanting him only for herself. Becky didn't like hiking and camping, and Michael couldn't go without her. She became the center of his life, but Maggie knew that he missed the good times they shared in the wilderness. Later he missed the wilderness so much that he moved back to Langston, giving up a promising career in the city.

Becky's voice brought Maggie's thoughts back to the present. "Well Maggie. You look businesslike. What brings you here?"

"Michael! I've been trying to reach him for two days, and I can't seem to get hold of him. Where is he, Becky? It's important that I find him."

"Yes, it's important that I reach him too, but I don't think he wants to be reached," she said.

Maggie looked at her curiously. "Looks like you guys had a fight. But I don't want to get involved in that. I need him for a story I've been working on, one that could affect us all."

"Oh, yes, I know all about that story. As for not wanting to get involved, it's a little late for that. You and Michael, and your boundless scruples! You have to be truthful and honest, no matter what the cost." She turned away, but not in time to hide the resentment on her face.

"What on earth are you talking about, Becky?" Maggie asked, completely bewildered. "Do you know something that I don't?"

"Maybe I do. But you'll have to ask Michael about that. Here, he left this message for you," she said, handing Maggie the note.

Maggie's thoughts raced as she read the contents of the note. Instead of clarifying things, the note only confused her. She was certain Becky knew something but wouldn't talk. In fact, she had been downright hostile. And why did Michael pick today to retreat into the mountains, for who knows how long, when he knew she needed that article for Wednesday's paper? But strangest of all, why should they stop drinking from their well? Could the acid rain be affecting their well water too? If he sent her a warning, there must be some danger. There were too many if's, too many unanswered questions. And now, she needed the answers.

Jake wasn't expecting her home for supper, but she knew he would be pleased to see her. He always was. Those years when she was away at college had been hard on them both though Jake had never complained. He was pleased that she would be returning home, thankful to Emmett Wilkins for helping her, encouraging her, and promising her a job. She had been excited about college and had learned much, experiencing life in the city. Emmett felt that was important for a reporter. He loaned her money for her education, to be repaid after she came back to work for him. She stayed in the city for a while after graduation, gaining experience, but always knowing she belonged with Jake, in the mountains. Now she was especially glad that she didn't wait before returning. Jake had aged greatly during the past year, and he was not well. It worried her, yet she felt helpless.

Maggie parked behind the woodpile and hurried inside. Jake was sitting in his favorite chair, the cane rocker with the pillow she had made for him one Christmas. She saw that he had been mending a snowshoe, weaving fresh sinew to replace the ones that were frayed, the way he had learned from his father. But now the snowshoe rested at his feet as he dozed, the late afternoon sun lending his skin an auburn glow. She stopped in the doorway to watch him, and to control the ache that rose in her throat. He looked so vulnerable sleeping there, suddenly grown old, and she felt protective toward him. She had never felt like that before, never needed to. He had always been the one to take care of her, to look after them both, ever since her mother had died when she was still a little girl. To her he had always been strong and invulnerable, someone she wanted to model herself after. Although he had missed his wife as much as Maggie had missed her mother, the bond between them had grown and strengthened as they came to rely on each other.

The changes in him hurt her deeply, like a physical attack on someone she loved. He had always been a compact and lean man, of medium height and weight, his body trimmed to the essential by constant physical use. His way of walking had always intrigued her, the way he placed his feet almost flat on the ground disturbing as little as possible underfoot. She had spent much time trying to imitate him. When he told her it was the way the Indians walked, the way his grandfather taught him, she was delighted. But over the summer he lost weight and grew measurably older, his back no longer straight, his step less than sure. He didn't do much walking now, and she frequently found him dozing in his chair. There was a tremor in his hand, a lack of confidence in his movements. Perhaps it was due mostly to his 70 years, but she didn't quite believe that aging could be so sudden and dramatic.

He opened his eyes as she crossed the room.

"Maggie! I didn't expect you back tonight."

"I know Dad, but something came up."

"What is it, child? You look mighty serious."

"I'm not sure what it means, Dad, but I got a note from Michael. He warned us not to drink water from the well."

Jake looked at his daughter questioningly. "Did he say why? I been drinking that water all my life."

"He didn't say, but I'm going to find out."

"What'll you do, Maggie?"

"I'm going to find Michael. He's gone up Marcy, heaven knows why. If he's trying to avoid me, he must have forgotten that I know the Marcy trail at least as well as he does. I'll leave early in the morning, Dad. I may be gone a couple of days."

"I wish I could go with you, Maggie, but I ain't up to climbing these days. Don't know if I'll ever see Lake Tear of the Clouds again."

She fought back tears at the meaning behind his words, then turned to him with her open smile.

"I came back early because I wanted to do something with you tonight, Dad. I want to go fishing down at Bullhead Lake. What do you say?"

The old man nodded, "I done a heck of fishing on that lake in my day."

It was growing dark as she drove the Jeep over the dirt road leading to Bullhead Lake. The road took them past the old mine. It looked like a home that had been used and deserted, but never tidied. Jake hated the site. He said it was a clear sign of how the land had been laid to waste, with no one having the decency to hide the wreckage.

"That mine site's been an eyesore ever since I can remember. The factory dumped its garbage there, and so did everyone else. The grass don't grow around it, and it's looking worse every year. You'd think at least them that worry about the tourists would do something about it," he grumbled.

Maggie glanced at her father. "You've always had a grudge against that mine, but you've never told me why," she said as they pulled up to the lake.

"Let's get the boat in the water first," he said. "Looks like there's some good bonfires along the shore."

Together they lowered the boat into the smooth water. It was one of the last true Adirondack guideboats, built for Jake to carry on his shoulders, but now she helped him with it. It was the boat he had used for most of his career as a guide, built much like his great grandfather's, seventeen feet long and pointed at the ends like a canoe but wider in the thwart, sturdy but light. Its copper and brass screws gleamed as they caught the light from the nearest fire.

Quietly Maggie slipped the oars into the dark, silky water and rowed toward the nearest bonfire while Jake attached bait to their hooks. August was the time for lazy fishermen to be after bullhead, or catfish, when the fish could be attracted to shallower waters by bonfires along the shore. It was a relaxed activity, unlike trout fishing in swift, icy, spring waters. But at no other time was a good catch more certain than late August on Bullhead Lake.

Small, expanding circles of light glimmered in the dark, opaque water whenever the oars broke its surface. The only sounds in the night were the occasional splashes and creaks of oars, the distant crackling of bonfires and the chirping of crickets that seemed to come from every direction. They fished in silence, allowing the peacefulness of the night and the lulling, barely perceptible motion of the boat to calm their thoughts. Further out in the lake dark shapes could be seen, indefinite and vaguely menacing. Maggie knew they were small islands with clumps of pine growing in isolated clusters, or large rocks that seemed to grow out of the very lake. Another boat passed them silently, its occupant nodding a soundless greeting. A nearly full moon rose behind them, its pale glow strengthened by the firelight. Five catfish lay smooth and silvery on the bottom of the boat when Jake laid down his pole and broke the silence.

"I guess you never heard the story of the old mine, Maggie; its time you did. It might explain some things to you about the Hughes's and the Langs, the feeling between us since we first came to the North Country."

Maggie sat up with interest, laying her pole beside her father's. "You've said that they see the mountains differently than we do, more as something to use for profit. And that we've always tried to respect and preserve the Adirondacks for the next generation."

"That's true, but there's more to it than that. Did you know that Jacob Hughes, who came from Ireland, discovered the old lead mine?" he asked.

Maggie shook her head, her interest piqued, as Jake continued. "Well, he did. Only he never got credit for it, not that he ever wanted any. This is how the story's been told in our family for over a hundred years."

Chapter 7

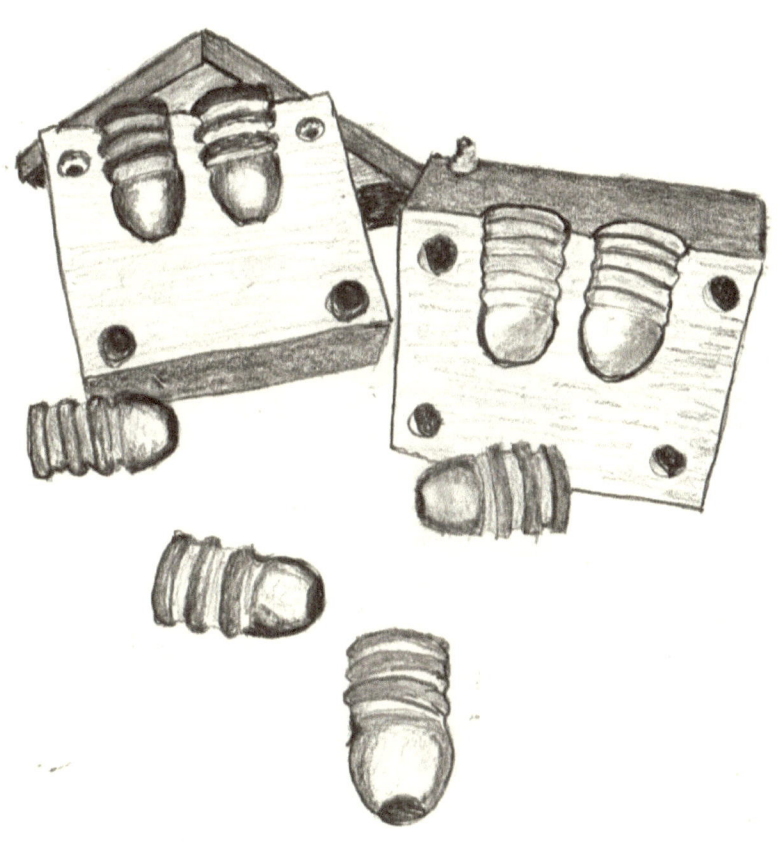

"Jacob and Oseetah didn't truck much with the white folks," Jake began. "Once a year they went to town for store-bought seeds to put in a garden. You see, Jacob taught Oseetah to farm. Oseetah couldn't see why they should grow plants when they was free for gathering all around them, but Jacob missed his Irish potatoes, cabbage, beans, and tomatoes, and soon Oseetah got to liking them too. He also bought hisself a few books and a jug of corn squeezings, which he shared with the Indians. But one thing he needed the town folk for was lead for his bullets. Jacob never could give up his gun in the wilds, though he was right good with a bow and arrow. Jacob and his gun were mighty close. He never left the cabin without his rifle loaded and primed. The city folk he guided felt safer with him carrying it.

"But Jacob feared running out of bullets. One winter the snow came early and he couldn't get to the trading post to stock up on stores. He heard stories that lead was found west of the Adirondacks and suspicioned that more was around for the finding. When he was a youngster back in Ireland, Jacob and a friend left their village to try their luck in the world. For four months they worked a lead mine. Jacob learned how to spot rocks with lead in them, and how to turn it into pure metal. So he was always on the lookout for the ore in his travels.

"Late in the spring of 1852, Jacob and his boy, Patrick, were setting a line of beaver traps in the marsh up near Sanford Lake when they spotted the fresh trail of a fox. They followed it through some rocks and into a crevice that widened into a shallow cave. When they lost the tracks on rocky ground, they gave up the hunt.

"As they were heading back to the lake, Jacob spotted a gleam coming from the dark. He ran his hand over a cluster of shiny rocks and studied them real close. In a minute he knew it was that rock called galena, the rock that contains lead! Lighting a candle he was startled by the glistening rocks in the walls of the cave, bursting out, trying to get free. Jacob marked the spot real careful-like in his mind, planning to return with his

82

tools. Lead is pretty easy to mine and separate out from the rocks. Jacob didn't need much, just enough for bullets.

"Jacob prized his good luck, but it also made him worry. He'd need to guard the secret of the lead carefully. He weren't selfish or greedy. He just knew what would happen to the land if his lead mine got found out. He remembered the mine back home in Ireland, and how the miners stripped the land, laid it bare. For some sixteen-odd years the family kept their private "bullet factory," a secret.

"A lot of folks wanted Jacob to guide 'em. He spent his summers taking men up the mountain and teaching his son all he knew about the woods. In time he built an extra cabin for the men he took hunting and fishing while Oseetah and their daughter, Dawn cooked for them."

Jake took out his pipe and lit it, drawing slowly on the aromatic tobacco. "I think you've heard the rest, Maggie, not just from me, but from the Langs and Ryans, too. Even if there's more than one telling of the story, there's only one that's truth."

They settled back at opposite ends of the canoe in comfortable silence, watching the night sink deeper into the murky lake. For a while they drifted quietly, allowing the motion of the water to carry them where it would. The secret noises of unseen nightlife around them lent Maggie a feeling of security, of not being alone. She inhaled the odor of Jake's pipe and thought over the events that caused the rift between her family and the Langs.

It was with a great deal of pride that Stuart Lang watched his son leave Langston for the university. Thomas was bright and promising, and he was to be the first Lang to have a university education. The lumber business was growing and growth brought complications. Thomas would study forestry, then return to help his father run the family business. But Stuart was to be disappointed when his son refused to apply himself to forestry with the same single-minded dedication that his father had turned toward lumbering. Thomas wanted to study engineering and mining instead. Finally, Stuart relented, but with the understanding that Thomas would return to Langston and come to work in the family business after graduation.

After working in the family business for several years, Thomas, who was an able businessman, saw that the forest was becoming depleted. At first Stuart refused to face that fact; he was content with his logging and lumbering operation, which he considered his life's work. Over the years he allowed his son a progressively greater role in running the company, and Thomas occasionally invited friends and business acquaintances on fishing and hunting trips, carrying out business in the relaxing atmosphere of the Adirondacks.

Jacob and Patrick agreed to take Thomas and his friends out for a week. They skirted Lake Sanford and hiked north along the Hudson, then followed Calamity Brook to Flowed Lands. From there they followed Opalescent and Feldspar Brooks to Lake Tear of the Clouds, nestled on the shoulder of Mt. Marcy. During the days the men hunted and fished and climbed mountains under Jacob's guidance. Patrick would scout ahead and set up camp at the next spot. In the evenings Jacob and Patrick prepared the game, cleaned their guns, and built temporary lean-tos of pine boughs by the campfire.

On the last night, they camped near the summit of Mt. Marcy. The week in the mountains had been an unforgettable experience, and they were reluctant to have it end. Thomas asked Jacob if he would guide them for another week. Jacob, reluctant at first, remembered that Stuart had lived up to their agreement, and Jacob was not one to go back on his word. So he agreed, but he told Thomas that first they would have to return to his cabin for fresh supplies.

What Jacob really needed was more bullets. One of the men was a remarkably poor shot and they didn't have enough for another week. He needed to make more in a hurry. Normally he would never risk it with strangers about, but now he had no choice.

Thomas and his friends turned in early back at the cabins, but Thomas couldn't sleep. He knew that the family business was in trouble, and he only had a few years to find a solution. The white pine and red spruce were being depleted in the Lang holdings. There were other trees, but they could not be profitably harvested like the pine and spruce. Thomas had wanted his father to diversify, but Stuart was not inclined to take the family business elsewhere.

Quietly he rose from his bunk and put on his clothes. Stepping out onto the narrow porch, he found the summer night soft and still, except for the tireless chirping of crickets. But his mind was on other things, not on the peaceful evening.

Thomas looked up in surprise at the sound of Jacob opening the door to his cabin. He was sure everyone had gone to bed. But here was Jacob slinking away in the night, a bundle under his arm. His curiosity aroused, Thomas followed the older man at a cautious distance. Jacob walked surely, picking his way through the forest with hardly a sound. Only Jacob's preoccupation kept him from hearing Thomas' clumsy rustling and stumbling. But Jacob was anxious to complete his task, wanting to put the danger of discovery behind him.

They crossed a meadow and headed for the low hills on the other side. Jacob walked past a cluster of rocks and disappeared into the darkness. Thomas waited a minute, then followed cautiously when Jacob didn't return. He saw an overhang and a crevice that melted into the darkness. From within the cave came the dull clanging of metal striking rock. The light of an oil lantern illuminated the entrance to the narrow chamber. Jacob was kneeling next to a rock wall covered with silvery, gleaming crystals. He was breaking the crystals off with a pick and gathering them into a woven basket.

Thomas pulled into the shadows trying to control his excitement as Jacob emerged carrying the heavy basket. Jacob started a fire in a heavy cauldron with wood that had been piled alongside. Thomas drew back into the darkness to keep from being seen in the light of the blazing fire. But he had to be sure; he wanted to see the process through before confronting Jacob. When the blaze subsided, Jacob added the basket of crystals to the hot coals. He stirred them periodically as he sat and smoked a pipe by the glowing embers.

When Jacob tilted the cauldron and blew away the ashes, Thomas saw a metallic liquid shimmering in the moonlight. Next Jacob laid out bullet molds on the ground and using a ladle, slowly filled them with the dense liquid. Jacob almost dropped the ladle in fright when Thomas stepped from the shadows, his suspicions confirmed.

Jacob tried to hide his secret, but he was too late. As he stood defensively before the cooling vessel he recognized Thomas and the emotions that played across his face in the moonlight. There was excitement and triumph, and something that awakened a fear--the expression of a coyote he had seen once guarding its kill. The two men stared at each other for a moment, their thoughts clashing in the silence, nearly audible in the surrounding stillness.

"Looks like you found us a treasure, Jacob," Thomas said, stepping closer to the older man.

Jacob moved away from the cauldron and sat down heavily on a nearby stump, his shoulders slumping. "As you can see," he said tersely. It would do no good to deny his discovery now.

"How long have you been mining this lode?" Thomas asked, eyeing Jacob suspiciously. "And why haven't you told my father about it?"

"I've been taking what I needed for a while, and my needs aren't much." Jacob refilled his pipe before continuing. "There isn't enough to bother with, no reason to tell you."

"No reason!" Thomas snorted. "No reason to tell us of a lead deposit you found on our land, a deposit that's probably worth a fortune?"

"No sir. This little bit of rocks will hardly be worth a fortune to you or your father." Jacob would take things slowly and calmly. There might still be a chance to save this land.

"And what makes you so sure that this deposit is worthless? I saw the galena you were digging out right near the surface. There must be much more deeper down."

"I don't doubt there is. But it can't be mined."

"And why not, for heaven's sake? It doesn't seem so inaccessible to me." Thomas was beginning to lose his temper.

Jacob grabbed a heavy branch and pulled himself up. He looked his adversary in the eye, with a steady, disconcerting gaze, until the younger man was forced to look away. "It can't be mined because it's on the land that's to be kept wild. You know the agreement I made with your father. "Forever Wild." Jacob appeared to grow under the eerie moonlight and midnight shadows. His spare frame straightened and his gnarled hand seemed to join with the branch on which it rested.

Thomas was startled, by Jacob's statement or by the effect he created in him, and hesitated before answering.

"When that agreement was drawn up my father didn't know that there were valuable minerals on his land. The land that's supposed to be kept wild is just that, wilderness, of no use to anyone. Naturally, we expect to use anything of value that we find. After all, it is our land."

Jacob knew he would be in for a fight, but didn't let Thomas guess his misgivings. Instead he only answered, "We'll see what your father has to say about this."

Stuart Lang didn't say much at first. When Thomas came to him with the exciting news, his initial feeling was that of relief. Here was hope that the Company could remain profitable in the Adirondacks, even after the last of the prime timber was gone. If the deposit was as large as his son suspected, he would invest the money he had accumulated over the years from logging and lumbering into a mine. Langston would remain a viable community, its future assured. The families would not have to move or look for work elsewhere. This was their home, and these were the mountains that did, indeed, provide their livelihood.

But despite his elation there was another thought that kept nagging at him, something that he hoped he would not have to face. When Jacob walked into his office, Stuart knew that he would not be able to avoid a confrontation. They were both old men now, and had developed a grudging friendship over the years, a friendship based on respect for each other's integrity and the subtler ties of their common roots. Of the two men, Stuart had changed more since their first meeting, from a restless, ambitious youth to an affluent and benevolent country gentleman. He was the most respected man in Langston. He was known as a fair man who had earned his success and was held up before the children as an example of what hard work, intelligence, and perseverance could achieve, even for immigrants like themselves.

At first glance Jacob was still the same man he had been years ago, his step sure and firm, his eyes dark with anger. He still tied his hair back with a leather thong, but it was steel gray now, and he walked with a slight stoop. Stuart's eyes wavered and dropped before his penetrating gaze, and he was thankful for the heavy desk that separated them.

"What are you doing, Stuart? How can you even consider breaking our agreement?" Jacob challenged without introduction.

"I wish you wouldn't take it like that, Jacob. You don't understand everything that's involved in this."

"I understand one thing, that you're going back on your word so you can make a few more dollars off the land you pledged to keep wild forever," Jacob said, slamming a hard fist down on the desk.

"When we made our agreement I didn't know that there were valuable minerals on this land. A mother lode that you kept secret from me, on my own land!" he added with a touch of righteous indignation.

"That doesn't matter. An agreement is an agreement! You ever seen what a mine can do to the land, Stuart?"

"But it does matter," Stuart said, ignoring his question. "There are some things you don't understand. The lumbering's going to be finished soon, and unless I find something for these people to do, Langston's going to turn into a ghost town. Everybody in this town is dependent on the Company for a living. If we close down, they'll have to leave, pull up the roots they worked so hard to put down."

"Jacob's gaze faltered, his will weakened for a moment, and Stuart pressed his momentary advantage. "You know what these people have had to go through to find a little security, make a home for themselves. You wouldn't want to take all that away for the sake of a few acres of wilderness when there's more left out there than you could ever need."

"Jacob sighed, then looked out the window past the town at the mountains in the distance. He knew he was defeated.

"The only thing I know is that I'll never trust you again on anything, Stuart," he said as he strode out of the office for the last time.

Maggie stirred out of her reverie as a cool breeze rippled across the lake, raising goose bumps on her bare arm. She slipped on her sweater, thankful for its warmth. They had drifted toward the opposite shore and Jake picked up his paddle to correct their course. When he spoke again, it was as if their thoughts had run along parallel paths.

"So you see, Maggie, Stuart and Jacob never spoke two words after that. In two years the mine was in full swing. The blasting chased off the game, until Jacob had to go farther and farther away to hunt. That winter Jacob got to hunting a long ways from home, in strange country. He was tracking a deer, not wanting to come up empty. A big storm was coming down from the north, and he knew they'd be snowed in for a while.

"It was near dark when he finished packing the better part of the buck in his pack basket. He headed back over a frozen stream he'd crossed while tracking the deer. He was hurrying, trying to beat the storm but the extra weight of the deer was too heavy for the ice and he slipped, crashing through. The icy water numbed him as he clambered for the shore. He felt no pain, but his legs wouldn't obey him, wouldn't move. He knew he'd broken his hip. He dragged hisself to shore and lay there, helpless. The storm broke over him, leaving him with no shelter or matches, his pack lost.

"They found Jacob two days later, froze to death, claimed by the land that fed him. Oseetah was thankful Jacob never lived to see the mine tear up the land, or the growing pile of waste rock around it. Patrick continued to guide, learning his sons what his father learned him. But the bad blood between the Langs and Hughes's never healed."

Jake began to paddle to shore as he finished his story.

"Maybe now you know better why we ain't never trusted the Langs and their promises, Maggie."

Chapter 8

Meanwhile, Michael and Rusty stopped above East River Falls for a breather, not because they were especially tired but because Michael had fond memories for that stretch of the river. The dog lapped greedily at the water while his master sat down and leaned against a tree. Michael knew the falls area in great detail yet never failed to be fascinated by it. He had spent many happy childhood afternoons there with Maggie, skipping stones, fishing, or daring each other to take frightening risks near its brink. As children they were drawn and fascinated by its power, by the roar of its water as it fell onto the rocks. They threw sticks and pinecones into the swift current above the falls and watched with held breath as their offerings were carried away, sucked under the white froth of the pool below. They waited, hoping to see the sticks escape from the turbulent pool and float calmly away down the river. But they seldom did. Each child imagined in private terror what it would be like to be carried away and trapped in such a powerful and merciless grip.

Although they feared the power of the waterfall, they were tempted to test themselves against it. In the spring floods trees were often torn up by their roots upriver and carried toward the falls, awkwardly turning and twisting in the raging waters. One spring day a tree became precariously entangled in the rocks and vegetation near the brink. Michael remembered how the tall pine had lodged against the bank, its roots emerging gnarled and exposed from the base. Halfway up the trunk it was wedged against a rock that protruded from the water, but several more feet of the narrowing trunk extended beyond this support, its flopping branches reaching helplessly toward the drop. The children had watched silently for most of the day while they played in the woods. They were intrigued by the tree, never completely taking their eyes off it. They thought the hapless tree would never be swept over the falls. Finally Michael had tested the log tentatively with one foot, then stood on it swaying uncertainly. Maggie said, "I dare you!"

Michael eyed the tree for a moment before replying, wondering how far he dare go. "I will if you will."

"Dared you first."

They exchanged a long, defiant gaze, daring each other to back down, but neither would. Their goal was to go as far out on the tree as each dared, without slipping off and being carried over the falls. After Michael reached his limit and returned, Maggie would try to best him.

Michael started climbing out on the fallen tree, crawling slowly over the slippery bark, making sure of each foot and handhold before proceeding further on the bucking log. Maggie watched from the shore, breathing hard, her eyes fastened on Michael's treacherous progress, a delicious terror and excitement playing in her eyes, her limbs taut with anticipation. Before he had reached the rock, Michael's foot slipped and plunged into the icy water. He pulled it out, his woolen sock and sneaker wet and his determination to continue dampened. He was sure Maggie could go no further, and slowly turned to rejoin her on the bank.

As Maggie started her climb there was only determination on her face, and if she felt any misgivings she hid them. She reached the rock without mishap and turned to present a triumphant face to Michael, but the motion shifted her weight, loosening the tree trunk until it began to buck under the force of the water. Maggie grabbed at the branches nearly losing her balance, and stretched her body along the trunk. The top third of the tree was underwater now, and with it the lower half of her body. Michael froze at the look of terror on her face as she clung to the swaying tree. For a moment he couldn't speak, then began to shout at her, his voice hoarse with fear.

"Start crawling back now, Maggie, but go slow! If you move too fast the tree might come loose! Hurry, before something awful happens!"

But Maggie just stared at him in panic and confusion, unable to move, fingers refusing to loosen their grip. Michael told her to go slow, then he was yelling at her to hurry, but she could do neither. Michael was almost beside himself on the

93

shore. He urged her on for a few long seconds with no result, then cautiously began to crawl out to her. She watched him fascinated, then regaining some of her composure shouted to him in a hoarse whisper: "Go back, Michael, or we'll both go over!"

But he kept crawling, slowly, steadily, his eyes focused on the swaying tree beneath him, avoiding the temptation to look at the terrifying water underneath. He stopped, shut his eyes for a moment and felt the tree lurch. He was certain that the tree had finally come loose. But when he opened his eyes he saw that the tree was still there, hanging perilously close to the edge of the falls. He only needed an arm's length to reach Maggie. In another moment he was prying her fingers loose, and coaxing her towards him. Then she was all right and following him along the tree as he inched his way backwards toward shore.

As they stepped ashore, the river claimed the fallen tree, as if their weight had been the only thing holding it on the rock. The children collapsed on shore, white-faced and trembling. They said nothing, but the look they exchanged needed no words. They lay on the ground until their breathing slowed and the color returned to their cheeks. They headed home reluctantly, and before parting they hugged each other. It was a quick, spontaneous hug but it made them both turn away in embarrassment.

Michael shook his head at the memory of their foolhardiness, at the unnecessary risks of their early youth. He was much more cautious now; probably Maggie was too, although she didn't seem to have changed as much as he had.

Rusty ran ahead to the suspension bridge, then stopped uncertainly as the wooden slats began to undulate beneath him. Michael laughed and reassured the dog. "It's O.K. Rusty, you can go," and the two crossed to the other side. Michael watched the clear water below them, an occasional silver gleam revealing the fish it contained, but his thoughts returned to the abandoned mine. Its story was an important part of the history of Langston, allowing the town to survive after the lumbering became less profitable.

It took a couple of years to develop the mine and build ore processing facilities. Lumbering didn't wind down right away, and additional men were needed to work the mine, so Thomas Lang brought in more immigrants, this time some Poles along with the Irish.

The galena ore was brought to the surface, then processed to separate it into its elements. The lead was then transported to the city where it was sold to manufacturers of ammunition, lead pipe, and glass.

By the turn of the century, Thomas was ready to retire. His eldest son, Randolph, assumed control of the Company, while Richard, ten years younger, was still learning his way. When war broke out in Europe the demand for lead rose sharply as ammunition production geared up. Some of the men from Langston were called up to fight, depleting manpower needed in the mine. Among the ones who joined up were Richard Lang and John Ryan, two life long friends who were learning the operation of the Company together. John was to become a foreman when he returned, and Richard would assist his brother, Randolph, who stayed behind to run the mine during those critical times.

During their year and a half abroad, the two young men matured as they saw their companions wounded and killed with lead bullets much like the ones produced with Langston lead. But despite the war, not everything was grim in Europe. During one leave, they visited Paris. There was drinking and dancing nightly in the bistros and dance halls, whose gray and crumbling facades spoke of sadness and neglect. Perhaps because of the outward drabness, the women dressed in bright, colorful clothes, lending an air of hope to the city, willfully defying the moral climate.

Richard Lang saw this and thought about it.

"This city sure looks like it needs some fixing up. Most of these houses could use a good coat of paint," Richard remarked.

John agreed. "I wonder what it's like back home. Probably not much better. There hasn't been much time or money for anything but the war, so I heard."

The two were silent but each thought about home, and the work they had left behind.

Richard broke the silence. "Something's been worrying me, John. Father writes that once the war is over, the demand for lead will go down and we may have to cut production."

John looked at his friend knowingly. "I've been thinking about that. We need to find another market for the lead, and I think I have an idea."

Richard leaned forward, as John continued. "Have you noticed how people around here love color? How the women love to dress up and party? Well, I'm willing to bet it's the same at home. Once the war is over, people will want some color in their lives again, and I think I know how to give it to them. Paint!"

Richard's face glowed with excitement. "Paint," he repeated to himself. "Why of course. It'll be the perfect thing."

As they had predicted, the demand for lead decreased sharply after the war as other industries converted from war materials production to manufacturing civilian goods. The mine had a capacity that greatly exceeded the reduced demand for its lead. It was the right time for the company to branch out, to develop a new market.

They started first by producing tough, flexible white lead. They then began manufacturing red lead, used in industry, for corrosion protection. In time they added chrome yellows and oranges that produced a wide range of hues in different combinations.

Richard Lang threw himself into paint manufacturing with the kind of enthusiasm and optimism that guaranteed the venture's success. While Richard became the leader of the paint operation, John Ryan provided the imagination and creativity. John designed the poster and proposed the name that was to captivate the attention of the new civilian market.

The poster captured the beauty of the Adirondacks in all its brilliant detail: a rainbow trout jumped below a waterfall, its multicolored skin shimmering in the autumn sunlight; bold hues of sugar maple foliage lined the stream's banks and white-peaked mountains towered in the background. The picture evoked a feeling of natural beauty that people came to associate with the colors of their paint. Across the picture were written words that summarized everything that the scene symbolized, including the origin of the paint. It read: "Opalescent Paints." The words were painted in rainbow hues, one pigment blending into the next, just as the colors of nature were delicately mixed. Before long, Opalescent Paints was known throughout the region, the poster reproduced in miniature on every can that was sold. Each customer felt that he was bringing a part of the Adirondacks' beauty into his own home when he painted with Opalescent Paints.

Over the years as the yield of the mine declined, the paint factory grew and generated a larger share of the Company's profits. By the time the mine closed, the future of the Company and of Langston had been entrusted to paint.

Michael continued along the river trail, keeping the river to his left until its junction with Upper Twin Brook. The most direct trail up Marcy followed along the brook, but before taking the familiar path, Michael paused. Rusty stopped too, and stood near his master sniffing the air expectantly. To their right stood the barely identifiable remains of the old logging camp. It hadn't been used for decades, and the forest was slowly regaining the land.

Michael paused as he envisioned life in the logging camp a hundred years before, remembering the stories he had heard from his grandfather, who had heard them from his father. What kind of men were they, who could spend the frigid winters of the North Country laboring in the open, pitting themselves against the forces of nature? They must have been rugged men accustomed to heavy physical labor and harsh lives. He remembered his grandfather talking about them with obvious longing, although he himself had been a little boy when the lumber camps had finally been abandoned. But Grandpa Morrison knew a lot about them, or so it seemed to Michael, since he had wanted to be a logger himself. It didn't work out that way though. Mining had replaced logging, bringing with it changes, making obsolete many of the old ways. As a child, Michael had been fascinated by stories of the river drivers, his youthful imagination caught up in their daring and fearlessness. In spring, when melting ice made the water run quickly, the river drivers drove or pushed the logs down river to the sawmill. Often the river became completely jammed with logs and had to be blasted free with dynamite. Crosses along the river still marked forgotten river drivers' graves.

Michael stood in the now quiet clearing, listening to the past around him. Rusty sniffed the bushes growing around the few rotten logs that remained of the buildings, disturbing grasshoppers among the tall grasses. A Monarch butterfly flitted among the milkweed blossoms, and the only sounds were those of insects humming and crickets chirping in the warming sun. The effect was timeless and peaceful, and Michael thought he heard the sounds of past lives that once filled the clearing. Beyond the sun-warmed grasses and young saplings he saw drifts of snow, giant white pines, snowshoes, axes, and the breath of horses rising in frosty clouds. He saw the men, their beards covered with white crystals as their breath exploded with each stroke of their axes. They were rugged and determined men, their lives a series of demanding tasks.

The five log buildings that had made up the camp had been almost completely reclaimed by the land; only a few rotting logs remained to remind the hiker of man's one time habitation.

Across the river was Twin Brook lean-to, a shelter he used frequently on his recent hikes with Rusty, as well as years ago with Maggie. Without encouragement the dog trotted across the familiar shallow place in the water and lay down in the shade of the lean-to, sure that his master would follow. Rusty thumped his tail on the ground and waited patiently for Michael to join him. Michael laughed and shouted across to the dog, "All-right boy, we can stop here if you like. There's no one expecting us anywhere."

The shelter was cool and fragrant with the combined odors of earth and pine. Michael placed his pack against the back wall and spread his jacket on the pine needles that covered the floor. The thick layer of needles was like a springy mattress. He leaned back against the pack and lit his pipe, allowing the delicious waves of relaxation from fresh air and physical exercise to flow throughout his body. For a while his dilemma was forgotten and he was supremely contented. He was aware of the mechanical tapping of a woodpecker, the sighing of the tall pines in a gentle breeze, and the beam of sunlight penetrating a crack in the lean-to wall, warming a spot on his leg. A sphinx moth crawled up the side of the lean-to, its gray patterned wings matching the bark. Two bluet damselflies mated on a blade of grass, their shimmering bodies undulating as they obeyed the laws of propagation. After a while Rusty came over and lay down, placing his head on Michael's shoulder, begging for attention. Michael opened his eyes and smiled, stroking the dog's silky head. "You did have to bring me back to reality, didn't you, Rusty? Well, I guess we do have to go on sooner or later, though I wouldn't mind stopping everything for a bit."

They sat there a while longer looking out the lean-to at the river. Michael was thinking of the mine, of the story his father had told him recently.

"It was in the late 30's that the mine became depleted and shut down. I was very young then, not yet in my teens," his father went on. "At first no one paid much attention to the old mine after it was abandoned. It was located far enough from Langston that it didn't offend anyone. The paint factory was thriving and the residents were glad of its source of income; none thought of complaining about anything connected with the Company. The townspeople were mostly descendants of the original group of immigrants who came to work in the lumber camps, the sawmill, and the mine so many years ago. They were industrious blue collar workers who depended on the Company for their living. The Company provided them with security, and they were ignorant of most things outside of the immediate vicinity. If the mine-site was an eyesore, it was ignored and avoided, something that was a necessary part of their lives.

"The Hughes's were the only ones who ever complained about the mine. That may be because they were probably the only Langston family that wasn't dependent on the Company in some way. They kept bringing up the old argument between Jacob Hughes and Stuart Lang, in which Jacob insisted that the land where the mine was located be kept forever wild. He claimed that Stuart had gone back on his word. And I suppose he had, although he set aside a larger piece of land to replace the land lost to mining. But I guess the Hughes's felt that if the Langs could go back on their word once, then none of the wilderness land was safe, so the doubt and the bitterness smoldered.

"There were two Hughes brothers when the mine was abandoned; Jake's father, Sean, and Brian. They always pointed to the fact that their great grandfather Jacob's predictions had come true, that the land around the mine had been laid waste and spoiled forever. They argued that the abandoned mine-site was a scar that remained to remind them of the wounds that development of the wilderness caused. And so the arguments continued, with blame and harsh words, though the Hughes's' complaints never convinced the Company to clean up the mine-site.

"At least not until some years had passed. I remember it so clearly, even this many years later. My brother, Harry used to play with Brian's daughter, Maura, who was about his age. They fished a lot and the woods near the Hughes cabin became their playground. One day their wanderings took them to the mine-site, and they decided to explore the mineshaft. It would be great fun. As children we often pretended that we were cave explorers, and the mine was nearly as good as a real cave.

"When they didn't come home that night the whole town went searching for them, but it wasn't until the next day that someone suggested the mineshaft. We knew right away that something terrible had happened when they found Maura's teddy bear at the entrance. The old rotten beams had given way and there had been a cave-in, trapping the children underground. It took two days to dig them out. They found Maura Hughes dead, and your Uncle Harry nearly so. Harry was rushed to the Company clinic and treated, and within a week he was as good as new. It was unfortunate that Maura was killed, for more reasons than one. If she had survived and been saved by the doctor at the clinic, the Hughes's might have softened up a bit, not been so adamantly against the company.

"After the accident something had to be done about the mine. My father was a foreman at the Company, and he worked out a hasty solution. No one objected, seeing as it was his son that was nearly killed as well. The mineshaft would be filled in with waste to prevent accidents in the future. Actually, it worked out well for the Langs; they needed a place to dump the waste from the increasingly productive factory, and the townspeople dumped their trash there as well. But the solution only aggravated the Hughes's' bitterness. They not only lost a child to the mine, but the land they had fought over for so many years was being increasingly desecrated by the accumulating waste."

It was nearly four o'clock when Michael finished his musings and continued along Upper Twin Brook. They still had about three miles of steep climbing before reaching Uphill lean-to, and climbing in the dark was foolish and unnecessary.

Chapter 9

Maggie shifted her pack as she paused before the suspension bridge. She had brought a lot of gear, probably too much, because she didn't know how long she would be in the mountains. If she couldn't find Michael, she would have to depend on herself, and she knew it was safer to be overprepared. She remembered what it was like to have others dependent on her in the wilderness, looking to her to look after them if problems arose. She had been young, though well prepared when she became certified as an Adirondack guide.

After graduation from college she returned home to be with Jake; at the time she thought for good. She had turned down a job offer from a city newspaper, feeling uncomfortable in a setting so alien to her, wanting the familiarity and comfort of their cabin on the river. At least that's what she told Jake, and he didn't question her, wisely knowing that she had to work things out on her own.

But there had been another reason for running home, an unhappy affair with a fellow student who had disappointed her. Only after spending lonely months in the mountains hiking or guiding occasional parties, was she able to level with herself. She could never have been happy with him because he was not the man she wanted. She wanted the friend she grew up with, the boy who shared her interests, loved the river and the mountains as passionately as she did, and roamed the wilderness with her. She wanted Michael. When she finally admitted her feelings, she stopped and laughed at herself with honesty and a touch of bitterness. All these years she had been looking for Michael, the Michael she had lost to Becky years ago, the Michael she could never have. They were married now and living in the city, and she avoided them. Once she understood herself she no longer needed to run. Although the mountains would always be her home she was not yet ready to come home for good; she had to get some experience elsewhere first. So she returned to the city, but with a new understanding of herself that complemented the deep love of her beginnings.

She stopped on the bridge and looked over the tops of the sugar maples that stood between her and Popple Hill. The summer morning was golden with sunshine, and only an odd rusty leaf hinted of approaching autumn. As she stood with her face to the sky, a familiar V formation of Canada geese, on the move earlier than usual, flew overhead, their nasal honking heralding the changing season. As confident as she was of her own abilities in the woods, she still wished for the companionship of a dog. Now that she was back to stay, she was seriously thinking of getting a replacement for Old Calamity. A dog would be good for Jake too, to keep him company when she was in town.

Maggie knew that Michael would follow the Opalescent River trail at least until it split at Upper Twin Brook, and she walked along without hesitation. As she passed Dudley Brook, memories of a trip up this stream to Loon Pond intruded upon her thoughts. She and Michael were only ten when Jake took them on the trip in search of loons. They had taken the guideboat, as usual, packed with gear and food, and Old Calamity. Only Calamity wasn't old then, wasn't even Calamity yet. He was just six months, a retriever of mixed parentage, with floppy ears and unpredictable personality. Mostly, he played with the children and was affectionate with Jake, but sometimes when out in the woods with them some ancient hunting instinct would seize him. He would put his nose to the ground and follow some mysterious scent, heedless of any orders shouted at him. He was not trained yet, so Jake was reluctant to take him on a trip where patience and silence were required. But Maggie wouldn't leave him behind, and the dog joined them eagerly.

The dog traveled well in the bottom of the boat sitting between Maggie and Jake, his senses alert to every change in the stream and the woods around them. When a trout jumped a few feet away, the dog leaped back startled, rocking the boat and making the children laugh at his intent expression as he searched the water for the elusive fish.

Jake told stories as he rowed them up the Opalescent River, stories of the Indians he had heard from his own father and grandfather. Maggie was proud of her Indian origins and exasperated that so little of it was apparent in her own physical makeup. She often sat before a mirror twisting her unruly red hair into braids, wishing for black eyes and dark complexion instead of the gray eyed and freckled face that looked back at her.

They had made camp by Loon Pond, near a stand of northern white cedars that edged its shores. Jake showed them how to use the shredded outer bark and the soft wood of the cedar to start fires, something he had learned from his grandfather who learned it from the Indians. After dinner they brewed tea from the flattened, scale-like needles of the cedar. Jake explained that the cedar was also called arborvitae, tree of life, because it had saved the lives of many sailors, protecting them from scurvy once they learned to drink its tea. They let the fire go out as they lay in their sleeping bags, listening to the soothing sound of waves lapping against the shore. The last thing Maggie remembered before falling asleep was the long drawn-out wail of a solitary loon.

At dawn the next day they were paddling softly along the shore, trying to conceal themselves among the marshy vegetation, searching for loons. As they emerged from the marsh into clear water, Jake quickly stopped the boat. He pointed to a nest built of reeds, grasses, and mud, resting on the edge of the shore, within a few feet of the boat. The nest contained two olive green eggs, but no loon. "We mustn't disturb the nest," he whispered. "Just hope we didn't frighten the mother away." Softly, he rowed into a concealing screen of cattails, then pulled in the oars and settled down to wait.

The dog lay still on the bottom of the boat, although his senses were alert to the myriad signs of life around them. They ate jerky and pemmican for their breakfast as they waited for the loons. The sun was beginning to burn the mist off the pond when they heard a loon laugh nearby. The dog sat up sniffing the air, his floppy ears straining to point upwards. They heard an answering call from the other side of the pond. The first loon appeared a short distance from them and began to swim toward the distant call. Soundlessly Jake eased the boat out of the reeds and followed the graceful bird.

As they neared the source of the call, Michael pointed to a group of eight loons ahead on the water. Jake pulled the boat behind a thick clump of reeds as the soft hoots of the loons reached them. They were close enough to see the red eyes and the white, shell-like markings on the loons' backs and necks. "Their eyes are red so they can see under water," Jake whispered. "You don't usually see this many loons together, except when they're getting ready to migrate."

Suddenly, one of the birds dove vertically into the water, vanishing beneath the surface. Hardly a ripple marked his disappearance. "He must have drowned," Maggie said after several minutes, but Jake shook his head. Finally the loon reappeared, rising up on the water and stretching its wings to their full five feet. "He's drying himself. They have very heavy bones, so they can dive real deep and stay there for a long time," Jake explained.

The group began to swim toward them, their bodies gliding through the water, barely disturbing the smooth surface. When the loons were within a few feet of them the dog rose from the bottom of the boat, and overcome by some primitive urge, coiled his muscles for a mighty leap toward the leading bird. Maggie lunged for him just as he hurled himself into the water. As the boat turned over, the birds scattered with a panicked whirr of wings and aggressive laughter. Two large males rose above the water and began to dance frantically with cocked wings, emitting a high pitched yodel. Jake hurriedly righted the boat, hauled in the children and dripping dog, and began to row away. "We gotta leave fast, so we won't scare the loons. If we don't, they might leave and never come back." After that the dog became known as Calamity, and was forced to undergo field training as punishment.

Maggie smiled at her memories of growing up, at the security of living with Jake and sharing his love and knowledge of the Adirondacks. And the warm, easy closeness with Michael that had held them together for so long made it impossible to think of him as no longer a part of her life. But, time changes everything, she thought, and smiled ruefully at the old cliché. Jake was ill and growing older, and Michael had been distant from her for a long time. Until his recent return, that is. Strange, how in the past few months, some of the old closeness between them seemed to return. But she knew she shouldn't delude herself. It could never be the same, for many reasons, especially Becky. He belonged to her now, was part of Becky's world, not hers. Even though at times she detected a feeling of dissatisfaction in him, even an attraction towards her. It was probably a longing for his youth, for the old carefree times they had shared. Maggie shook herself, willfully redirecting her thoughts. There were other things to consider now, work to do, the problem they shared that must be solved. She would be content to be friends again.

Maggie hesitated as the trail split into two branches, uncertain which Michael had taken. Both trails led to Marcy. The right trail followed Upper Twin Brook, the steepest and most direct route to Marcy. The river trail continued along the Opalescent to Hanging Spear Falls, Flowed Lands, and Lake Colden before rejoining the Upper Twin Brook Trail. Was Michael pushing to reach the summit or was he following the longer but more scenic river trail?

Just ahead on the left was the old lean-to, and she decided to check it for clues. She saw the tracks of a dog and a man's boot in the soft earth in front of the shelter, and a reddish-gold tuft of hair caught on a protruding nail. She was sure it was Rusty's. A small plug of partly burned tobacco had been spilled on the floor, its aroma the same as the one Michael favored. She sat down to think, but an odd feeling of excitement seized her, and she couldn't remain still for long. She had the feeling that she was making contact, that she was getting close to the answer to her questions. And there was something else mixed with her feelings, something less clearly defined or easily accepted. She started off in the direction of Flowed Lands, but soon noticed that despite the muddy trail, the tracks had ceased. She frowned, annoyed for a moment at making a mistake in the woods. She retraced her steps to Upper Twin Brook Trail and within a few yards found the sign she was looking for--dog spoor and the familiar tread of a boot along the path. Confident now, she walked on at a steady pace.

The climb became fairly steep as the hardwoods gave way to conifers. Footing was sometimes tricky, the occasionally slanting corduroys wet and slippery. After about three miles of steady hiking the trail leveled off. Level walking was a relief to Maggie. She was starting to get a blister on her right foot. She stopped, removed her boot and attended to the swollen blister. With a sterile needle from her first aid kit, she punctured it, drained it and dressed it for protection. Relieved, she looked up at Cliff Mountain. Its slopes had been logged before she was born, and were now covered with a second growth of birch, mountain ash, and other sun-loving hardwoods. She wondered if she would live to see the next growth, the eventual return of the firs and spruces that preferred shade.

She put on a dry pair of socks and her boots and continued on the now level trail. Soon the trail headed gently down over more corduroys, rejoining the Opalescent Trail. A little over a hundred yards past the junction was Uphill lean-to.

She saw that Uphill lean-to had been used recently. A fire had been thoroughly doused, the ground still wet around it. She smiled, remembering how particular Michael was about putting out fires, unlike many modern campers. Inside, pine needles had been piled up for a bed, something they had learned to do after a few uncomfortable nights on rocky ground. Michael had spent the night there, she was certain. He was moving slowly, probably without a specific goal, just wanting to be alone with his thoughts as she had often wanted to be. She felt she understood his need, and part of her was reluctant to intrude, but she had questions that needed answers.

After half a mile the trail to Marcy took a sharp turn to the right and climbed steeply alongside Feldspar Brook. The trail ahead went to Indian Falls and Adirondack Loj, but Michael had said he was going up Marcy. The Opalescent gained much of its strength from Feldspar Brook. Here the river was strewn with glacial erratics, boulders dropped during the ice age and differing in composition from the rocks around them. There were no fish in Feldspar Brook. Its grade was too steep, the water too acid, and the spring runoff too violent to sustain the aquatic insect life on which brook trout fed.

Maggie continued toward Lake Tear-of-the-Clouds. She had always loved that name. It sounded like the lyrical names the Indians used in their legends. She checked the Lake Tear lean-to. It was empty and cold. Michael usually avoided it, with its swarms of mosquitoes that came up from the lake on warm summer nights.

It was just a gentle quarter mile hike to Four Corners lean-to, the last shelter this side of Marcy. Michael would either be camping there or on the other side of the mountain. As she approached the lean-to she could see signs of habitation. A short-handled axe rested on a stump, its blade buried in the wood, and she recognized the plaid shirt hanging on a nail at the entrance. Her heart beat a little faster as she came closer, expecting Rusty to run to her with his exuberant welcome. But there was no sign of the dog or his master; only their belongings advertised their presence somewhere nearby.

A blackened coffeepot and frying pan, a cup, a plate, and a set of utensils were neatly stacked on the entrance log of the lean-to. Michael's bedroll and pack were inside, and a canvas bag probably filled with food hung from the branch of a nearby tree. This was one precaution they almost always took when camping. Maggie smiled as she remembered the time they did forget, many years ago, and were visited by a hungry black bear in the night. The bear dragged their packs out into the clearing and tore them apart while she and Michael cowered in the furthest corner of the lean-to. After satisfying himself on their provisions, the bear lumbered off into the forest.

She removed her pack and unlaced her boots. Most likely Michael had climbed Marcy and would return soon. They had often made camp at Four Corners lean-to, then climbed Marcy without a heavy load and returned before dark. Darkness seemed to be falling earlier, she thought, then glanced at the sky. Storm clouds were moving in from the west, the weather changing rapidly as often happened in the high peaks. Well, that only meant that Michael would return sooner. She made sure there was dry wood in the shelter in anticipation of the coming rain, then settled down to rest and wait.

When Michael had risen that morning the sun shone brightly, promising a beautiful view from the top of Marcy. He had made a cup of coffee then quickly packed, not forgetting to douse the coals of the fire. Rusty wouldn't let him eat until he prepared a bowl of dried dog food, moistened with a little water from the heated pot. Rusty was finished before Michael could sit down to his breakfast of hard roll, dried fruit and cheese.

They hiked quickly and silently to Lake Tear. He paused at Feldspar Brook, the last source of water on the trail. Here was the highest source of the Hudson. Lake Tear's waters flowed through a marsh, emerging as Feldspar Brook, the water starting on its long journey to New York Harbor, far to the south. Lake Tear was a rapidly aging body of water. It was becoming dry land, perhaps even in his lifetime. He couldn't imagine Lake Tear not existing some day, although the change was taking place before his eyes. With every heavy rain and spring thaw, more silt and plant debris washed down from the slopes of Marcy and Skylight into the shallow basin. Each year the reeds and grasses inched farther out from the shore. Eventually they would carpet the surface, turning the lake into a marsh. He stepped over the thin ribbon of cold mountain water, his boots sinking into the soft ground.

He shed most of his equipment at Four Corners lean-to, not wanting to carry anything extra the last steep mile to the peak. He unpacked his backpack, setting his mess kit out to dry. He was hot in the late morning sun, so he took off his plaid overshirt and hung it on a nail to air. He was sure he'd be back well before he would need it again. In his haste, he almost forgot to hang the food bag in a tree.

Michael wanted to be at the peak, to feel the wind whip at his clothes and hair, to know that he was the highest person for miles around. Looking down from the top of Marcy let him see the world from another perspective, at a distance from which nothing could touch him. Above all, it gave him a feeling of peace.

After leaving Four Corners the going became tougher and steeper, the trail less clear. He was on the last leg of his climb, and he was glad that he had kept himself in shape. Mostly spruce and hemlock surrounded him now, and the trees were stunted and farther apart. A large raven croaked at him from the top of a weather-bent branch, its harsh tones whipped away by the wind. Rusty bristled at the rude challenge, a low growl in his chest. Michael savored the loneliness of the mountain, something he treasured after his years in the city.

Just below the top dwarf balsam were the only trees remaining, a stunted caricature of their cousins found at lower elevations. The top of the mountain was in the arctic zone. There were no trees here, only rocks and shrubs, and tiny, delicate Alpine plants clinging to the rocks with a show of tenacity and determination. Most were past their bloom but he recognized them nonetheless--the rust-speckled, leathery leaves of the Lapland Rosebay, the thick clusters of Diapensia leaves, the evergreen leaves of Labrador Tea with their dense, brown, woolly coating underneath. He saw tufts of cotton grass or Hare's Tail, although its cottony seed heads had long ago been dispersed by the wind.

At the peak he climbed on a rock and looked down at the valleys and forests below. To the southeast lay Panther Gorge. Looking into the gorge was like looking down from the top of a roller coaster. Sheer rock extended down as far as he could see. No trees or shrubs to break one's fall. The wind pulled at his hair and clothes, drawing him forward, towards the drop. With an effort he looked away.

In the distance, streams and ponds were but small, reflecting mirrors. He could see no sign of man in any direction, and here, with the wilderness surrounding him, the problems of the people he had left behind became less important. He sat there for nearly an hour feeling the keen air on his skin and listening to the incessant howling of the wind. The trees around him grew as they had for eons, and the rocks crumbled and were rebuilt with the regular rhythm of time. Here nothing seemed to change, yet slowly, imperceptibly, everything did. He felt sadness, then an acceptance of the inevitability of change, an acceptance of his role in it. Like it or not, change would come to Langston far quicker than it did on the mountain, and he was responsible for the direction of the change. He would follow his conscience, even though the outcome wasn't clear yet. Somewhere in the depths of his being he knew that in the next few days he would know what he needed to do.

"It's going to be all right, Rusty," he said and patted the dog lying next to him. Then he glanced at the sky, and sat up, startled. Storm clouds were moving in quickly, blocking the late afternoon sun, lightening streaking across the rapidly darkening sky..

"How could I have ignored the storm warnings? There's no way I can get to camp before this storm breaks, but we'd better get off the mountain fast," he muttered to himself. Rusty, sensing his master's anxiety, got up expectantly. Michael checked the sky one last time, then started down the trail at a trot. Being at the top of a mountain during a thunderstorm could be fatal. He was annoyed at himself for abandoning caution and good sense, for allowing his thoughts to distract him. There was nothing he could do now but get off the mountain as quickly as possible. He had brought no supplies or tools with him, expecting to return to camp well before dark. He was going to get wet and cold.

In a few minutes the clouds closed over his head and darkness fell. A low rumbling filled the air. Suddenly the rain came, in large, heavy drops, striking his face with cold, stinging regularity. He hurried with head down, swearing under his breath as a rivulet began to flow down the back of his neck under his shirt. Rain turned the ground muddy and brown as it struck and carried some of the soil downhill with it. Soon the trail was impossible to follow, slippery and unstable underfoot. He tried to stay on rocky ground but that wasn't always possible, and he slopped his way through the deepening mud. Still he continued, hurrying toward the shelter of the lean-to and the comfort of his dry clothes.

Suddenly the ground gave way under his feet and he was hurtling down the side of the mountain, blindly grabbing for something to slow his slide. Then there was nothing under his feet, and his stomach lurched in panic. He only fell for a second or so, landing heavily, his legs jammed into a crevice in the rock. He wiped the mud from his eyes with his right hand, then tried to free his left arm, which was wedged against a rocky wall. He leaned back from the wall, reaching his right hand out to brace himself. He felt nothing but air, could see nothing in the dark and the driving rain. Suddenly a bolt of lightning illuminated the scene around him. In the flash that lasted no more than a second, he saw Panther Gorge yawning under him. In horror he realized that he had fallen through a gap in the cliff. He had lodged in a narrow cleft that closed below him, gripping his legs. His left shoulder rested against the rock wall. He dared not shift his weight to free his arm. He felt overhead with his free hand, encountered nothing but smooth stone made slippery by the rain. On his right the wind whipped up at him from the gorge, driving the cold water through his clothes.

The cleft through which he fell was some fifteen feet above him. He could make out Rusty's head, watching him and whining softly. Willing his panic under control, he called to the dog: "It's O.K. boy, I'll find a way out. Just let me think a moment."

Michael forced himself to think slowly, clearly, logically. He spoke his thoughts aloud, concentrating on them. "There must be a way out; there is always a way out. If I calm down, I'll find it," he lectured himself while feeling around for a ledge with his feet. Then he explored the walls of his prison with his free hand, searching for a handhold, a root or a branch, anything. But there was only the hard, dripping rock that defied his grasp, infuriating him with its slickness. After a quarter of an hour he gave up and rested his throbbing head against the cold stone. The pain eased somewhat, and he realized that he hadn't even been consciously aware of it. He touched his aching forehead and his hand came away bloody. He stared at the blood, his mind blank, despairing. Could it be that there was no way out? It happened almost every summer to some inexperienced, overconfident camper or hiker. But how could it happen to him? He was always so careful, so methodical. He had known this mountain all his life, why had he let his guard down, then compounded it by rushing? He felt around him once more, then looked up at the opening. Rusty was still watching expectantly, lost without Michael's direction.

"Go Rusty! Get help!" Michael commanded the dog. The dog stood up and began to pad uncertainly back and forth before the opening. Michael summoned all the authority he could into his voice and commanded the dog once more: "Go, Rusty, get help!" This time the dog turned and headed down the trail, leaving Michael totally alone. It was his only chance. Michael tried not to think how long Rusty would take to find someone. They hadn't passed any hikers on the trail; he would probably have to go back to Langston for help. And with the trail so wet and slippery it would take someone even longer to get back to him. Michael closed his eyes and tried to blank out his thoughts. He could do nothing but wait.

Chapter 10

Maggie had been in the lean-to for an hour when the storm broke. At first she was concerned that Michael hadn't returned before the rain started, but he must have sought shelter elsewhere from the storm. The beating of rain on the open roof and the aroma of wet earth and leaves were soothing to her. In another hour the storm was over. Great glistening drops hung from the branches and leaves of an overhanging tree outside the lean-to. A rustling sound from the trail up Marcy caught her attention. Was it Michael, returning wet and tired from the half-shelter of a tree? The sound was moving nearer, and she sat up, expectant. In a moment Rusty ran into the clearing and stopped to shake his wet, reddish coat. He looked around, and seeing Maggie, eagerly bounded into the lean-to.

She stroked the dog's ears, waiting for Michael, expecting him to be following behind. Five long minutes passed without him. She looked more carefully at Rusty and noticed that he was acting strangely. He refused to settle down and alternated between running out onto the trail as though looking for his master, and returning to tug at her sleeve as he did when he wanted her to play with him. "What's keeping Michael, boy?" she murmured.

Once again Rusty ran toward the trail, and this time she followed, expecting to see Michael's familiar figure walking towards her. But there was no one within sight, and the dog seemed to be leading her somewhere. Suddenly, with a flash of insight, she knew that something was wrong. It only took her a moment to decide what to do. Calling to Rusty, she ran back to camp and started throwing things into her small day pack. Axe, knife, rope, first-aid kit, matches, canteen, flashlight, a blanket, some dried fruit and a few granola bars. In a minute she was ready, following the dog up the trail in the fading twilight, trying to make time over the muddy terrain. She needed to find Michael before night fell; even in good light the wet trail was risky.

It was nearly dark when Rusty veered off the trail and disappeared into the night. For a moment her heart stood still.

Had Michael fallen? She remembered the steep drop into Panther Gorge. She heard Rusty barking nearby and reached for her flashlight. Cautiously, she felt her way through the low brush and loose rocks to the edge of the cliff. As she looked out into the total darkness, she heard Michael's voice. He was trying to reassure the dog, but his voice shook.

Maggie called to him quickly, undoing her pack as she spoke: "Michael, I'm here. Rusty found me."

There was a moment's silence, then his voice, a mixture of hope and disbelief, reached her from a somewhere below. "Maggie? Is that really you? For a minute I thought I was hallucinating!"

She talked to him as she worked, uncoiling the rope, looking for a sturdy tree or boulder to tie it to. "Are you hurt, Michael? Can you slip a rope under your arms?"

"I'm not hurt. At least I don't think I am, but I am stuck. Toss down the rope and I'll try to tie it around my chest."

Maggie attached the rope to a dwarf balsam, in the process driving a splinter of wood into her left palm. Ignoring the pain, she then tested the rope with her weight. Satisfied that the tree was firmly rooted between the rocks, she threw the free end of the rope down to Michael. The hard wet rock bit into her knees and the sliver was making her palm throb, but her thoughts were on Michael and she held her breath while he struggled with the rope.

Rusty wagged his tail, running between her and the cliff face, expecting a reward. "You did your job well, Rusty. Later you'll get all the treats you want, but now I've got to get Michael off this cliff."

"Ready," Michael called to her. She sat down, bracing her feet against a rock outcrop. She wrapped the rope around her back and using both arms pulled in the slack, carefully increasing the tension. Together they would try what neither could accomplish alone. Slowly Michael found a handhold, and with Maggie supporting most of his weight, he was crawling up the cliff face. She was leaning back now, away from the edge. The sound of his labored breathing, the changing tension and the increasing length of rope at her feet were her only clues to his progress.

Her mind raced crazily as she sat, straining with all her strength, frantically trying to gauge the amount of rope she had retrieved, edging him upward, thinking of all that could go wrong. He could slip and pull them both over the edge. Or the knot could give way and he could fall, who knows how far. In her imagination she heard his hollow scream trailing off in the darkness, and shuddered. Sudden panic nearly forced her to turn to check the knot she had tied, but the cool, rational Maggie sat still, pulling in the rope, knowing she couldn't move until he was out. Half the night seemed to pass before his hand appeared. In another instant he was over the edge and lay panting on the wet ground beside her. She fell next to him, nearly as exhausted.

In a minute she was up again, kneeling next to him, examining his scrapes in the beam of her flashlight, searching out his bruises with her own bruised hands. He lay with his eyes closed, exhausted, giving himself over to her care. She checked his forehead first. His hair was matted with blood, but since the bleeding had stopped, cleaning it could wait. He could have a concussion, got to keep him awake, she thought. Her numb fingers struggled with the buttons on his shirt, as she laid bare his chest beneath the narrow beam of light. A large red welt ran across his left side where he scraped against the rock as he fell. She stared at it as her hand brushed the light covering of hair hesitantly, hovering over the injury. At the lightness of her touch his eyes opened, searched her face, but it was hidden in darkness. She pulled back, turned off the light, drawing into herself. Rusty lay down next to his master, tail anxiously thumping the ground.

"The bruises don't seem to be too bad. But you're all wet and tired, and we'd better be careful you don't catch pneumonia.

You may have a concussion, so we've got to keep you awake. Can you walk?"

"I think so." He got to his knees, and although dizzy, managed to stand up.

"Sit under that overhang while I make a fire," she directed.

He obeyed, shivering, while she gathered some squaw wood and coaxed a small fire to life. "We'd better stay here until daylight. Going back down in the dark would be asking for more trouble," she said.

He nodded, too tired for words, as she spread the blanket over their shoulders. Her hand brushed his damp hair and the denim shirt that stuck to his skin in wet patches, and unexpectedly her tears came.

"Oh, Michael, I thought you were dead. It was so awful, I couldn't imagine life without you." The words came from somewhere deep inside her, from a secret place hidden for so long. The sensible Maggie was shocked and tried to stop the flow, but a different, emotional Maggie was taking over her words. Overwhelmed, she no longer cared. Her whole body shook with great, gulping sobs as she sat, arms clasped around her knees, rocking gently next to him.

He reached for her shakily, pulled her to him in a hug as he had so many years ago by the waterfall. But this time neither pulled away in embarrassment. Her trembling slowed in his returning warmth. "You know, Maggie, hearing your voice was a miracle. But I wasn't really surprised, not in the deepest part of me. I was almost expecting you. Strange, after all these years, that I should still be expecting you to be there for me." He paused, frowning at the strangeness of his thought. "And there was something else. I prayed that before I died I would see you once more." He stopped, embarrassed and confused, then turned back to look into her eyes. They were the same clear, honest gray he had known and trusted, but now there was something in them he hadn't seen before. It was as if he were seeing into her for the first time, and what he saw was soft and warm and inviting.

He searched in his pocket for a moment and brought out something small, indistinguishable in the darkness. He held it closer to the fire, and she recognized the polished golden rock encircled by bands of amber. It was her tiger eye, the one she had prized above all in their rock collection. She reached for it, caressed the smooth stone, enjoying its texture between her fingers.

"I've carried it in my pocket ever since you gave it to me before my first hockey game in high school. It's always brought me luck, just as it brought you to me tonight," he said.

She didn't answer, only continued to gaze at the stone in her palm, its fiery eye hypnotizing her.

The damp wood sputtered in the fire throwing off sparks that rivaled the reddish glow of her hair. He touched the unruly locks that he had pulled when she was a little girl, but his hand trembled unexpectedly. Here was Maggie, his old, familiar playmate, yet she was not the same. She who had been his closest friend, his confidante for so long, was suddenly a stranger. She had let him see only what he wanted; she had been merely the friend he needed. He looked at her more carefully now, studied her sharp profile in the flickering firelight as the flames drew dark shadows across her face. He ran his finger over the freckles and caressed her cheek, tracing her pointed chin.

A gust of wind made the fire dance and sent a shiver over them in their damp clothes. He pulled the blanket closer around them and felt the heat of her body next to his. How many times had they huddled together as children by a campfire, keeping each other warm, telling stories in the thick forest night? Now there were no stories, no words even, only a silent language between them. He was keenly aware of her breathing, of the rhythmic rise and fall of her breast pressing against him, and her hair, which smelled faintly of chamomile. When she rose to feed the fire he reached for her without thinking.

"Don't go, Maggie."

She turned, half surprised, taking the hand he held out to her. She sat down again by his side, their fingers intertwined, staring into the dying fire. So much like those nights spent on windy mountaintops around a campfire, with Jake telling long spun tales of terror, their delicious fear intensified by the moaning of the wind. They knew that they were safe as long as they held hands, and nothing bad could enter the fire's circle of light.

When Michael finally spoke, the words were a continuation of her own thoughts, so that she scarcely knew when they started talking.

"How long has it been since we've sat by a fire like this, Maggie?"

"Years," she answered, "more than ten. It was just before high school graduation. We wanted to go camping once more before going away to college, before having to grow up. Do you remember?" she added softly.

"Yes. It was late spring and there was water everywhere, melting snow running down the trail in little rivulets so that we hiked through mud everywhere. We dried our boots out at night by the fire and piled pine branches under our sleeping bags to keep the dampness out."

She nodded, continuing on with her memories. "Do you remember when we took that shortcut by Flowed Lands and were completely covered with mud? We jumped in the lake to wash off but the water was icy cold..."

"..and we couldn't stand it more than a minute at a time. We took turns plunging in and shivering until we were reasonably clean," he finished for her. "Then we spent the rest of the day drying off by a fire, our teeth chattering." They laughed, then he became more sober.

"But I had to go back early," he continued. "Becky was angry at me for going at all, so I couldn't stay as long as I wanted."

She moved away to tend the fire, her back to him, feeling suddenly self-conscious. She poked at the coals longer than necessary, all the time feeling his eyes on her. His voice was subdued when he spoke again, and a little wistful.

"Those were good times, Maggie. I've missed them."

She didn't look at him when she returned, sitting down a little distance away. But his eyes were compelling, forcing her to meet them, to read his message.

"I've missed you, Maggie."

The fire snapped and a piece of wood rolled toward their feet. They both rose with one motion to kick it back among the coals, then stood facing each other, one side warmed by the flames. Only a few inches separated them. Confused by exhaustion, the heat of the fire and the cool of the night, it was a boundless distance one moment, then a gap closing so swiftly it made her mind spin. She stepped back, wavered giddily as he caught her with one arm. Then there were no more words, no more hesitation.

He felt her body against his. The body he had only known as hard and sinuous was now soft and yielding. He kissed her slowly, wonderingly, savoring, exploring the newness of her. She returned his kiss fiercely, almost angrily, and he was amazed that in all the years of their closeness he had never known her like this. Then she was unbuttoning his shirt, fingers impatient and clumsy. The fresh night air stroked his skin, leaving little shivers in its wake. Her fingers touched his chest, traced the bruises she had nursed earlier. She stepped back, and he stood trembling, watching as she removed her shirt, all shyness gone.

She stood before him and he caught his breath. This time he reached for her with more urgency, pulling her down on the blanket beside the dying fire, feeling all of her hungrily, regretting all the time they had wasted. Willing, sobbing, she cried out for him. As they moaned together, joining the secret sounds of the night, only the mysterious reflecting eyes of tiny nocturnal creatures witnessed their release.

Chapter 11

"Michael?" It was her first thought upon waking, her first word as she felt the empty place beside her. Concerned when he didn't answer, she awoke fully and threw off the light wool blanket that had been pulled up around her shoulders. She was wearing her khaki trousers and shirt; she could vaguely remember waking up cold in the middle of the night and putting them on. He had been asleep, his face turned towards her. She had sat watching him, wanting to remember him like that always.

That night on the mountaintop was theirs, belonged to them alone, but even at the height of her joy there had been a little sadness. The knowledge that this couldn't last, couldn't continue. He didn't belong to her, never had. She reminded herself of this now, sternly, practically. Yes, he had loved her last night, she knew that beyond doubt. But would he love her today? Stop dreaming, Maggie, you have work to do, she told herself. That's why you came up here, after all. Or was it because you saw a chance to be alone with Michael again after all these years?

She stepped out from under the overhang. The sky had cleared from the previous night's storm. Only a few wisps of clouds hung high over the mountaintop, the sun rising on a world freshly cleansed. Here the vegetation grew close to the ground, and the raindrops that still clung to leaves and branches could have been morning dew. Soon, they too would be gone, dried by the sun as it shined down on them unprotected. The song of a chickadee filled the brilliant morning around her, and she stopped for a moment to listen, closing her eyes. When it ceased she did not move, but continued to luxuriate in the peaceful silence of the high peaks.

Rusty ran towards her from behind a boulder a few yards away, greeting her exuberantly. She smiled and petted the dog. He ran back to the boulder and she walked resolutely after him. Michael was watching the sunrise, leaning against the rock, his back to her. She came up beside him quietly, suddenly shy. The practical Maggie laughed at the thought of her being shy with Michael; the other, new Maggie held back, suddenly unsure of herself. Michael turned and saw her, saw the love in her eyes she hadn't had time, or perhaps the desire to hide. There was love in his eyes too, but he was troubled, she could tell from the creases around his eyes.

"Maggie."

She felt his tension as they embraced, and his gradual relaxation as they held each other. Her doubts were gone again, and she marveled at her own fickleness.

"Maggie, I didn't realize how much I've wanted you."

"Part of me has always been incomplete without you, Michael. But it is too late for us; we have other obligations now."

He turned away from her, troubled again. "Maggie, we need to talk."

"I know. That's why I followed you, why I've been leaving messages for you all week."

They moved to a flat rock and sat facing the rising sun. Its early warming rays promised another hot August day. She sat next to him, unable to ignore the nearness of his body, disturbed by his closeness, vaguely aware of longings that had been stirred but not fully satisfied. She sensed him pulling away, turning into himself. Sensitive to his moods, she became alert, waiting.

"How did you know where to find me?" he asked.

"Becky gave me your note."

"Then you know about the water?" he asked cryptically.

"Know? Know what, Michael? All I know is what you wrote in the note. But I don't understand. Has it got something to do with your studies on acid rain?"

"Yes... and no! My studies found that the river is being contaminated with lead. I think I know what caused it, and it wasn't acid rain or any other such act of God. I know what I should do, but no matter what I do, a lot of people are going to get hurt."

She stared at him, not understanding his words but hearing the pain in his tone. He stood facing her, the sun at his back, hiding his face in shadow, but she knew the pain was there. Seeing her puzzled look, he knew it was time to explain.

"You know that I've been avoiding you, Maggie. I'm sorry if you were hurt by it; it was so unlike the openness we've always had between us."

"I thought you were angry because I printed that story about the acid rain," she interposed.

"No," he shook his head. "I wanted to know what I was going to do before talking to you. That's why I came up here, to sort things out. But you found me before I was finished sorting. If you hadn't found me I would probably be dead and the problem would have been buried with me."

She felt his struggle and reached out to him: "Well, I'm here now, Michael. You know I'll help you if I can, but you must tell me what this is all about."

He took the hand she offered and sat next to her again. She was the one person he had always counted on, but would she understand this time?   He envied her certainty, the clearness about duties and principles that she always seemed to have.

"You know that when I was helping Steve Harper with that project on acid rain we found high concentrations of lead in the Opalescent," he began.   "As your article said, most researchers believe that acid waters have been leaching toxic metals from soils and rocks in the Adirondack watersheds. But I was bothered that all the high concentrations were found around Langston. All the samples up in the watersheds were below detection limits, even using that sensitive equipment Tom Lang donated to the school. It seemed that in the river just below your cabin the concentration of lead suddenly rose."

Maggie had been listening intently, and suddenly she was ahead of him. "The lead is coming from the mine!" she interrupted excitedly. "But why now? That mine's been there for over a hundred years!"

"Yes. But it's not the mine itself, but the wastes that were buried in it. As for how long it's taken, groundwater doesn't move all that fast, maybe a few feet a day. And metals move a lot slower than that because they get tied up on the soil. I don't know how long ago the lead reached the river, but the concentration is increasing. In a few years, we could really have a problem."

"Dad's always hated the mine. He said it's been an eyesore and a blot on the landscape ever since he could remember. Now it's even spoiling our river!"

He took her hands and looked into her face, now flushed with excitement. "Maggie, I'm afraid it's pretty serious. Once I knew for sure, I had to warn you. But Jake's health is at stake, and maybe yours."

"Jake's health? What do you mean?"

"Your well had extremely high concentrations of lead, and I don't know how long it's been that way, though I'd guess it's been a while. Jake's been ill for several months, hasn't he? I didn't suspect it at first, but after testing your well I knew. The intestinal cramps, headaches, weakness--they're all symptoms of lead poisoning."

She stared at him blankly while his words settled into her consciousness. They settled heavily, like the lead she could almost taste in her mouth. As she absorbed their meaning, exploring their implications, a torrent of emotions engulfed her. He saw thoughts and emotions follow one another across her face, each rapidly claiming significance, then yielding to another equally disturbing one. She struggled with horror, disbelief, denial and finally, anger. It was indignation and rage that finally found expression.

"Jake poisoned by his own well! And by that hateful mine, the mine that had already killed his cousin, Maura. Now it's killing him, too! Well, I won't let it!" Her dilated eyes looked through him, past him. She was searching within herself, gathering her strengths, preparing for a battle.

"The Company did this," she went on. "They'll pay for everything they've done to my family and to our mountains. For a hundred and fifty years they've been spoiling the wilderness, cutting down the trees, tearing up the earth with their goddamn mine, polluting the land with their garbage, and now poisoning our water. They must be stopped, so we can salvage the little that's left!"

She spoke with conviction, her words a jarring contrast to the timeless beauty surrounding them. The air was fresh and clear. The sun sparkled on tiny pools of water that formed in the centers of delicate alpine leaves. The birds repeated their endless song to the sky. But for the moment she could sense none of this, her thoughts only of outrage and pain, her need for vengeance overwhelming. He watched her, concerned, feeling her anger and hurt, yet restraining his own emotions. He smoothed the tangled mass of her hair, pushed it back from her face that was distorted with fury.

"Of course, we'll do something, Maggie. But there are other things we need to consider."

She stared at him, not understanding his words. What other things? What else could matter? Wasn't it obvious that the Company was at fault? Wasn't it clear that they had to be stopped?

"We need to think about the Company and its importance to Langston. And I must think about Becky and Tom Lang."

She pulled away from him, her body suddenly tense, rejecting his touch. "How can you think about the Company after what they've done? And the Langs are the Company! They're responsible for everything that's happened!"

"Listen to me, Maggie! This town owes its existence to the Company. There is hardly a person in town who isn't somehow dependent on the Company for their living. Tom Lang is not a bad sort, and I owe him a lot. He's done an awful lot for the town, and you know how Becky looks up to her father."

"I don't care about the Company," she shouted. "They must suffer for what they did to my family. If you won't help me, maybe the EPA will. They won't be intimidated by this town's petty politics!"

"Maggie, wait! Do you know what could happen if the EPA is called in? They could authorize a massive study of the site that could cost millions without really cleaning anything up. The Company would go bankrupt and shut down. Then hundreds of people would be out of jobs, would need to look for work elsewhere. There would be no Langston without the Company!"

"I won't listen to this, Michael! What do you want to do, let my father die, have all these same townspeople suffer from lead poisoning because you're married to Tom Lang's daughter?" She did not wait for his reply but turned and fled down the mountain.

She ran down the trail, sliding over loose rock, anger propelling her, tears blurring her vision, obscuring the way. So this is how it would be, Michael loyal to Becky and Tom Lang, leaving Jake and her to battle alone. Their family always had to fight the Company alone. I won't give up, not even if I have to fight the whole town, she vowed. There's got to be something I can do and I will, by God. Tom Lang won't get away with this!

She heard Michael's heavy footfalls behind her and ran faster, trying to put distance between them and their night on the mountaintop. Her foot caught on a root exposed by the rainstorm. She fell hard, scraping her hands and face on the rough ground. She sat huddled on the ground sobbing, rubbing her ankle, her tears making dirty streaks as they ran down her face.

Then Michael was on the ground beside her, holding her in his arms. She went limp, defeated. He stroked her head gently, enjoying the texture of her hair, then brushed the dirt from her shirt and cleaned her scrapes, washing them with water from her canteen. He had thought to stop and pick up her pack.

When her tears finally stopped she felt drained, the impotent rage that tore at her stilled. It felt good to be with him, having him take care of her, allowing herself this weakness. And yet she felt ashamed, as if she had betrayed herself and all the Hughes's before her. She took a shaky breath and pulled away a little, so that she could look at him. She wanted to hate him, wanted to see the hateful face of an uncaring enemy. Instead she saw concern, and a hurt that mirrored her own.

"Please listen to me, Maggie. I want to get the mine-site cleaned up as much as you do. But I want to do it in a way that won't harm a lot of innocent people. I have decided to go directly to Tom Lang and ask him to clean up the site. If he agrees, and I think he will once he understands, the problem will be solved. It will cost the Company a lot of money, but it could stay in business, and Langston would be spared."

"And if he doesn't agree?" she asked, searching his face.

"Then we'll go to the EPA. Your welfare, Jake's, and the townspeople's health are more important to me than all the jobs in Langston. I know that now. But I need your help to solve this problem, and we will solve it one way or another. Please believe me."

She believed him. She believed him because she wanted to, and because she had to. He couldn't lie to her, wouldn't deceive her any more than she could him. Suddenly she felt that there was no need for talk. They would work together and solve the problem. No matter what happened, they would always be there for each other because it couldn't be any other way. She marveled at the irrationality and the truth of this.

It was still early in the day when they set off for Four Corners lean-to. The hike down the mountain was quiet, uneventful, yet wonderfully soothing for both of them. Where the trail was wide they walked together; where it narrowed to a couple of feet hugging the steep mountainside, one of them took the lead and the other automatically fell behind. It was almost like their hikes when they were children. There was a special honor in being the first on the top of a mountain. They had had to draw pine needles to determine the leader.

The sun was hot before they reached the shade of the forest. Michael took off his shirt as he led the way over a boulder that had fallen into their path. Maggie admired the supple movement of his muscles under the tanned skin, the graceful motions of his athletic body. He hadn't changed much physically since high school, only matured; his body filled out. He had been much admired by the girls in their class, considered a prize, and many vied for his attention in those days. He had an adolescent's emerging masculinity that was so vulnerable to flattery. So he picked Becky, or rather she picked him. Becky with her flirtatious ways, silky hair and innocent blue eyes. Everyone said they looked so perfect together.

Maggie shook her head. Becky had once been her best friend, though even now she wasn't sure why. They really had nothing in common except for Michael. She paused, reflecting. Perhaps Becky had envied the bond between her and Michael, envied what he shared only with Maggie. Then, little by little Becky drew him away from her, from those interests that she didn't share. The thought that Becky might have been competing with her gave Maggie a rush of satisfaction. It had never occurred to her that she could have been competition for

Becky. Back then she had been flattered that Becky had picked her for a close friend. It wasn't until much later that she recognized the wedge Becky had forced between her and Michael.

They all left for college after graduating from Langston High. Michael went to Newgate on a hockey scholarship, and she enrolled at the State University in the same town. Becky went to a more prestigious private college downstate. For a while it was almost like old times, Maggie and Michael taking long walks, studying together, talking late into the night. But on long weekends he always returned to Becky, and in time a distance developed between Maggie and Michael. She was hurt and puzzled, blaming herself for his increasing coolness. She hardly saw Becky anymore, and when she did there wasn't much left between them. Christmas of their senior year Becky and Michael were engaged. Maggie went to the wedding, though not the reception. She felt she didn't really know them anymore, and it hurt her to think of losing Michael that way. She never stopped missing him. But she kept her distance from him, out of pride as much as from instinct.

After that summer she took a job with a city newspaper. She got the experience that she needed, but she never really adjusted to the city with its dirt and soot and noise, and especially lack of space. After three years, she was ready to take the job that Emmett Wilkins had offered her.

She breathed more freely in the mountains, knew she belonged in Langston, moving to the slower rhythm that was more closely tied to the cycles of nature. Then Michael had returned, reminding her of days long past and of a friendship deeply missed. She knew sensibly that it was irrational to expect the old closeness, but something in her couldn't be convinced. All that mattered was that Michael was back in Langston, in the mountains they both loved. He and Becky were building a house, she knew that, but somehow he was changing, acting more like the Michael she remembered.

He had spent the years in the city too, first as a graduate student, then working as a young engineer. But city life didn't suit him, just as it hadn't suited her, and when the opportunity came he returned to teach at the high school. Some thought he was giving up a more prestigious and promising career. Even Becky did at first, although she was happy to return to her social position in town and was soon caught up in furnishing their new house.

Maggie frequently ran into him around town. Sometimes she would see him at the high school, and lately he had been stopping by to visit her at the newspaper office. He visited Jake on the weekends. Becky was rarely with him. One time, when they were together on the old cabin porch watching the summer sunset, Jake whittling a stick endlessly and Michael lounging on the step with Rusty at his feet, Maggie was reminded of those summers long ago when her world was perfect. Jake still had his health, she had Michael and Old Calamity, and together they all had the wilderness and their futures stretching before them. With the innocence of youth, she never thought those times would end.

The sun was high when they reached Four Corners lean-to. Michael threw Maggie's pack inside and they sat at the entrance and removed their boots. Carefully, with complete absorption, they examined their feet for blisters. Moments later, Maggie raised her eyes to see Michael watching her, laughing silently. "How many times have we done this, Maggie?"

"Countless," she laughed. "No matter what, when we return to camp we must always examine our feet," she said with mock seriousness. "I see you haven't forgotten the basic rules of camping."

They sat for a moment smiling at each other, and at memories of other moments. "I think we need a swim, Maggie. I haven't been this dirty in years."

For the first time Maggie noticed her dirt-stained clothes, felt the sting of her scrapes where she had fallen, and the sweat matting the hair at her temples. Although she had removed the sliver from her palm after tending to Michael the night before, her hand still ached. She picked at the dirt under her fingernails and remembered how only a few hours in the woods could make her feel incredibly grubby. But it was dirt she didn't mind, for it smelled of earth and moss and pine resin.

They put on their camp moccasins and headed down the trail to their favorite swimming hole on Feldspar Brook. There the water formed a deep pool where the bottom had been hollowed out by some natural event long ago. The bank rose steeply, forming an overhang with bluebells and asters leaning over the stream to catch their own reflections. Maggie ran ahead, jumping in without her clothes, enjoying the cold water on her overheated, bruised skin. In a moment Michael joined her, and they were splashing and diving, scattering a pair of small frogs into the tall grasses. The tension and fatigue washed away with the dirt, leaving them carefree and relaxed in the healing water.

He dove under and caught her around the waist and felt her weightlessness as she brushed against him with the movement of the current. They stayed in the pool for what seemed an eternity, keenly aware of the sensuous stroking of the water sending little shivers of pleasure as it flowed around them. When Maggie finally climbed up the steep bank he followed her, the invitation in her eyes pulling him.

They went to a small clearing that had been their secret place. It had a narrow grassy opening and was surrounded by tangled bushes, hidden from others but always exposed to the summer sunshine. Here they lay in the tall grasses and moss, breathing in the fragrance of wild raspberries and herbs that surrounded their hiding place. The grass was pleasantly rough underneath them. A frightened insect ran confusedly across their bodies before finding its way back to its own path. Cooled and refreshed by the brook, they welcomed the sun, their skin tingling pleasantly with the evaporating moisture. There was no time, no noise, no demanding outside world, just the incessant droning of insects and the occasional call of a bird. They had been there before, the same two people, telling each other their secrets, hiding from the world, from everyone but each other.

But they were not the same, Michael thought as he looked at Maggie. She was lying on her back sunk into the barely moving leaves of grass that brushed and outlined the lightly tanned contours of her body. He thought she was beautiful, unique, and very special. How was it that he had never seen her like this, open and loving yet vulnerable? Of course, because she had never been this way, had never let him see this part of her, and he had never bothered to look. He sighed with regret for what they had missed, and remembered the emptiness he had felt for a number of years. But that was gone now, he had found Maggie again after so much time, a new and different Maggie who left him breathless.

She smiled with her eyes closed as he traced her cheek, her neck and shoulders, and ruffled the wisps of hair that were beginning to dry around her face. She reached for him, pulled him down until he felt the heat of her body rising toward him, felt the longing within himself. He kissed her gently, felt her rapid breathing and the tiny tremors that shook her body. There was only the tremendous tension, unbearable yet sweet, and the essential release, their cries mingling with the chirping of a cricket, the scent of pine, the feel of sunshine on a bed of ferns.

They lay on the crushed carpet holding each other, unwilling to let go, to acknowledge the end of the moment.

"Maggie, you were the part of me that was missing all these years. I thought I only needed the mountains, that I would be whole again when I returned, and in a way I was. When I was out at the cabin with you and Jake, I was happy the way we were years ago. Things were almost right, but not quite. I didn't want to admit to myself that I'd made a mistake in marrying Becky."

She looked into his face and saw all that she wanted; she loved him with all the feelings she had repressed for years.

They had always belonged to each other, but it had taken them this long to realize it.

She smiled, kissing him lightly. Then her eyes turned serious. "What are we going to do? You and Becky are still married."

He continued to stroke her gently, but the smile left his face. "I don't know, Maggie. I don't know yet, but we'll work it out somehow."

Chapter 12

Michael and Maggie spent that day and the following night at Four Corners lean-to. It was a time without pressures, demands, or interruptions. Tacitly, they agreed to allow themselves those hours to enjoy and rediscover each other. They talked about their lives and about old times, remembering other days together on Marcy. They had a need to strengthen their new bond and old friendship, span the years with talk, make up for lost time. Worry about the mine was suspended, but because both knew that the problem couldn't be postponed for long, their time alone on the mountain was all the more precious.

They left Four Corners early next morning, wanting to return to Langston to begin the work ahead of them. They stopped at the edge of town where their paths took them in different directions. Maggie would take the road to Main St. and the Gazette office, and Michael would head toward Yellow Birch Trail and home. They separated reluctantly, yet with a certain impatience to get on with it, to solve the problem that lay before them and put it to rest.

"I want to go home to check on Jake, but I have to stop at the paper first. I need to call that reporter from the Times, see if I can stall him," Maggie said. She lingered for a moment searching Michael's face, reading his emotions. He was still troubled, she could see it in his eyes, but his thoughts eluded her.

"I have to talk to Becky first, tell her what we've decided to do. Then I'll go see Tom Lang."

A tightness formed in her chest as she felt his struggle, wanting to share it, but knew instinctively that this was something he needed to do alone. They embraced and he held her hard, almost desperately as she closed her eyes and marveled at her happiness at finding him again.

"It'll be OK, Michael. We're together now, and we're doing the right thing." With that the tension fell away, and she knew intuitively that as long as they were together her world would be all right.

"I'll come to your room tonight," he said, shouldering his pack and calling Rusty to his side. She watched him disappear behind the birches, then turned toward town as the noon whistle sounded at the factory.

Michael was unaware that the noonday sun was burning the back of his neck, oblivious to the air shimmering over the road before him or of the coolness of the pine woods through which he and Rusty took their usual shortcut home. He didn't notice the dog chase a squirrel up a tree, then sit at the bottom, tail wagging, while it chattered its annoyance at him. Usually attuned to his surroundings, now his thoughts were turned inward, thinking of Maggie and Becky, Jake, and Tom Lang. Their lives were all deeply entwined with his own. To each of them he owed a part of what he had become, and his responsibility to them weighed more heavily on him than the pack he carried. But their needs were in conflict, and he must choose between them.

He knew he loved Maggie and didn't want to live without her. Yet he had also loved Becky once and wanted her, although for different reasons. And Jake. Even in his moments of doubt he knew he couldn't turn his back on Jake, a man he loved and respected more than any other. Jake had taught him most of what he knew about the mountains; secrets shared with very few. Michael admired Jake's self-sufficiency and integrity, wanting those qualities in his life, too. Tom Lang had been good to him, had welcomed him into his family when he and Becky had become engaged. He was generous and fair, but hard-nosed when anything threatened his family or his business. He just hoped that Tom would listen to reason.

The front door was unlocked, but Becky was not in the house. He dropped his pack in the hallway and went into the kitchen for a glass of ice water. Rusty emptied his water bowl, then lay on the cool tile, panting. Michael sipped the water in the glass reflectively, savoring its sweetness. How often did he

143

stop to think about it, how often does anybody? His generation and even his father's, took the safety of their drinking water so much for granted. It wasn't always like that, yet stories of waterborne epidemics of the last century seemed somehow unreal. Families, whole communities had been devastated by cholera or typhoid. It had even happened in Langston once; more than a third of the population died in a few weeks. He set down his glass, took a deep breath, and walked to the back patio.

Becky lay in a lounge chair facing away from him, a towel over her eyes. She wore a green striped bikini, revealing her golden skin glistening with suntan oil. The straps of her swimsuit had been let down, and he could see the cleft between her breasts from where he stood. Again he admired the perfection of her delicate, rounded body, but for the first time she left him cold.

She stirred at the sound of his steps, removed the towel from her eyes, and half-turned to see him. Her face was guarded as she waited for him to speak. He placed a lawn chair across from her, not too near, and sat down. A moment of strained silence followed. He looked down to focus his thoughts, but was distracted by the sparkle of her diamond ring in the sunlight. It aroused vague, uncomfortable feelings in him, a sense that things began to go wrong between them when he had finally bought her the diamond.

At the time they had been married four years and living in Mount Kisco. He couldn't afford a diamond when they were engaged, and Becky had been very sweet about it, thoroughly understanding. There were other priorities such as finishing graduate school and repaying his student loans. The ring would have to wait until he started a job and they were clear of debt. She never complained, although it wasn't easy for her to be the only girl at her school who was engaged without a diamond.

Later, when they moved to Mt. Kisco, she changed. At first it was just little things, minor dissatisfactions, complaints that led to arguments or sulking on her part. She was tired of

144

waiting, tired of doing without things. As Tom Lang's daughter, she had never had to wait for things before. She had grown up with money, and expected more than what Michael could give her in the early years. He reminded her that there was still a year left on his loan, that she had known things would be tight in the beginning. But that didn't convince her. He finally bought the ring, borrowing the money from Tom Lang. Michael always regretted it. After that Tom started pressuring Michael to return to Langston and join the Company, and support his daughter in the manner she had been raised to expect. He looked up to see Becky watching him.

"I've made my decision, Becky."

She sat up, alert. His tone warned her that something unpleasant was coming.

"I'm going to your father to ask that he clean up the mine-site," he continued. "I have no choice. Not if I want to live with myself or the people I care about." He paused, waiting for her reaction.

She rose from the lounge chair and threw the towel at him. Her round eyes were narrowed like a cat's and her voice shook with anger. "The people you care about! What about me? What about Daddy? Don't you care about us?"

"Of course I do!" he answered defensively. "But there are other people to consider, too. Jake's well is already contaminated; he could die of lead poisoning if I don't do something."

"Jake!" she cried with contempt. "It's always Jake! How many nights have I sat home alone because you had to go see Jake? And now you're going to ruin my father because of him!"

Her words wounded him but he forced himself to remain calm. "Listen to me, Becky. Tom won't be ruined if he takes responsibility for cleaning up the mine-site. Maggie and I agreed that we'd give him a chance to clean it up on his own before calling in the EPA."

"Maggie!" she flared. "I should have known she'd get mixed up in this somehow. When did the two of you hatch this scheme?"

"She followed me up Marcy and we worked things out up there." His face had darkened at her words, but he managed to keep his voice under control.

"Oh, yes, the note. I should have known she couldn't wait to take off after you. She always had her eye on you, ever since we were kids. Not that she ever had a chance," she added maliciously.

Michael got up from the chair and turned away from her. "I'm going to see Tom now. I'll be back late."

Something in his manner made her stop. She stepped in front of him, blocking his way, and searched his face. She saw tension and anger, and something she couldn't quite identify, an aloofness that was new and disconcerting. With an impatient shrug he turned aside and walked into the house.

Since it was Sunday Michael drove to the Lang's house, assuming that he would find Tom Lang at home. Carolyn, Becky's mother, answered the door. No, Tom wasn't there, but he was expected home shortly. He had gone into the office to look over some papers. She invited Michael to wait, but Michael didn't feel like making small talk with Carolyn. He would find Tom at the factory.

The offices of the paint company were located within the factory fence, separate but overlooking the plant. The guard at the gate recognized Michael and waved him through. It was a new two-story building, the front attractively landscaped with tall bushes lining the flagstone walk. Michael walked toward the entrance resolutely, head bent forward as he contemplated, unseeing, the irregular stones under his feet. He had not bothered to change for the meeting, hadn't even thought of it. The matter was too urgent; he felt that it couldn't wait another minute. He was determined now, his resolution hardened by Becky's words.

Tom Lang's door was open and Michael entered before realizing that Tom was engaged in conversation. Michael apologized, momentarily confused, forced to hold back his prepared words. Tom was leaning back in his chair, sleeves rolled up in the summer heat, hands clasped behind his head. At the sight of Michael he unclasped his hands and beckoned him into the room.

"Michael! What brings you here?" he asked with a broad smile.

"I'm sorry to interrupt, Tom. I see you're busy, I'll just wait outside," he said formally.

"Nonsense!" Tom said. "This is Don Harrison; Don, Michael Ryan. The fellow who stole my Becky away from me," he added, chuckling. "Don's our best customer. He's a distributor for hardware stores in southern New York, Connecticut, and Long Island. He's up here on vacation and wanted to stop in."

Harrison was a middle aged, paunchy, ruddy complected Irishman. Michael walked over and offered his hand. "So the paint poster made you want to see the real thing."

Harrison grinned broadly. "Yeah. That picture sure sells a lot of paint. Opalescent is my best selling brand. The stores all put it out real prominent at the end of their paint aisles. In fact, one of the reasons I'm here is to convince Tom to send me a couple of extra truck loads before the end of the summer fix up season."

Tom Lang chuckled again. "You've got it."

As the two businessmen completed arrangements for the new order, Michael walked over to the window of Tom's spacious office. A leather sofa and several chairs were arranged to give the impression of a luxurious sitting room rather than a conference area. A marble topped bar stood to the side, its mirror reflecting Rotary Club plaques, honorariums, and a framed picture of Tom breaking ground for the new hospital wing on the wall behind Tom's heavy oak desk. The thick carpet was a rich cream color, and for a moment Michael regretted his muddy boots.

The room contrasted with the man who occupied it. Tom seemed more natural telling stories with boots raised before a fireplace than giving orders to lawyers and accountants. But Michael had learned that Tom Lang's down-home flavor masked the same shrewdness that had kept the family business thriving through the generations.

A framed photograph of Becky at eighteen was his prized possession. He kept it proudly angled toward the door so any visitor, no matter how casual, would see it. It captured Becky at her best, fresh and young, glowing with the certainty of her innocent beauty. Becky had given her father a new picture, her wedding picture, a wreath of orange blossoms in her hair, the pride of a conqueror in her eyes. But Tom kept the old photo on his desk saying, "This is how I want to remember my Becky always, when she was still my little girl." Michael smiled wryly. She still was Tom's little girl and always would be.

Michael looked up as Harrison rose to go. "Thanks, got to go find my wife before she spends all our money at the souvenir store." He shook hands with Tom and Michael, and left. Tom Lang turned his attention to his son-in-law.

"Becky tells me you've been in the mountains again. Looks like you just got back," he said, looking at Michael's crumpled clothes and muddy boots. "You know, you shouldn't leave Becky alone so much. I know she never cared for mountain climbing, but I'm sure there are lots of other things the two of you could enjoy together."

Michael was momentarily at a loss for an answer. He didn't want to start an argument, especially not about Becky.

His tone was serious as he began. "I went up into the mountains to think. I want to talk to you about something, Tom."

Tom sat up, suddenly concerned. "What's the matter, Michael? It's not Becky, is it?"

Michael failed to hide his annoyance as he shrugged off the question. "No, of course not. She's fine. It's something else, and it's pretty serious," he added after a pause.

"You know that I've been testing the water in the area this summer," he continued. "Well, I've found alarmingly high concentrations of lead and finally traced its source to the old mine-site." He stopped, waiting for the information to register on Tom's open and friendly features.

"We've never had a problem with the old mine since we closed it up. What makes you think the mine's causing a problem now?" Tom's manner did not change; he continued to lean back in his chair, but his face became guarded.

"Upstream from the mine the concentrations of lead were below detection limits, whereas just below the mine, lead concentrations increased dramatically. I tested a groundwater sample between the mine and the river. It tested out hundreds of times higher than the safe drinking water standard. There is no question of the source," Michael explained.

Tom didn't reply immediately. He appeared to be considering his options. Then, "Just where did you find this dangerous concentration of lead?"

"In Jake Hughes' well. In fact, Jake is already showing some of the symptoms of lead poisoning."

Tom appeared to perk up. "Only in Hughes' well? That should be easy enough to fix."

"You don't understand, Tom. This problem is more widespread than just Jake's well. It takes lead a long time to move through the soil. I believe the high concentration has only

149

recently reached the well. The river is still safe, but in time high concentrations will also reach the Opalescent, Langston's source of drinking water. As you know, the Opalescent flows into the Hudson, and there are millions of people downstate who don't want that river polluted any more than it already is." Michael was standing now, leaning over the desk that separated the two men, his voice low with intensity. "You must do something before that happens."

"What do you propose we do about this?" Tom asked.

"Find out exactly how far the contamination has gone, treat the contaminated water and clean up the mine-site."

Tom interrupted. "How much is all this going to cost?"

"I don't know."

"Are you positive the water will be unfit to drink?"

""Yes. I'm just not sure how widespread the problem might be."

"Do you have a plan?"

"Not yet. We need more..."

"How can you expect me to commit to spending our money, risking the financial health of the Company, when you don't have a definite plan, don't know how much it's going to cost, don't even know for sure that there is going to be a problem?"

"You really have no choice."

"Don't be such a worrier, Michael. We will do something when it becomes necessary. For now, let's just worry about the immediate danger, Jake's well." Tom came around his desk and put his arm reassuringly over Michael's shoulder.

Michael fought an urge to shake off the arm, wanting to shake the man out of his complacency instead.

"You did say it takes lead a long time to move through the soil, didn't you? Well, then we have plenty of time to figure out something. After all, it has taken this lead fifty years just to get to Jake's well."

Michael started to protest, resenting his patronizing tone, but the other's presence filled the room, his voice full of reassurance and authority. "Stop worrying, son. I promise you I will take care of it. Don't I always? You just go back to your experiments and leave the rest to me." He was a man used to giving orders.

Michael turned toward the door, swallowing any additional arguments. The other man's will guided him, forced him away from a territory that wasn't his own. He would have to trust Tom, at least until he had stronger evidence. He owed Becky that.

Michael came in through the back door and went directly to his den. He sat in his favorite chair and stared vacantly at the papers on his desk. But his mind was elsewhere, and he didn't feel at ease. The matter still lay unfinished, unresolved. Tom Lang said he would solve Jake's problem, but somehow his attitude left Michael uneasy. Michael should have pressed him more for a commitment, should have discussed specific plans. Instead he had been overwhelmed by Tom's will and self-assurance.

He needed to do something, something that would make Tom see the urgency of the situation, something that would convince him that the site could be cleaned up without bankrupting the Company. His eyes rested on the paper nearest him. It summarized the results of tests he had run at different points along the river when he was trying to pinpoint the source of contamination. Some of his latest tests needed to be added to the summary. He thought he was already beginning to detect a trend of increasing lead concentrations in the river south of the Hughes cabin. He needed to include the latest data. He would evaluate the data now, and see Maggie in the morning instead.

Before beginning, he telephoned the newspaper office to tell Maggie about his conversation with Tom Lang. The line was busy. He hung up and started to work on the data. Soon he was immersed in the numbers and forgot about the time.

He had been working an hour, perhaps longer, when he finished. He stood up, agitated, hardly able to concentrate on the numbers that confirmed his concern. The lead concentration in the river was increasing faster than he had expected. Jake's well must have been contaminated for quite a while. There wasn't much time, for Tom Lang or for Langston.

His feelings alternated between fear and rage. He feared for Langston and the people he loved. The rage stemmed from a feeling of impotence at having his hands tied by obligations to Becky and Tom Lang, when there was work to be done and little time to lose.

He was deep in thought as he rose from his desk, his plan only half-formulated, but his need for action propelling him. The late afternoon rays of the sun shone through the window obliquely, making the dust motes dance in their path when he looked up and saw Becky standing in the doorway.

Her face looked soft, vulnerable, childish in the shadows as she looked up at him.

"I've been waiting for you to come upstairs, Michael."

"I'm very busy."

She reached out a hand and touched him on the arm, lightly, tentatively. "I don't want us to fight, Michael. I just want us to be together again."

Michael looked at her, annoyed, perplexed, but mostly impatient. He didn't want to deal with her right now.

"I'm going to New York for a couple of days. I have to pack a few things and I'll be on my way."

Her hand lingered on his arm and she turned her face up so he could see the message in her eyes. "Can't you wait 'til morning?"

He stared at her for a moment, mesmerized, then shook his head. "No, I can't just sit still waiting to see what'll happen. I need you to do something for me, though. When Maggie calls, tell her I've gone to New York. I'll be at my old firm, trying to find a good way to clean up the mine-site. Tom is in way over his head, and he's going to need help, whether he admits it or not. I'll wait a few days to see how he handles it on his own, but then I want to be ready with some answers. He's going to have to move fast."

Becky's hand dropped and she drew back against the wall. Her face was turned in profile as he passed her, her mouth pulled down. She no longer looked soft and vulnerable, just childish.

Michael threw his duffel bag into the Jeep and climbed behind the wheel. As he was turning around in the driveway, a thought occurred to him. It surprised him, came to him unbidden. He had nearly forgotten about it, yet it must have been carefully stored in the back of his mind over the years, in case he ever needed it.

Once, while playing hide-and-seek with his sister, Eileen, Michael ended up in his father's study. When he heard Eileen's steps in the hallway he ducked into the closet where his father kept his papers. His elbow bumped something, and a stack of notebooks and papers came crashing around his head. The children stared at the mess in consternation. They were trying to straighten things when their father walked in. He was angry, and made them sit on the couch while he surveyed the damage.

They stared anxiously at the objects on the walls, waiting. On one wall hung a sketch of the old logging camp, drawn by some logger who filled his evening hours drawing by the fire. Next to the drawing hung an axe, its handle well worn, its blade dull and rusty now. They said it belonged to Liam Ryan, who had been the first foreman in the sawmill. On the corner of the desk stood the miner's lantern that had been used by John's grandfather when he was foreman of the lead mine, and framed on another wall hung the Company's first paint label.

John sat down at the big desk and placed the stack of notebooks and yellowed roll of drawings in front of him. The top notebook was covered in marbleized cardboard, and filled with writing in black ink. Here and there an inkblot obscured a word, but most of it was legible. It looked like a diary of some sort, with daily entries spanning a number of years.

"You don't know what these are, do you?" John asked his children.

The children shook their heads.

"I'll tell you, then maybe you'll learn to be more careful around them," he said with unaccustomed sternness. "They're mementos from my grandfather, Hugh Ryan, who was foreman at the lead mine when it opened. He kept an extra set of drawings of the mine and a daily diary. When you're older you can read it and learn what life was like for a miner back then. I even have his old ledger that he used to record the daily yield of the mine."

Michael stood beside his father and looked obediently at the faded drawings and the notebooks that chronicled the miners' daily progress, their failures and successes. It was a unique look into the past, but at the time Michael was more concerned with the future, and he soon forgot about them.

His parents' house was on Amberwood Lane, and Michael slowly drove along the comfortable, shady street where he had lived most of his childhood. He had learned to ride his first bike here, and could point out the spots where he took his worst spills. He passed Mrs. Smithfield's bright yellow house. His first home run had gone through her front window, and had cost him his allowance for a month.

154

He parked in front of the light gray house with dark gray trim. His parents had built the house when Michael was three, planned it with love and care as their lifelong home. The garage door was open, and a neat stack of kiln-dried lumber lay in the driveway. John Ryan always had improvement projects for the house, putting in shelves or finishing a room. When Michael was twelve years old, his father had converted the family room into the perfect teenage boy's room. A long counter extended along one wall with drawers and doors below and shelves above it, stretching almost to the ceiling. This room had been his first chemistry lab, study, and dark room. His father had even included a sink in the corner. There was a glass case for his trophies, the baseball he had caught at Yankee Stadium.

Michael walked into the garage, past his father's wood working tools neatly lined up in the shop area, and into his room. Since Michael's marriage, his father had reclaimed it, extending his working area. Traces of Michael still remained in the room: a poster of the 1980 Olympic hockey team, a few honor certificates from high school, sports letters, books he had read but was reluctant to give away.

He started up the stairs that led to the main level of the house just as his father opened the door above him.

"Michael! I thought I recognized your Jeep out front. Good to see you." His father greeted him enthusiastically, wiping his hand on his overalls before offering it.

"Hello, Dad," Michael returned the greeting, shaking hands. His father's hand was rough, and his handshake firm. "What are you working on now?"

Before his father could answer, Michael's mother pushed past him on the stairs. "Hello, dear," she said, giving Michael a kiss. "Come and see what your father's making for me."

Michael followed the small, energetic woman into the kitchen. There she stopped and swept her hand over the room, pointing out the new pine cabinets below the counter and along one wall. Her pleasure was evident as she glanced fondly between husband and son. Michael smiled at her with affection. He thought her pretty, standing in the middle of her domain, cheeks pink with excitement, a wooden spoon in her hand.

"They're beautiful, Mom," he said, opening a cabinet, feeling the soft, oil-smooth finish and admiring the concealed hinges. He looked at his father, who was smiling self-consciously. "You really outdid yourself this time, Dad. What fine workmanship!"

John Ryan scratched his bristly head--he sported one of Ed's trademark brush-cuts--and stuck a pencil behind his ear. "This project was way overdue. I've been promising your mother new cabinets for five years."

"Can you stay for dinner, dear?" his mother asked, bending over to check the roast in the oven. "We're eating rather late tonight. The Morgan's grandchild was baptized, and they had a little party afterwards. We got home later than usual," she explained.

He watched his mother as she checked the meat with a fork, her flowered dress protected by a crisp apron, and thought how natural she looked. She was usually busy in the kitchen when he came to visit, but she never lost track of what he was saying. The aroma of the roast blended pleasingly with the smell of freshly finished wood, and for a moment he wavered. Then he shook his head.

"I'm sorry, Mom. I wish I could. But I'm on my way to New York and can't stay."

"Well, you'll have a cup of coffee, won't you?" she asked, ushering them into the living room.

"Sure. Actually, Dad, I'm here to ask you for something," Michael said, sitting down in a low easy chair.

The furniture in the comfortable living room was arranged around a large picture window that looked out onto the street. A side wall had built-in shelves, containing photographs of their children and grandchildren. There were graduation and wedding pictures of Eileen and Michael, photos of him playing hockey, a large wedding picture of his parents, looking young and uncomfortable. The photos were kept carefully arranged and dusted, each displayed to its best advantage.

John had been very proud of his son's academic and athletic successes, but was even more pleased when Michael returned to Langston to teach. Helping the town was almost like helping their own family.

"Is Becky going to New York with you, dear?" his mother asked.

Michael hesitated before answering. "No, she's not. I'm going on business, and that wouldn't interest her."

Something in his tone made his parents look at him, making him turn away uneasily. He was not ready to talk about Becky.

"I'll go get the coffee," his mother said, getting up.

Michael turned to his father, "Dad, do you still have those drawings of the old mine and the ledgers and diaries that your grandpa Hugh kept?"

His father nodded. "Sure. Why do you ask?"

"I'd like to borrow them. I'll make some copies so the originals won't be damaged."

His father got up and headed toward the den. "Let's go get them while your mother's making the coffee."

John Ryan opened a drawer in the great roll-top desk and took out the notebooks and drawings. As Michael studied them, his father watched him curiously. "What do you want with these?"

"Oh, I'm helping one of my students on a science project," he said vaguely. "I'm looking for information on the old mine."

John picked up one of the notebooks and began leafing through it. "Grandpa Hugh kept a pretty detailed diary. You can get a real good idea of what life was like in the mine if you read these." He began to read one of the entries aloud: "We hit hard rock and digging was difficult... Very little progress made. The men were discouraged." He turned the pages and read another entry: "We ran into crushed rock today. It was easy digging, and we made good progress. The yield was higher than usual." The third entry made them both pause for a moment. It was written unevenly, with many inkblots, a contrast to the neatness of the other passages: "There was an accident today. Part of the roof fell in, and three men were trapped. I helped dig them out, but it was too late for Maynard and the O'Dell boy. We got Sullivan out, but don't know if he'll make it. May God have mercy on their souls!"

Soberly, Michael took the notebook from his father. "It must have been a hard way to make a living." Then, brightening, "But these are just what I'm looking for."

Margaret returned with the coffee and poured for the two men. Michael was careful to set his cup away from the drawings. "These drawings and Hugh's descriptions in the notebooks, along with the ledger, will help me estimate the volume of the mine." He sipped his coffee, lost in thought.

"Why would you want to do that?" John asked.

Michael looked up. He didn't want to discuss details, didn't want to alarm his parents until he had a solution to the lead problem. Yet he couldn't lie to his father; they had a mutual respect for each other, despite differences of opinion on certain subjects. Michael suspected that this might be one of those subjects.

"I want to find out how much waste is buried in the mineshaft."

"For what purpose?" his father persisted.

Michael stood up and paced the room a couple of times before answering. His mother had been about to offer him a biscuit, but now her hand stopped in the air holding the plate, as she watched his face.

"Mom, Dad, the problem I'm working on is pretty serious. It concerns all of us, everyone in Langston."

His mother looked frightened. His father said, "Let's hear it." They both sat up straighter as they waited for his explanation.

"There is lead leaking out of the mine. It has to be cleaned up before it contaminates our drinking water," Michael said in one breath.

"Well, I'm sure that the trash in there must have some lead in it. After all, most of it is factory waste," John said. "But how is it getting out?"

"I'm not sure how, yet. But I'm trying to find a way to stop it."

"Is that dangerous?" Margaret asked.

"It can be, if it gets into the drinking water," Michael answered, turning to his mother.

"Hold on a minute, there, Michael. How much lead are we talking about?" John asked.

"Well, the maximum safe drinking water standard is 0.05 parts per million. And Jake Hughes' well already has 6 parts per million, over a hundred times the safe limit."

"Only 6 parts per million?" John laughed. "Why, at the factory we deal with concentrations thousands times that every day."

"I know, Dad, but you make sure that the men are well protected from it, don't you?"

"Of course," his father said, offended. "I wouldn't think of letting my men work under dangerous conditions. If I ever felt that they were in danger, I'd talk to Tom Lang immediately. I haven't had one of my men sick from the lead yet," he said proudly.

"I know how responsible you feel for your men, Dad. I feel responsible, too, for the safety of the town's drinking water."

John shook his head slowly. "I can't believe such a small amount of lead could do any harm."

"But it can. If you drink it, it builds up slowly in the body. Tom Lang has got to take care of the mess the Company left at the mine-site."

"I think you worry too much about the environment, Michael. Just what do you expect him to do?"

"Clean up the mine-site. Put in barriers to keep any additional lead from getting into the groundwater. Clean up the groundwater that has already been contaminated. There are different possibilities."

"Have you talked to Tom about this?"

"Yes, but he's stubborn. He needs more convincing. I'm going to New York now to get some advice. I want to have a plan of action, along with cost estimates to present to him when I get back."

"What kind of costs are you talking about?"

"A lot. Could be millions."

John Ryan whistled. "No wonder Tom is reluctant. He can't afford to spend money like that on just your say-so. There are some things you don't know about running the Company, and one of those things is the money involved."

"That's why I'm going to my old firm to get a better estimate to present to Tom. He will need to realize that the longer he waits, the more it will cost. And that if he cleans up the site himself it will be less costly in the long run, than waiting until he is forced to do it."

John Ryan shook his head doubtfully. "I hope you're wrong about this, son. But if you're not, and it turns out that the town really is in danger, I'll be the first to support you."

"I know, Dad." A long look of understanding passed between the two men. They were, and had always been, on the same side, Michael thought.

Margaret disappeared into the kitchen as Michael rose to leave. She returned with a small package that she handed to Michael.

"Take some of this pumpkin bread I just made, dear. You know you always liked my pumpkin bread," she said, smiling.

Michael hugged her, thinking how he always took a part of her with him, along with the pumpkin bread or the cookies she urged on him so frequently.

Chapter 13

Maggie was exasperated. She had tried to reach the reporter from the Times all afternoon, without success. She must reach him and stall him before he left for Langston, must tell him some plausible story to gain time for Michael to convince Tom Lang. She felt dirty and sweaty, wanted to shower and change her clothes, but instead she sat by the phone in the stifling newspaper office, stale air ineffectually whirled around her by a noisy fan. At five o'clock she couldn't wait anymore and went down to the cafe for a cold drink and dinner. Before leaving she left word with the Times to have the reporter call her at her room.

After dinner Maggie went to her room to shower and change, and wait for Michael. She put on her silky lounging pajamas and brushed her hair dry before the mirror. It shone auburn in the light of the shaded lamp and she smiled approvingly at her reflection. The dark rose of her pajamas warmed her complexion, and she reached into a drawer for a tube of coral lipstick. She put it on quickly, then glanced into the mirror self-consciously. She was not used to paying attention to her appearance, but what she saw pleased her. Her eyes seemed larger, clearer, with more depth to them. Suddenly she saw herself with Michael's eyes, and a pleasant warmth ran through her as she felt his lingering gaze.

Her favorite classical radio station was playing Ravel's Bolero, and Maggie lay down on the couch to listen and wait. She wanted to talk to Jake, to explain what was happening, but there was no phone in the cabin. And she didn't want to leave her room since the Times reporter might return her call and Michael would be arriving soon.

She must have fallen asleep, because when she opened her eyes it was ten, and the announcer was giving the evening news over the radio. There would be no call from the Times tonight. She stretched, wondering what had happened to Michael. Something important and unexpected must have kept him, but he would surely come in the morning. Maggie toyed with the idea of calling him, but didn't want to talk to Becky. She sighed, wiped off her lipstick, turned out the light, and went to bed.

Maggie was awakened the next morning by sunlight streaming through the window. Tired from the previous day's hike and the emotions of the past two days, she had overslept. She dressed hurriedly, grabbing a cup of instant coffee and doughnut on the way to the paper.

Emmett wanted her to follow up on a couple of stories in town, so she got ready to leave the office for the morning. But first, she dialed the Times office and left a message. She would try to call the reporter around two; he was not to leave for Langston before talking to her. She also left a message for Michael in case he called or came by while she was out.

Maggie returned to the Gazette after lunch and dialed the Times office, waiting impatiently while her call was put through to the desk of the reporter. This time he was in, and her spirits lifted as she delivered her message. No, don't come this week. It's just that the tests aren't conclusive yet, they need to be rerun. Yes, I will call in a week or so when I know something more. Good-bye.

After hanging up she looked for a message from Michael. Finding none, she sat down to type up her stories. Emmett left her to finish the layout for that week's paper, and it was late before she noticed the time. Quickly she locked up and ran down the outside stairs to her waiting Jeep.

It was early evening but the summer twilight lingered, reluctant to give way to night, when she turned down the dirt road to the cabin. A fat porcupine lumbered across her path, oblivious to danger. Maggie swerved to avoid hitting the animal. She remembered the one time Old Calamity tangled with a porcupine. He was still young, and had much to learn about wild creatures. He wanted to play, but the porcupine was not interested. Calamity circled it, barking, tail wagging and nose close to the ground, edging closer. The porcupine was trapped, and misinterpreting the dog's friendly advances, swung his tail in a wide arc, swiping Calamity's nose with dozens of sharp quills. Surprised, Calamity retreated, but too late to avoid the blow. Then he was lying on the ground, whining, nose between his front paws, uselessly trying to pull the quills from his tender snout. Maggie was frantic. Jake only laughed as he firmly but tenderly removed the quills with a pair of pliers and soothed the pain with some secret ointment. Old Calamity learned his lesson well, first-hand and painfully, as most young things do. From then on he was cautious around unfamiliar wild animals.

As Maggie pulled up to the cabin, Jake was nowhere in sight and the cabin was dark. No smoke issued from the chimney. Maggie shook her head; Jake probably hadn't bothered to cook himself a decent meal, and had fallen asleep without lighting a lantern. She parked by the woodpile near the well, then started in amazement. She saw in the headlights that the ground around the cabin was covered with ruts, as if heavy machinery had been operating there. She jumped down from the Jeep, puzzled and concerned, to examine the signs of this rude intrusion. At the well she stopped and stared--there was no well. The hand pump had been removed and the hole filled with concrete. Their source of water for generations wiped out.

For a minute her mind refused to work, to make sense out of this outrage. Then slowly the possibilities dawned on her, worming their way into her thoughts as she tried frantically to drive them away. She wanted to turn and run toward the cabin, to find Jake and an explanation. Jake would make it allright, Jake would make sense of this, and lay her suspicions to rest.

She stumbled over the uneven ground as she ran, and was nearly at the door when she saw something that made her draw back in alarm. The door had been boarded up, nailed shut. She stood looking at the cabin dumbly, uncomprehending, her mind unable to make sense of what confronted her. Over and over she read the sign that was nailed across the entrance:

In a fog she walked to the window and looked in at their darkened home. Jake was obviously gone. The cabin was very quiet; it had an air of sadness and abandonment. The kitchen table with dishes that hadn't been cleared, Jake's cold pipe sitting by his favorite chair, the snowshoe he had been repairing--all were merely objects in an empty house. But in her mind they were also intimately connected with Jake, a part of him. He had given them meaning and life.

A shiver went through her. Where was Jake? What had happened to him? Her head spun as she considered the possibilities. Then with an effort she tried to control her anxiety. Wherever he was, he was not strong, not well enough to look out for himself. She needed to pull herself together, clear her head before she acted. If she were to look out for him, she would need to be strong for both of them, for now there was no one else to rely on.

As she turned to go, she stumbled across a pile of boards that had been left lying by the path. Tears of anger and vexation stung her eyes as she fell, scraping her hands and knees on the rough wood. She sat on the ground sobbing, unable to see the splinters that had driven into her palm. Wiping away her tears angrily, she leaned her wet face on her knees. She was angry with Tom Lang for what he had done to their cabin and their well, for stealing their land. And she was perplexed and uneasy, unclear about Michael's role, no longer so sure of him. Why had he let this happen? She forced the thought away but it kept returning: could he have been a part of this atrocity?

Her heart wanted to say no, but she couldn't deny the evidence around her. A great lump of bitterness rose in her throat and she sighed, pulling herself up. She untied the kerchief from around her neck and wiped her face with it, then twisted the blue cotton in her fingers. Michael had lent it to her just yesterday. She had kept it, unable to give it up, wanting to keep a part of him with her. She looked at the kerchief and found herself still unwilling to part with it, as she was reluctant to give up her hopes and belief in him. She must listen to him first, let him explain. Perhaps she was grasping at air the way a falling climber grabs for an impossible handhold, hoping that somewhere there was a logical reason she had missed, something that could erase this fearful mistake. Nonetheless, she must give him another chance, she must find Michael.

Maggie knocked on the door and waited. She heard Rusty's bark inside, signaling her presence. Her heart beat faster, expecting Michael to open the door in a moment, and she summoned all of her anger at the recent outrage to support her. She must be strong; she would not be swayed by his charms. If she were to trust him again it must be because the betrayal she feared was a mistake, a misunderstanding.

When Becky cracked the door open, Maggie's heart sank. Rusty was behind her, pushing his nose through the crack toward Maggie, greeting her excitedly. Becky pushed him back with her leg. She recognized Maggie, but made no move to open the door further.

"Maggie." Her tone was cold, even hostile. Her face was in shadow, the hall light behind her.

There was no time for niceties, and Maggie was too preoccupied to notice Becky's manner. She spoke quickly, urgently. "Hello, Becky. I need to see Michael. I need to ask him about my father."

Becky stared at Maggie without moving, slowly taking in her distraught appearance. Maggie grew uncomfortable under her gaze. Self-consciously her hand moved to her hair, which was tangled and wild, and unsuccessfully tried to smooth it. Her nails were rough and broken, and she became acutely aware of the dirt and stains on her clothes where she had fallen near the cabin. For a moment she felt rough and ugly opposite Becky's near perfection, like a trick reflection in a fun house. With a feeling of annoyance she pushed the thought away. Those feelings didn't matter now; whatever inadequacies she may have felt next to Becky were irrelevant.

"He's not here," Becky said.

Maggie stared at her blankly, her mind still forming the words she planned to say to him. "Please, Becky. It's very important that I talk to him."

"Well, you can't. He isn't here," she repeated.

Maggie looked at Becky more closely and noticed the barely disguised malice in her face. "How much do you know about the problem of the old mine?"

"Enough to know that you've been setting Michael against me and my father. That you're trying to convince him that the Company was responsible for making your father sick. That he should risk everything because of you. But it won't work; Michael knows that his family is more important than a childhood friendship!" she added triumphantly.

169

"Where is he, Becky? I want to hear it from him!" Her voice shook slightly and she raised her trembling hands to the kerchief at her throat.

"He went to New York on business. Said he'd be back in a few days. Maybe he'll see you then, but don't count on it," she answered complacently.

"Do you know what Tom did with my father?"

"Oh, he's in Greenbriar Hospital. I'm sure he's getting the care he needs. My father will see to that," she added with a touch of pride.

Maggie sighed; at least one question had been answered. Jake was getting medical attention, something she was having trouble convincing him to do. But what about the cabin, the land? "Why was our well filled in and our home boarded up?"

Becky shrugged. "My father was taking care of the problem like he promised Michael. They had a long talk yesterday and agreed on what to do. Michael seemed pretty satisfied when he left for the city," she added smugly.

"Solving the problem by taking away our home and water? He had no right to do either! He was stealing our land!"

Becky's eyes narrowed. She hesitated as she focused on Michael's blue kerchief. Then she struck, swiftly and instinctively. "Your home! My family has only allowed you Hughes's to keep your shack on our land out of some sentimental feeling for the past. If it were up to me, I would have removed it long ago. It's nothing but a useless eyesore." Her words cut as deeply as they were intended.

Maggie stepped closer, forcing Becky to retreat. For a moment she saw Becky's face clearly. There were many emotions reflected in it, power and triumph and spite, but also an underlying fear. Then Maggie turned, speechless with rage, and fled out into the darkness.

Maggie waited impatiently for the floor nurse to answer the telephone. She would drive over to the hospital tonight, but she stopped to call first to make sure Becky's information was correct.

"Yes, Jake Hughes was admitted today," the nurse answered her query. "Dr. Irving is taking care of him."

"May I speak to him?"

"He is gone for the night and won't be in until morning."

"Can you tell me what my father's condition is, then?"

"He's been given a sedative and something for pain. We'll start the detox program in the morning."

"I'm coming over to see him," Maggie decided. "Can you give me his room number?"

"Visiting hours are over now. Anyway, he's asleep; it wouldn't do you much good to come until morning."

Maggie hung up, exasperated. Suddenly everything seemed to be going wrong and she didn't like sitting around and waiting; she wanted to do something about it.

She couldn't sleep much that night. What little sleep she had was filled with dreams that skimmed the surface of her consciousness, confusing thoughts and fears, worries and unreality. She saw the cabin in the woods razed, the land laid waste around it. Dead fish floated in the stream with Jake among them. She awoke with a gasp, to a night alive with crickets and bullfrogs unaware of the threat surrounding them. In another dream she was looking down into the crevice where she had found Michael. She called to him but he didn't answer. In her panic she leaned too far over the hole and fell into a black, bottomless abyss. She awoke in a sweat, as the first cold streaks of dawn threw bands of light across her bed.

She couldn't go back to sleep, nor did she want to, for her restless dreams were more tiring than wakefulness. She boiled water for tea, then sat by the window looking out at the slowly awakening town. Since their cabin was boarded up, she had stayed in her room in town. Now she wished she were at the cabin, chopping wood or carrying water. She needed mindless, physical work that would tire her muscles and allow the sleep that would give her mind the rest it craved. Instead she drank the tea and shivered, pulling her feet under herself on the couch. She had one goal for the day, to see Jake, but visiting hours at the hospital wouldn't start for hours. She dozed again. For a moment she was with Michael once more, alone under the fragrant firs, lying atop the springy needles in the lean-to. They had hung a blanket at the entrance for privacy in case a chance hiker passed by. The sun broke through between the logs of their shelter in bright, joyful streaks. They were happy in the old way and the new, loving and discovering each other. His touch lingered for a moment after she awoke, and the sharp contrast between dream and reality made her pain more poignant.

There were some signs of life in the street below now, a few men hurrying in the direction of the paint factory, arriving early for the day shift. Young and old, hurrying toward the heart of Langston, toward the institution that provided their living, defined their lives. At the same time this essential and benevolent institution was secretly poisoning them, subtly draining away the very life it had given them. All at once Maggie felt sorry for the factory workers as well as contempt for the mindless labor they performed in the factory that would prove their ruin. She wanted to warn them, to shake them out of their complacency, but her mind was lethargic, tired. What she really wanted was to find Jake and take him away from the town and its pollution, away from the Langs, who held the townspeople and even Michael in their power.

The factory whistle shook her out of her stupor, and she quickly drank the cold and bitter tea that remained in the bottom of her cup. She dressed in jeans and a camp shirt, and began

172

the drive to the hospital. The wind in the open Jeep whipped her hair into her eyes, and she searched for something to tie it back with. Her hand fell on Michael's blue kerchief, and without thinking she tied it around her hair. At the hospital she insisted on seeing her father, although visiting hours weren't until late afternoon. She hurried down a white corridor where efficient nurses ducked in and out of rooms on silent rubber soles, ministering to private miseries behind closed doors. Hospitals always gave her a queasy feeling with their strange smells, mixtures of food, medicine, urine and stale air. But today she ignored them all, intent on her mission.

She found Jake in a room by himself, a small room with a window that looked over the highway, and beyond that toward a hill covered with birch and aspen. She entered softly, not wanting to wake her father, yet hoping that he would be awake. He lay in the bed very still, breathing deeply and evenly. His pallor, surrounded by the bleached whiteness of the sheets frightened her, made him seem suddenly very old and vulnerable. His right arm was strapped to a padded board and was hooked to an I.V. bottle. The blue vein in his arm stood out sharply against his pale flesh as the foreign liquid was being forced into his body.

Maggie experienced an overwhelming need to wake him, to hear him talk, to know that he was alive. Tentatively, she whispered his name, then touched his hand. He stirred slightly, then resumed his even breathing. She called to him more urgently when a nurse entered the room carrying a tray of medication.

"You shouldn't try to wake him," she said. "Anyway, it won't do you much good. He's been given a sedative and it won't wear off for another hour."

"A sedative? What for?"

"He was having severe cramps when they brought him in. He's very weak and he needs rest. He's got more lead in

173

him than a number 2 pencil, and it'll take a while to clean him out. He should've been brought to the hospital long ago."

Maggie looked at her, frightened. "He'll be all right, won't he?"

"That depends. He seems pretty strong, and we're doing everything we can to help him. We're giving him something in the I.V. for cramps, and we're deleading him as fast as we can. It'll take time, and we have to let him rest between treatments."

"How much time?"

"At least three weeks. But it'll be a while after that before he gets his strength back. Did you know that Mr. Lang brought him in?" she asked in a gossipy voice.

Maggie stiffened at Lang's name and turned away from the nurse. "Oh? Did you talk to him?" she asked.

"Just for a moment. He told us to be sure to take good care of your father, that he would pay for everything. He even insisted that your father have a private room. Mr. Lang's a real gentleman, always looking out for other people."

Maggie swallowed her bitterness and struggled to hold her tongue. Tom Lang did bring Jake into the hospital and made sure that he was getting the best medical care. But Jake wouldn't need to be in the hospital at all if it weren't for the Langs and their damned mine.

Maggie stared out the window, not wanting to look at the silly nurse anymore. Like most of the people of Langston, she held the Langs in awe. All they saw was the power and wealth, and the occasional donations that the Langs contributed to the town, always with much ceremony and publicity. They couldn't see beyond the superficial actions to what lay beneath.

The nurse waited for Maggie to turn around, perhaps to join her in praising Tom Lang. When she didn't, the nurse shrugged and left the room muttering just loud enough for

Maggie to hear: "Some people don't know a good thing when they have it, just don't know how to be grateful."

Maggie let out the breath she had been unconsciously holding as the door closed. Then she sat in a chair by Jake's bed, stroking his hand, waiting for him to wake up. With an effort Jake opened his eyes and tried to focus on Maggie, then drifted off again for a few moments. He made an attempt to clear his groggy mind of the dulling pain killer, but his reactions were sluggish, his speech slurred.

"Maggie darling, I hate for you to see me like this," he mumbled.

"Nonsense, Dad. I'm glad that you're finally getting some help. You should've gone to a doctor long ago."

Jake made a rueful attempt at humor: "You know me, Maggie. What I can't cure myself ain't worth curing." Maggie smiled and nodded.

Then she became serious. "What happened, Dad?"

Jake passed his free hand over his eyes trying to wipe away the cobwebs that still clouded his mind.

"I hardly know. I been feeling pretty bad since you left, weak and tired and headachy. Then I began to have these awful cramps. I drank some herb teas, but it just got worse. When Tom Lang came to the door I was in no shape to argue."

"What did he say, Dad?" she asked carefully.

"Something about our well being poisoned by lead, though he didn't say how. Said he was worried about me and wanted to make sure I would get help."

"Did he say how he found out about the well?"

"It seems that Michael told him. They're working together."

At his words Maggie looked up, then tried unsuccessfully to hide her expression. "Did he say what they were going to do?"

"No, he didn't." Jake paused, studying his daughter thoughtfully. "What is it, Maggie? What's troubling you?"

"Nothing, Dad. Really."

He reached up and cupped her chin in his roughened hand. "Now, Maggie, you know better than to keep things from your old man. I ain't so old and confused that I can't tell something's the matter."

Maggie looked into his eyes full of concern and love, and suddenly all her pain and rage overflowed.

"Oh Dad, you don't know what the Langs have done to us. They filled in our well and boarded up the cabin. They've even posted our land as their own!"

Jake watched her in shocked silence.

"And the worst of it is that Michael is part of it!" she sobbed.

"Michael? Are you sure?" Jake struggled to sit up, then sank back into the pillows.

"There's no question about it. Lang told you he was working with Michael, and Becky said the same thing."

"What about Michael? What did he have to say?"

"Michael made me promise to give Lang a chance to clean up the water before doing anything. Now he's gone to New York without talking to me. You see, the lead is coming from the old mine-site; it's slowly leaching into the river and will eventually poison Langston's drinking water. We were the closest to the mine so our well water was poisoned first."

Jake sat up, agitated. "I should've known it had something to do with the mine. That site's been a curse ever since it was first discovered. But Michael--I can't believe he'd be a part of it."

She sat up, smoothing the hair out of her eyes and her hand fell on the blue kerchief. She slipped it from her hair and crumpled it in her fist as she answered, "I couldn't believe it either, not after everything. But it's true.

Well, they are digging their own graves," she sighed. "Tomorrow I'll call the Times and the Friends of the Wild. Nothing can stop me now."

Chapter 14

Michael left Langston late in the afternoon, hoping to reach New York by midnight. Below Sanford Lake where the Opalescent joined the Hudson, he left the river, choosing a route that occasionally returned to cross its path again. He drove through the town of Minerva, then passed the North Creek Ski Bowl on his left, signalling the approach of the Hudson once more. He turned northwest for a couple of miles and drove to the lookout at North River where the river came closest to the highway. Between Newcomb and North River the Hudson passed through wilderness, unpenetrated by roads. This stretch of rapids was the most spectacular on the Hudson, attempted successfully only by those with much canoeing experience.

Michael got out of the Jeep and leaned on the railing overlooking the river. Two canoeists had just reached the bank and were dragging their craft out of the water. Michael watched them pull the canoe onto the shore and lie down beside it, exhausted. Michael could feel their exhaustion, the marrow-deep fatigue that comes from sustained tightening of nerves and muscles fighting the river, conquering the angry white waters of the rapids.

It had been years since his trip down this wild stretch of the Hudson with Jake, but the memory was still clear. He and Jake were both aware of the dangers, but that knowledge, combined with a realistic confidence in their own abilities prepared them for the challenge. At Newcomb they launched Michael's nineteen foot Grumman canoe into a placid pool. They glided over a smooth, black lagoon, through the morning mist that covered the surface of the water. From somewhere ahead, around a bend in the river, the stillness was disturbed by a muffled rumbling sound, like distant thunder. As they paddled closer, the volume increased. Rounding the bend, the river exploded with a thundering roar. Deep, standing waves stretched across the width of the river, marking the beginning of Long Falls.

Jake wanted to study the white water from shore before committing themselves to the flume. Ahead, the water thundered down a natural staircase and disappeared under a cloud of silver mist. Jake reviewed the rules of white water canoeing with Michael. "If I say, `back-paddle,' you back-paddle hard, but if we can't stop, let's try to get the nose straight before we go through. If we swamp, stick with the canoe, but keep away from the front. The water pushing against a heavy canoe can pin you against a rock."

They pushed off and paddled into the flume. Instantly the canoe was lifted high on the crest of a wave. Jake yelled: "Back-paddle!" and they back-paddled hard, slowing their momentum as Jake steered between a pair of submerged boulders. For Michael time stopped, then rushed forward again as they were carried down the roaring chute. He caught his breath, then his brain swirled with a surge of adrenaline as they plunged nearly vertically down the falls. Michael felt the power of the rushing water in the seat of his pants. The thrill, uniquely composed of fear and exhilaration, was unlike anything else he had ever known. Even Jake, who had run these rapids many times, was shouting in excitement as he maneuvered the canoe from the back. When they came to rest in a quiet pool Jake looked at Michael, who was breathing hard, his eyes dilated, and said, "The river's like a fiery woman. She wears you out, but she makes you want more."

Drifting down the now placid water, they entered a scenic valley. Wood ducks, surprised by the canoe's sudden appearance, took off in a shower of spray, hurling insults at the intruders. Thick pine and cedar forests covered the river banks. Long stretches of slow moving water alternated with short, easy rapids.

Eventually the valley narrowed and they began to pick up speed as the grade steepened. At the base of Cedar Mountain, Cedar River joined the Hudson, increasing the river's flow. As they danced along the crests, Michael let out a loud whoop of joy.

Just past the sportsmen's camp on the gently sloping right bank, the Hudson turned sharply eastward, joined by the

Indian River, entering a deep gorge with walls that towered above them. Dark holes and long pools followed each set of rapids, allowing short periods for rest. The water flowed over a series of ledges that dropped off, one after the other, resulting in almost a mile of continuous, heavy, rolling waves. A stiff wind sprayed the tops of the whitecaps into their faces as they fought to stay upright.

The river curved smoothly to the south. Blue Ledge loomed before them, swallowing up the river, a magnificent precipice rising eight hundred feet from the water's edge. Exhausted, they pulled their canoe out of the water on the opposite bank and pitched camp. Silently eating their food, they watched the sun set across the river. Tomorrow they would face Big Nasty Rapids, the most difficult stretch of rapids on the Hudson, but tonight they would savor the adventure behind them.

They prolonged their last day in the wilderness, staying at the campsite longer than necessary. It was beautiful here; a wild, inaccessible spot, protected by the walls of the canyon and difficult rapids above and below. They carefully packed the canoe, strapping their waterproof bags tightly to the thwarts, covering them with an oilcloth, and pushed off into the current. Soon, they were fighting for their survival. The water threatened to turn them sideways, but Jake's skilled hand on the paddle kept them straight. Time slowed, and what was actually less than 30 minutes seemed to last a lifetime. The river twisted through the gorge, the walls rising steeper on the sides as the canoe plunged down the furious rapids. Then, without warning it was over; they were pushed out of the gorge and into a quietly flowing river.

Michael remembered that the remaining five miles to North River were uneventful. He now looked at the placidly flowing river that began at 4,293 feet on top of Marcy, fell to 1,550 feet at Newcomb, and in another thirty miles of rapids lost 550 feet. Only 1,000 feet of elevation remained to push the water the rest of the distance to New York City.

Michael checked his watch, then reluctantly returned to his Jeep and retraced his route along the river to North Creek. Here the river and Route 28 diverged for ten miles. At The Glen Michael crossed the tracks of the Delaware and Hudson Railroad, then crossed the river, and followed it south for a few more miles. Before long he reached Warrensburg and the Adirondack Northway. The southern tip of Lake George stretched below him, only hinting at its magnitude. At Glens Falls the waters dropped over a fifty foot ledge, creating a scenic falls. Just below Glens Falls the Hudson turned sharply to the south and continued in that direction for the remainder of its course to the Atlantic.

By early evening he had left the mountains behind and the landscape assumed a different character. The countryside was gentler than the Adirondacks, still wooded but interspersed with open fields and rounded hills. Here and there a farm bordered the highway, its weathered wooden buildings alight with the setting sun. Occasionally the trees of an apple orchard lined the road, their branches heavy with ripening fruit.

Although he couldn't see the river from the freeway, he continued to think about it flowing parallel to him, gathering other rivers to it, growing on its journey south. At its source it was but a small trickle that emptied into Feldspar Brook. It gained strength when it joined the Opalescent, and then gathered itself into the full, flowing waters of the Hudson. The river had many aspects. The northern half was a thing of beauty, a means of recreation, and a wild habitat. As it travelled south, the river attracted the small towns to itself, growing as the population along its banks increased. From Troy south to the ocean, the river was wide and deep, an avenue of commerce and trade. The cities of Troy, Albany and New York itself drew sustenance from this dependable trade route, although they had also abused it as well, using it as a convenient sewer.

Michael crossed the Mohawk River just as a barge steamed below the bridge pushing its heavy load. Just five miles downstream at Troy, the Mohawk joined the Hudson, forming a major segment of the Erie Canal. By linking east and west, the canal stimulated business and trade, and was greatly responsible for the growth and development of New York City as well as the state. As Michael drove over the bridge watching the dark greenish water below him with its promise of life, he was thinking of the mine-site north of Jake's cabin, and it's threat of adding further to the pollution of this mighty river system.

Michael decided to stop at an Albany exit to call a friend in Mount Kisco. He knew Ben would be happy to see him. They had been close friends during Michael's years in the city, working for the same engineering firm, sharing the commute each morning between the quiet, sleepy town and the vibrant life of New York.

A third lane joined the Northway as it reached Lake George, and traffic became thicker, more rushed. Billboards beckoned to him, hawking Vodka and cars and insurance, all the things seemingly necessary for urban life. As a car passed on his right, tires screeching, the driver rolled down his window and tossed a burning cigarette in Michael's direction. It flew against Michael's windshield and was whipped away, leaving tiny sparks in its wake. Paper and beer cans littered the shoulder, sometimes an old sneaker adding variety to the rubbish. Where was its mate, he wondered.

Ben was glad to hear from him, and of course Michael could stay as long as he wanted. He would put a key to the townhouse under the mat so Michael could let himself in.

Michael took the New York State Thruway south, and an hour later he was passing through the Catskills. It was dark now, and the lights of sleepy towns shone in the distance. The mountains were outlined in the bluish light of the moon that played hide and seek with the clouds. Four miles or so to the east was the Hudson, barely above sea level, reversed daily by tides surging from the ocean one hundred miles to the south. The Indians called this section of the Hudson "The River That Flowed Two Ways."

At West Point he began to look forward to the end of his trip. The thruway turned east to cross the Hudson where it widened to form the Tappan Zee, or Tappan Bay. He drove across the 2.8 mile long Tappan Zee Bridge, a feat of construction he had always admired. He arrived in Mount Kisco before midnight, winding his way through the familiar streets by instinct. Finding the key in its hiding place he let himself in, not wanting to disturb Ben. They would have time to talk tomorrow.

Michael noted few changes as they walked to the train station the next morning. The two mile walk was pleasant. Michael had always preferred walking to the train when he had lived there, having few other opportunities for exercise. Often Ben joined him, as he did this morning.

"Don't you miss it, Michael?"

"Sometimes. There isn't a single good Jewish delicatessen in Langston and the big show is the senior play at the high school," he said smiling. "I miss the challenge of solving a client's problem. But I also remember the long commute and the even longer hours working on environmental impact statements for projects that should never be built. Like that highway plan to jam another hundred-thousand people onto the Manhattan streets. Besides, right now I have enough challenges to deal with in my own life."

His friend looked at him curiously, then went on. "I couldn't live without the bright lights. Don't you remember when we first started work, how excited we were, how full of energy? What a heady experience it was to be living and working in the city? How eager we were to start, to explore during our off hours. Each day was an adventure. Remember, the night we were in Chinatown for their New Years festival? We sneaked in and played the dragon's tail, and you got a string of firecrackers caught in your cuff. Becky and Fran laughed about that for days."

"Yes, we had some good times. My years in New York were an experience I'll never regret." Michael smiled, slowing

185

his steps for a moment. He remembered the early days when he felt a vitality in the Big Apple, what people called the heartbeat of the city. It was almost tangible when you walked the streets or rode the subways, or looked down from the seventieth floor of an office building on a city pulsing with activity below. The city's neighborhoods teemed with all varieties of humanity, from newly landed Afghan refugees whose communal households were redolent with the odors of exotic spices, to wealthy natives that retreated to their penthouse sanctuaries far above the crowded streets. New York unleashed his imagination, fired his curiosity. And it offered things that a small town never could: concerts, plays, lectures, and especially the museums. He spent hours poring over the dinosaur bones at the Museum of Natural History, imagining life in the primeval rain forests. Ben was always tempting Michael to return to his old job.

"Frankly, I expected to see you back here before now. The way I see it, once a person's known the city, nothing else will do."

Michael shook his head. "It wasn't for me, Ben. Not really, not where it counts. There are some things I miss, but not enough to come back to stay," he added.

They walked the rest of the way in silence, each occupied with his own thoughts. Michael noted two recently completed houses built in a style similar to the old homes surrounding them. The architect had intended harmony with the older style, but the effect was that of an imitation antique that just missed fooling the eye. Perhaps it was the unfinished landscaping; the houses needed the trimming of old trees and ivy to truly fit in.

They arrived at the station at seven, in plenty of time for the usually late train. The long platform was filling with commuters, mostly businessmen with freshly shaved faces, wearing gray or blue pin-striped Wall Street suits, carrying briefcases and folded newspapers. At 7:05 a few late comers raced into the station, driven by haphazardly dressed wives in curlers, pajama clad children in the back seat. The commuters stood on the platform reading their newspapers, occasionally glancing in the direction of the expected train and checking their watches.

This daily ritual was familiar to Michael, having once been a part of his routine. Now as an outsider, he noticed the faces around him for the first time. Most wore blank expressions that hid their emotions, while a few revealed their boredom or irritation. Surprised by this discovery, he surreptitiously ran a hand over his face, searching for signs of his emotions. Most of the men were silently awaiting the approaching day. It was still early but the August air already lay wet and heavy over them, portending the heat and humidity of mid-afternoon.

Finally, the tracks began to buzz and whine, and the low rumble of the train could be heard in the distance. The commuters crowded to the edge of the platform. Michael often wondered why someone wasn't pushed off the platform into the path of the train more frequently.

They were waiting for the 7:07. Except for one stop, this was an express train to Grand Central Station. Once, Michael made the mistake of getting on a local and suffered a maddening extra half-hour as the train stopped at every town between Mount Kisco and Grand Central. The train roared in with a shrill whistle, and its brakes emitted a tortured metal-on-metal screech. They found seats in the front of the coach and opened their newspapers to read. The constant rattle of the train filled their ears, and they did not try to talk. Michael rested his elbow on the windowsill, picking up a streak of dirt on the sleeve of his light jacket. He saw trees and greenery covering the rolling hills along the tracks as they passed through the northern suburbs of New York. It always amazed him how there could be so much greenery and open space that close to one of the world's most populous cities.

They pulled into White Plains five minutes behind schedule. More commuters jumped on, scrambling for seats, their mood for the day often determined by their luck at finding seating.   The train system in New York always impressed Michael; its miles of subways providing rapid and affordable transportation for millions.   During his sophomore year his engineering class took a field trip to New York. He marveled at the maze of subway tunnels carved out of the granite core of Manhattan Island, the majesty of the Brooklyn Bridge, and the soaring dignity of the Empire State Building.

This trip reinforced Michael's conviction to make civil engineering his major. He balanced his love of hockey with a determination to train for a profession that he could practice after he finally hung up his skates.

Shortly after he got out of his cast, one of Michael's professors offered him a job, helping out on a research project. The professor believed that rainwater leaking into the existing dumps would pick up toxic metals and organic compounds, carrying them into the groundwater, the largest source of fresh drinking water. He hired Michael to assist him in testing his theories. Michael relished finally working on a real problem, although it bothered him that it represented a conflict between technology and nature. He resolved to enter a career where he could help protect nature from the negative side effects of technology.

Growing up in the Adirondacks, nature seemed too powerful to be threatened by man. Except for a few careless tourists neglecting to put out campfires, the remote forests remained unchanged, protected by the "forever wild" provisions of the state constitution. Other parts of New York State were less fortunate. Suddenly Love Canal exploded in the national headlines. Major centers of industry, those cities located in the midst of progress and development, were the ones with the problems. It was easy for him to think that these problems could not touch his home in the mountains.

Michael took two courses from the professor he was working for, and found out that a masters degree was required to specialize as an environmental engineer. Once his goal was established, he completed his senior year on the Dean's list and graduated with honors. With his advisor's recommendation, he was accepted in the graduate program at Columbia University, with a fellowship.

He and Becky were married and moved to New York while he completed his masters. After graduation he accepted an offer to work for Garrison and Connely. By then he'd had enough of the crowds and the concrete lined streets where the only trees grew from little holes cut in the sidewalk. They moved out to Mt. Kisco, to the quiet, pleasant suburb where old oaks and maples lined the sidewalks.

Working at Garrison and Connely was exciting. He was constantly learning new things, feeling useful. There was never a shortage of work, in fact sometimes they had to turn down jobs. New York and New Jersey seemed to have a great need for their services. Michael was happy and interested, and learned quickly. After three years, he was made project manager for the cleanup of a hazardous waste site in New Jersey. Carl Garrison noticed the good job he did in developing a cleanup plan that was less expensive than the client had originally budgeted. From then on, Michael had his pick of assignments, and usually picked the most challenging ones, the ones that more timid engineers avoided.

He had been project manager for a few years when things no longer seemed right. He began to feel that he was running in circles, facing an endless series of problems. Before one was solved another arose, and they were always racing, never seeming to make headway against the environmental problems of the city. He began to feel like the clown that followed the elephants at the circus, and the elephants were multiplying.

Soon, the daily commute began to bother him. Each day when he left Becky, he entered a world totally isolated from Mt. Kisco. The train ride to New York, nearly an hour each way, seemed more and more like an artificial link between worlds that had nothing to do with each other. Whereas before he had spent the train ride to work looking out the window, curious about his surroundings, now he withdrew into himself, like so many others, burying his face in the daily newspaper. In the city he found himself becoming irritated by the constant noise, and the people that jostled him and hurried by mindlessly.

More and more frequently he worked late to avoid the crowds and stopped for a drink at the station. And the more frustrated he became, the more he missed the mountains. It was as if a part of his life was missing, a very important part. At first he thought about transferring to another office, or even switching to a firm that wasn't based in the city. But he realized that successful environmental companies had to be where the problems were, in the midst of a large city with its industry and dense population, and myriad sources of pollution. So he carried on for a while, tolerating his situation. Then he and Becky visited Langston for two weeks.

He spent time with Jake and it was like the old days again. They hiked the familiar trails, fished among the reeds where only wild duck and bullfrogs kept them company, and carved sticks on Jake's old porch as fireflies signalled to each other in the fading twilight. They didn't talk much, but Michael found a long missed satisfaction in the older man's company. During those days he felt more complete, more peaceful, than he had in years. His senses cleared. Once again he found himself drinking in the subtle sounds, smells, and sights around him, instead of screening out the overpowering stimuli that assaulted him in the city. Here the morning arrived with the freshness of dew and the scent of pine; often the only sound was that of wind in the trees or bumblebees among the honeysuckle.

After a week he wanted to stay, but couldn't think of a possible way. He spoke to Jake about it. They were on the porch at dusk, waiting for the stars. Jake smoked his pipe while Michael paced back and forth, now kicking the old boards aimlessly, now leaning against a post with hands buried deep in his pockets and looking out into the approaching night. He sighed a few times until Jake sensed his anxiety and broke the silence.

"Sit down, Michael. Something's troubling you. Care to talk about it?" he asked, pipe clutched between his teeth.

Michael glanced at the older man with a sense of relief, and sat down on the porch next to his friend. He hadn't realized how much he wanted to talk to Jake. "I've been having doubts, Jake."

Jake nodded. "We all have doubts at times."

"I suppose so. But I'm just not comfortable with my life." He paused, looked up at the evening star directly above them. "A few years ago I saw my future so clearly. I would become an environmental engineer and protect nature. And I suppose I'm doing that. But it seems so hopeless. The problems keep coming faster than we can solve them." He sighed, and pulled himself up.

"But that's only part of it," he continued. "Lately I find myself becoming resentful. In order to do even the little that I can, I have to live and work in the city, and that is becoming more and more difficult." He turned toward Jake and studied the craggy profile, the weathered skin, the intricate lines disappearing into his shirt collar. Then Jake faced him, and only his eyes were clear in the semidarkness.

"You're thinking of coming home, aren't you?" Jake asked simply.

"Yes. But how can I? I've worked hard to be an engineer, and I can't just abandon it. But, during these last few days I've been happier than I've been in a long time. Not since years ago, since before college. Sometimes I just want to leave everything and come back here, to your kind of life." He spoke quickly, painfully, the words uttered as much to himself as to Jake.

191

"Listen to me, Michael. You can't live my kinda life. My life suits me, not you. You gotta find your own way. It'd sure make me glad to see you come back. But you can't do it 'til you decide it's right for you."

It was dark now, and the evening star very bright. He couldn't see Jake's face, but felt his eyes burning into him, heard the truth in his words.

After that, things fell into place quickly, so fast that he hardly had time to weigh the consequences. The science teacher at the high school was leaving before Christmas, and they had no one to take his place. The principal approached Michael tentatively, with little hope that Michael would accept the position. But, to his surprise, Michael jumped at the chance. He would have three months to give his notice and wind things up at work. All the while he was finishing his life in the city, he could barely control his elation and excitement. Whenever he was disturbed by doubts, something within would laugh, drowning out his negative thoughts. I am going home to the mountains, to the beauty and freedom I've missed so much! I know that is my place and my life to shape the best I can.

Tom Lang was happy to see them return, although not so happy with Michael's career choice. He had wanted Michael to come to work for him, to take a responsible role in the family business. But his little girl was back to stay, and he showed his joy with a generous gesture. He would build them a house as he had planned if they ever returned to Langston. So Michael returned home, with few regrets and many plans.

When they reached the Bronx the train gained elevation until it was traveling 20 feet above the street. Michael saw ample housewives in flowered dresses idly staring at the moving cars, their faces reflecting the boredom of the commuters. Sullen young men and embittered older ones sat on the fire escapes, perhaps suffering a hangover from the previous night's cheap wine. Sometimes a dark eye flashed at him with what he imagined was resentment and hate, perhaps a challenge.

Laundry swayed in the breeze overhead, strung on lines connecting tenement windows.

They travelled over the Harlem River into Manhattan and came to a stop at 125th St. The buildings around them were dirty and crumbling, housing liquor stores, used clothing stores, pawn shops and run down Woolworths. Aimless men loitered in the doorways or leaned against graffiti-covered walls. They passed used car lots and the boarded-up shells of abandoned buildings.

Soon the train went underground and they continued on in the dark. Other trains passed them, their windows flashing squares of light like the frames of an old motion picture. A dull roar consumed all other sounds, dazing him with its ceaseless monotony.

When Michael finally walked through the massive stone archways into the main concourse of Grand Central Station, he stopped under the blue, soaring ceiling that suggested the sky, the open air, all the things that Grand Central wasn't. The sound of hurrying footsteps on the stone floor echoed hollow in the cavernous space. He tried unsuccessfully to make eye contact with someone, but the grim, blank faces passed around him without recognition or interest. When he finally turned away, disheartened, Ben was waiting for him at the exit, tapping a newspaper against his leg with a short, jerky motion.

Chapter 15

From Grand Central Station they took the escalator directly up to the Pan Am building. The Garrison and Connely offices were located on the 45th floor. In the main lobby, two guards were sitting at a semicircular desk that served as the building control center. A third guard, one that Michael recognized immediately, walked toward them from the revolving doors of the 45th Street entrance. Joe was something of an institution, having worked in the building since before anyone could remember. They stopped to exchange a few words with him before heading for the elevators. People in business suits poured into the lobby, lining up before the parallel banks of elevators, waiting their turn. There were several Japanese men, who worked for companies that had offices in the building. Michael and Ben were the last to squeeze into an elevator that served the 45th floor.

The tan hallway carpet muffled their steps as they entered the reception area of Garrison and Connely Environmental Engineers. Michael stopped and turned to his friend.

"You go ahead, Ben. I'm going up to the top for a minute."

"All right. Remember, lunch at noon."

Michael took the elevator to the top of the building and opened the door to bright sunshine. It was a shock moving from the temperature controlled environment and artificial lighting to the warmth and humidity of an August day. At least here on the top there was air movement, and the noise of the city only reached him as a faint, confused hum. He moved to the railing and looked down. Far below miniature buses honked madly at tiny cars that were impeding their progress and at insignificant people who darted between the gridlocked cars, hurrying to who knows what crucial appointment. To his left on the East River he spotted a tour boat, while to his right the Hudson stretched to the Jersey shore. Barely visible in the distance, the Statue of Liberty held aloft her golden torch. He stood for a moment taking it all in, feeling the beat of the city below. Unconsciously a part of himself responded to the low thrumming that was the life of New York, its heartbeat and breath.

Carl Garrison's office was furnished in sleek, polished teak. He had bought the minimum furniture necessary for efficient, brisk meetings and undistracted work. A large potted palm stood in one corner by the window, his only concession to unnecessary decoration. A single large painting on the near wall, a Rockwell Kent, complemented Carl Garrison's minimalist style with its simplified lines and stark colors. The landscape was harsh and revealing, reducing nature to its most basic elements. Michael had influenced Carl's decision to buy the painting.

Carl Garrison rose when Michael entered his office and walked toward him with hand outstretched. He was a lean man of average height, with light brown, receding hair, forty-three years old. His appearance was unremarkable, but his manner was not. His every movement, every expression was charged with energy. As he smiled at Michael his blue eyes lit up and his face became animated. His energy and enthusiasm were contagious, and were the driving force behind his firm. As they shook hands, Michael thought once more that this was a man who accomplished his goals.

"Michael! It's been nearly two years! Are you coming back to work with us?"

Michael smiled, remembering the pressure Carl had exerted when he announced his resignation. For awhile all of his energies were brought to bear on Michael to convince him to reverse his decision. But when these attempts failed, he accepted Michael's decision with grace. Carl had let Michael know that a place would always be open for him if he ever changed his mind.

"No, Carl, I'm just back for a visit, and for some advice."

"Well. How're things in the country? I must say, you're looking good. Life must be agreeing with you. Do you ever miss us here in the big city?"

As they sat down next to each other at the conference table, Michael smiled at the other man's habit of bombarding one with questions . It used to leave him at a loss for words, not knowing which to answer first.

"Yes, I do miss you all, and sometimes the work. But not the life."

Garrison leaned forward, his nervous fingers tracing the lines of a marble ashtray.

"You know, sometimes I don't blame you for leaving. Sometimes I think, how lucky you are to be in the clean open spaces of the Adirondacks. How fortunate to be away from the crowds and pollution. It must be a different world up there, away from all this." He made a sweep with his hand toward the window, encompassing all that lay beyond.

Michael hesitated before answering. "I'm fortunate to be living in the Adirondacks. In many ways it's a different world up there. Things are slower, people more rooted. There's a continuity about life in the mountains, a timelessness. There's a feeling of peace I can't describe, knowing the mountains have been there for millions of years and will be there for millions more. But there are problems, too. I'm afraid that environmental problems aren't restricted to the city. In fact, that's why I'm here."

The older man sat up, his interest piqued. "Oh? Something happening up north that we'd be interested in?"

Michael leaned forward and gazed at the carpet for a moment. "Yes. As I said, I'm looking for some advice."

"You've got my interest. Tell me what's going on."

"All right. A certain company disposed of their solid wastes in an abandoned mineshaft. Lead leached from the waste and contaminated a private well near the mine. The well's owner is showing symptoms of lead poisoning. Traces of lead have also shown up in a nearby river. Two miles downstream, a town of a few thousand people depend on the river for their drinking water."

Garrison studied Michael. "Do you have a personal involvement in this as well?"

"Is it that obvious? Becky's father is the company president."

"I see. Go on."

"I have a number of questions to work on. First, what is the most cost-effective method for cleaning up the groundwater and eliminating contamination of the river? Second, how can the mine-site be cleaned up or the contaminants contained in place? And finally, approximately how much will the cleanup cost?"

"Is that all?" Garrison asked, a thin smile on his lips. "As you know, those are the typical questions we face at a hazardous waste site. Hundreds of thousands if not millions of dollars can be spent in coming up with reasonable answers to them. Did you know that over two hundred million dollars has been spent on Love Canal and a permanent solution hasn't been found yet?"

"Yes, I did. But, right now, I only want to come up with a reasonable cleanup method and develop a cost estimate in sufficient detail and accuracy to convince my father-in-law, Tom Lang, to take action."

"Is he looking for engineering services?"

"Not yet. First I need to convince him that the problem is urgent, and that the cost of cleanup is affordable, or at least cheaper than the option of waiting for the EPA to declare it a hazardous waste site."

"Yes," Carl agreed. "You want to keep the EPA away unless absolutely necessary. The EPA Superfund program is a major source of revenue for our firm, but I know our friends at the EPA would agree that every time the program is used to clean up a site, it represents a failure. They would much prefer companies to clean up their own wastes. The purpose of the Superfund program is to handle `orphan' hazardous waste sites, those that have been abandoned by their responsible parties. Much of the cost of the program is for gathering evidence against the responsible parties and for developing cleanup methods that will be defensible in court and be acceptable to the general public. The companies end up paying many times more for these analyses than what it would cost them if they would have cleaned up on their own. They pay for the EPA study team and also for their own experts to advise them on the cleanup. The biggest cost is for the lawyers to handle the eventual litigation."

"That's what I've been telling Tom Lang, that delay can be very costly. If he would get going and perform his own engineering study, he would save a lot of time and money."

"So what are you looking for from me?"

"I can handle the groundwater treatment. I would like to brainstorm ideas with one of your hydrogeologists on developing a containment or removal strategy for the waste that's in the mine."

"Why don't you go and talk to Nate Maguire. Come and see me after you've talked to him, and we'll take it from there."

"Thanks, Carl. I was hoping you'd say that."

Michael met Ben for lunch at the Zum Zum Room on the second floor of the Pan Am building. Sitting at the counter on the high stools, amid the steam of sauerkraut mingled with the sharp odors of beer and mustard, Michael felt at ease. This was a familiar place, one frequented by many commuters. Often, after work he would stop for a beer and a hot dog to fortify himself against the crush of people outside and the long commute home. Also, it had been a means of slowing down, of closing the gap between the two facets of his life.

It was only one when he left the Zum Zum, telling Ben not to wait for him after work. He had talked to Nate Maguire, the company's chief hydrogeologist earlier, at Garrison's urging. Nate suggested meeting for a drink at four to discuss Michael's problem. Michael had worked with Nate before and found him helpful and creative. He hoped that Nate would help him find a feasible solution to Langston's problem.

Until four his time was free, and for a few moments he was at a loss. The midday sunshine blinded him as he stepped through the revolving doors from the climate controlled environment of the Pan Am building. Shafts of brilliant light were scattered in sudden bursts from the chrome of moving cars and the tinted glass of skyscrapers and shop windows. Heat assaulted him from all sides, radiating from the tall buildings around him as well as the pavement below. The air was oppressive, making it difficult to breathe. He headed north on Park Avenue, toward Central Park. He walked past several apartment buildings with tasteful awnings and liveried doormen at the glass doors. Small, exclusive boutiques that catered to the residents of these buildings displayed designer scarves and fashionable jewelry in their windows. At 51st Street he cut over to Fifth Avenue, passing St. Patrick's Cathedral and the Museum of Modern Art. The stores along Fifth Avenue always impressed him, although he never shopped in them. They were the ones with classy names, Bergdorf's and Henry Bendel, and he stared with fascination at the mannequins with stylized features and polished heads modeling clothing in impossible poses.

He stopped before a jeweler's window and looked at the glittering display of gold and diamonds. They were beautiful and impressive, but they left him cold. He preferred warmer stones, the ones that looked more like they came from the earth, like jade and turquoise, and Maggie's tiger eye. He reached into his pocket and took it out, moving it in his fingers, admiring it as the sunlight reflected off its different points. The stone looked satiny with vanishing bands of light gliding over its surface. A passerby bumped his arm, nearly causing Michael to drop the stone. Alarmed, he returned it to his pocket and rejoined the pedestrians swirling around him in their endless hurrying, their need to rush, he didn't know where. He, too, hurried the last few blocks, caught in the rhythm of the city, entering Central Park with a feeling of relief.

He walked past the pond toward the zoo, staying on the main path most of the time. Lawns and benches lined the path, with shady, wooded areas further away. A nanny pushing twins in a double stroller passed him. An old man sat on a bench tossing popcorn to pigeons milling on the ground. Their gray feathers gleamed purple or green as they caught the sunlight. A family was eating a picnic lunch near the pond, watching the ducks splashing in the murky water. The sounds of traffic were dulled here, reaching him through the insulating barrier of trees and shrubbery.

Central Park, although imperfect, was an oasis in the middle of the city. It was here that people came to escape the noise and confusion of the streets, when they needed the sound of flowing water or wind in the trees to calm their overwrought senses. In Central Park, many of the city's children made their first contact with nature. During his first months in New York, Michael explored the abandoned paths, obscure trails overgrown with vines and shrubbery from lack of use. They reminded him of the Adirondacks, the woods he had hiked all his life.

Familiar, mixed odors met him at the entrance to the zoo. The smells of popcorn and hot dogs from the vendors' carts combined with ammonia and hay from the animal houses. Balloon vendors stood next to souvenir stands as sparrows fought over the undigested grain in the piles left by the horses from the buggy rides. He looked at his watch, then swatted at a fly that kept landing on the back of his neck. The air felt muggy and his shirt stuck to his back. Deciding quickly, he climbed into one of the horse and buggy rides going north. He would visit the Metropolitan Museum of Art instead, and spend an hour among its rare and beautiful treasures until his meeting with Nate.

Michael stopped in the doorway of the Copter Club at the top of the Pan Am building, waiting for his eyes to adjust to the dim lighting. He scanned the room with its comfortable chairs and intimate atmosphere, searching for Nate Maguire. It was still early, and only a few men sat around the low tables, relaxing or winding up business. The club was exclusive, for members and guests only. It was insulated from the sounds and heat of the city, the sunlight filtered out by heavy tinted glass. Nate lounged in a leather easy chair by a window overlooking Park Avenue, sipping on a Dewar's. He was a man in his forties, with thick, unruly hair, who looked like he would be more comfortable wearing an old sweater than his well cut suit. They shook hands and exchanged greetings while the waitress took Michael's order.

Nate broached the subject without ceremony. "Carl told me a bit about your dilemma, Michael. Just what kind of a problem are we facing here?"

"First of all, I'm going to have to ask you to keep what I say to you in confidence. The situation is delicate, and I need time to negotiate a resolution without outside interference."

"OK. Although if its about a site we're working on for the EPA, I'm going to have to stop you."

"No, it isn't. I already cleared that with Carl."

"Go on. I'm listening."

"A certain company operated a lead mine in the Adirondacks during the early part of the century. This company manufactured paint after World War I to market their lead.

When the mine played out in the thirties, they continued to manufacture paint, getting their raw materials elsewhere. After closing, the mine-site was filled in with the company's and the town's solid wastes. Needless to say the company's wastes contained lead."

"Carl said that there was some lead contamination of a well and a nearby stream. You know that lead contamination of groundwater is pretty rare."

"Yes. It seems that this is the exception. A well located about a quarter mile from the mine-site had lead concentrations above 5 parts per million. The owner of the well is showing symptoms of lead poisoning. The Opalescent River, about a hundred yards from this well, is showing lead concentrations approaching the drinking water limit."

Nate looked up sharply. "The Opalescent? I went fly fishing on that stream a couple of years ago. That's a pretty clean river, to my knowledge. And I know of only one town on that stream." He paused to take a long sip of his drink. Then, "Well, what do you need from me?"

"I'm trying to convince the company's president to clean up the site and protect the river and groundwater from the pollution. I need to prepare a reasonable cleanup plan with a rough cost estimate to present to him. I'd like your ideas and suggestions on how to do this."

Nate ran his hand through his hair and stared out the window over Park Avenue for a few minutes. The hostess asked if they needed their drinks refreshed, but he didn't notice. Michael ordered another round, not wanting to interrupt Nate's thoughts. When she returned with their order, Nate took a sip of his fresh drink and leaned forward in his chair.

"A lot of times the best way to control a problem is to imitate nature. Finding out how the contamination occurred may help you to come up with a cure.

"As I said before, it's unusual to have groundwater contaminated with a metal like lead. At neutral pH, lead is not very soluble. An acid water would be needed to dissolve lead. Soils tend to be alkaline, which would neutralize most acids. Dissolved lead would precipitate, forming solids that would be filtered out by passage through soils. Fine grained soils like silts and clays also adsorb highly charged metals like lead, providing further protection for the groundwater. Obviously, both of these barriers must have broken down."

Michael broke in. "The Adirondacks have been greatly affected by acid rain. Researchers at some of the remote lakes have measured pHs below 5. In fact, I was originally testing a theory that metals are being leached from the Adirondacks by acid rain. That's how I stumbled on the high concentrations of lead in the Opalescent.

"Also, the mine was used to dispose of a mixture of garbage and industrial waste. As you know, over time, the decay of garbage produces organic acids that can dissolve metals."

Nate finished Michael's thought: "The acid rain could have reduced the alkalinity of the local soils, or the water could have found a passage through fractured rocks, rather than through the soils.

"You will also need to determine the extent of the contamination to come up with a cost estimate for clean up," he continued. "The best way to do this and at the same time evaluate cleanup alternatives would be to drill a number of soil borings and wells and analyze soil samples and groundwater for lead. We could then use our computer model to determine the extent of contamination, and test alternative cleanup or containment strategies."

Michael interrupted. "I'm trying to persuade the company president to have that done. However, I can't convince him to go that far without some idea of the potential cleanup methods and probable costs."

"You don't believe in making things easier for me, do you?" Nate laughed. "Well, lets work with what you can find. I'll need detailed information about the local geology: soil types and distribution, soil alkalinity, depth to bedrock, presence of fractures in the bedrock. I also need information on local rainfall and its pH. Oh, and find out if there's been a groundwater study performed for that area. If you can get as much of that information as possible,

than maybe we can make better guesses than we can just by looking at the ice cubes in these drinks. Even so, we're going to have a wide range of uncertainty."

"I know. Where do I start?"

"You could try the Columbia library, but the best place is the Geological Survey library just outside of Washington, DC"

"I'm on my way. I was wondering if you could look over this material while I'm gone," Michael said, taking out the notebooks and sketches he had brought along from his briefcase. "They're copies of some sketches of the old mine, the ledger of ore production and diaries of my great-grandfather who was foreman of the mine. I have a feeling they could be useful to us."

Nate nodded, taking the papers Michael handed him. The two men finished their drinks quickly, each anxious to get on with his own particular assignment.

Chapter 16

Maggie sat on the grass next to Jake's wheelchair. Weak as he was, he had wanted to come outside and be a part of the balmy summer day, to get away from the sterile whiteness of his hospital room. They sat in the late morning sunshine, facing the hills across the highway.

"Are you feeling any better today?"

"Yes. The cramps ain't so bad now. Must be the medicine they're giving me. But I'm weak, Maggie, weaker than I've ever been in my life. Those nosy nurses won't let me do nothin' for myself anymore, and I'm too weak to fight 'em off." He tipped his head toward the sunshine and closed his eyes for a moment.

She studied his drawn face with concern. "The weakness will pass once they get the lead out of your system. Your job is to rest and cooperate with the treatment."

"How long, Maggie? I don't know how long I can stand it in that hospital."

She looked up sharply. "Aren't they treating you well?"

"Oh, well enough. It ain't that. It's just that I never been shut up. I didn't know how bad it was to be shut inside like this, away from everything that's important. The trees and the mountains and the river, and my own strength to count on. I'm so high up in that hospital that I can't even hear the birds singing."

"I know. It must be awful. But in another three or four weeks you'll be ready to come home."

"Home? It seems that we ain't got a home no more. What can I look forward to? A room in town?" He spoke with bitterness and despair.

Frightened, she looked at him, saw only resignation in his face. It's only fatigue, she told herself. It's not like Jake to give up without a fight.

"It seems that the battle is over," he continued. "After all these years the Company's won. It took a hundred years to force us out, and they finally did it. Now there won't be no one to fight 'em no more. They can take over the mountains and ruin them and leave 'em when they're through. I'm glad I'm old, Maggie. I don't wanna be around to see what happens to the Adirondacks."

Alarmed, she knelt before him, looked straight into his eyes, wanting him to share her outrage, to gain strength from her anger. "Don't talk like that! It isn't over yet. The company can't take our land without a fight. I promise we'll get it back. And I need you to help me!" They had only each other now, and she needed him. They were the only Hughes left to continue the fight.

Through her tears, she saw that Jake had dozed off. She watched him tenderly for a moment, then her expression hardened. I guess I'm on my own, she thought. Then out loud, "I'll give them the fight of their lives."

Emmett Wilkins was sitting at his desk amid the smell of ink and dust and the whirring of the fan when Maggie entered the newspaper office. He sipped his coffee noisily, then set it down on a stack of papers. Maggie greeted him, agitated. She went to her desk, but was unable to settle down to work. When she turned to him, her face was troubled.

"Something serious is going on in town, Emmett. I want to write about it, but I need to talk to you first."

"Well?"

"It has to do with the Company, and I know how you feel about saying something negative about the Company. It's just not done. But they finally did something that can't be covered up, something that can't be made right by making a donation to the hospital."

"Well, what is it, Maggie? You know we have to tread softly where the Company is concerned."

"I realize this'll put you in a difficult position. But I also know that you believe in printing the truth, no matter who is involved."

Emmett nodded, waiting for her to continue. She took a deep breath, then turned her chair around to face him.

"You know that the Company dumped waste in the old mineshaft years ago?"

"Yes. It seemed to be a good place at the time. The mine needed to be filled in to prevent accidents. We got rid of an eyesore and we've never had any problems with it."

"That's just it. A problem has developed that no one was aware of, except for the Company, I suspect."

"What problem are you talking about?"

"The waste they dumped in the mine contained lead."

"So?"

"Some of that lead has seeped from the mine into the groundwater and is beginning to contaminate the Opalescent. As you know, the Opalescent supplies our drinking water. In time, we'll all come down with lead poisoning if something isn't done about it."

Emmett sat up, open-mouthed. "How do you know all this?" he asked sharply.

"I know because my father's in the hospital, poisoned by drinking from his own well." Her voice shook and she turned her face to the window.

"What? Jake?" Emmett stood up, overturning the coffee cup in his haste.

Maggie nodded, staring as the spreading coffee stain soaked the papers. Emmett gaped at Maggie, oblivious to the mess before him. "Is he going to be OK?"

"You know Jake. Tough as an ox. But he's not as young as he once was, and it hit him pretty hard. Worse, he seems to be losing his will to fight."

Emmett walked around the desk and looked hard at Maggie. "How do you know all this about the lead?"

She hesitated before answering. "Michael told me. You know that he worked as an environmental engineer before coming home to Langston to teach at the high school. He was studying the effects of acid rain and came across high concentrations of lead in the river, below our cabin. Then he tested our well and traced the problem back to the abandoned mine."

"Is he sure that it's coming from the mine?"

"Yes."

"But how come it took this long for the lead to reach your well?"

"Apparently it takes years for a metal to travel through soil. Our well is closest to the mine, so it reached us first."

"Does Tom Lang know what's going on?"

"Yes. Michael talked to him, tried to convince him to do something about it."

"And?"

"He did. He filled our well with concrete and threw my father off our land. Our well! And our land, the land that's been ours for generations!"

Emmett's initial disbelief shifted to concern for Maggie as he began to understand her pain. He thrust his hands into his pockets and began to pace the room.

Maggie continued. "I'm going to notify the EPA, Emmett. I've already talked to the Friends of the Wild and they're sending someone out to talk to me on Thursday."

Emmett shook his head. "Wait, Maggie. We must be very careful. The EPA could be more trouble than this town needs. More than it could survive. We've got to talk to Lang first, get his story, then see if we can make him come around."

"Emmett and Maggie! Come in, come in. Good to see you again. What brings you here?" Tom Lang slapped Emmett Wilkins on the back as he directed them to a pair of easy chairs facing the wall of glass overlooking the woods. The last time she had talked to him was during an interview in the spring. Tom Lang had made a major contribution for the expansion of Greenbriar Hospital. Maggie wrote an article that praised his generosity as so many articles had done before. She studied him closely now, his broad, open face, the smile that rarely left his features. He seemed genuinely happy, satisfied, and he wanted those around him to feel the same. She looked for signs of guilt or uneasiness, some indication of discomfort at seeing her, but could detect none.

"Tom, we've come to talk to you about the problem at the old mine-site," Emmett began. "We wanted to hear your side before putting something in the paper."

"Problem? Oh, that. Nothing to worry about. I've already taken care of it."

"Taken care of it? How?"

"By making sure nobody drinks from that well again." He rose from the leather couch and walked briskly to the gleaming bar. "How about something to drink?" he asked, looking from Emmett to Maggie.

Maggie jumped up, incredulous. "You solved the problem by filling up our well and throwing my father off his land?"

212

Tom turned toward her, surprised at her outburst. "Why Maggie, I didn't expect you to see it that way. The well was making your father sick, so we had to seal it up. I'm very sorry about that, but I've made sure that Jake is getting the care he needs. We'll find another place for him to stay when he's better." He said condescendingly, turning his attention to the bottles on the counter and tossing ice cubes into three glasses.

Maggie's voice rose as her face turned white. The morning sun lit up strands of her hair like melted bronze. Her eyes were dark as she spoke, reflecting the tone of her words. "Another place? You can't just throw him off the land that' been in the family for over a hundred years. That land was given to Jacob Hughes by your great grandfather, Stuart Lang! It was part of an agreement that our family has always honored. Jake isn't just an inconvenience, a nuisance that can be cast aside on a whim. He has rights to that land, and you can't cheat him out of it!"

Her words stung him, and for a moment competing emotions struggled in his face. He set down the bottle of seltzer water and fixed her in his gaze before speaking. "I'm not used to being accused of dishonesty, Maggie, and I don't appreciate it. As far as the land goes, it was never given to the Hughes. We've allowed your family to live on it, but it still belongs to us. Now I can't allow that to continue, because of the problem with the well. After all, it wouldn't be safe for anyone to live there with the water contaminated," he added defensively.

Speechless, Maggie looked to Emmett for help.

"What are you going to do to clean up the water?" Emmett asked, returning to the central problem.

"Do? I've already done it. We've closed up the well that had the lead contamination, and we'll find a new place for Jake to live. I can't see that there's much more to be done right now."

"Aren't you concerned that the lead is moving toward the river and could contaminate our drinking water?"

Tom Lang waved his hand dismissively. "Oh, that lead's been there for a long time, why should it start to bother us now?" He sank into the leather cushions and sipped his drink.

"It has already reached the river! And it won't be long before it affects Langston!" Maggie cried.

"That remains to be seen. There'll be time enough to do something about it if that happens," Tom said, facing her squarely. "I didn't expect you to turn on us like this, Maggie. Why, you and Becky grew up together, you were practically one of the family. And didn't you and Michael play together as children? He's a part of my family now, too."

"I know that only too well. Michael warned me of the danger we're all facing from the lead contamination!"

"Apparently he has more faith in my judgment than you do, since he left it to me to take care of the problem."

Emmett shook his head. "The time to do something is now, Tom, before it's too late. If you wait until the river is contaminated, it may mean the end for Langston, and for the Company, I might add."

Tom Lang rose, all trace of hospitality gone from his voice. "I think I know my business better than you. I'll do something when I feel it's necessary. Until then, why don't you two stick to reporting local gossip and let me handle my own affairs."

"We'll have to do just that, Tom. If that's your last word, we'll have to write it up for tomorrow's paper," Emmett said, rising.

"Write what up? You'd better watch your step, Emmett. You know what an article like that could do. There's no need to upset the town," Tom said cautiously.

Emmett paused, studied Tom Lang's face as it vacillated between concern and some other, less defined emotion. "You know me better than to think that I'd print sensationalism in my paper. What I aim to write is the facts, as I know them."

"Well, let me give you a few facts, just between you and me. If you make a big deal of this in the paper, it could cause trouble for the Company. And trouble for the Company means trouble for this town. You know I've always dealt fairly with the people of Langston, always tried to help them. And that's what I'm doing now, trying to protect them."

"By hiding the threat to their drinking water?" Maggie broke in with sarcasm. "It seems that you're trying to protect the Company instead!"

"That's pure supposition, Maggie. Until you have facts, you'd better be careful with statements like that. But you're right, I am trying to protect the Company. That's how I can protect the town and the people. Without the Company there is no town, no jobs for the people of Langston."

Emmett stepped forward, his words a final appeal. "Tom, we know that you're concerned about Langston. You've proven that many times. But you can't keep something like this secret. You must let the town folk know the danger they're facing. You must face it yourself and do something before it's too late!"

"As I said, I'll do something when it's time. And I'll judge when the time is right. So if you know what's good for the town, you'll leave this out of the paper," he repeated stubbornly.

"Is that your final word?"

Tom Lang nodded and ended the interview, quickly ushering the reporters toward the door.

They drove back to the newspaper office in silence. Emmett was deep in thought. Maggie watched the conflict in his face. He was struggling with something, trying to decide on an issue that was critical in many ways, involved many people. Once, when she was just starting out as a reporter he had told her: "Never take your work lightly, Maggie. What you write, and

215

how you say it, can be more important than you think. It can influence lives, change the course of events. Most of the time you'll only be reporting trivial events, especially in a small town. But every once in a while there'll be a story whose significance you'll barely even suspect. So always be very responsible in your reporting for you never know when you may be held accountable for your impact on the lives of others."

He didn't speak to her the rest of the morning, but when he returned from lunch he stopped at her desk and said, "OK Maggie. Go ahead and write your story."

Her fingers were poised over the keys, and they wrote almost of their own accord:

LEAD FROM ABANDONED MINE THREATENS WATER SUPPLY

There is reason to believe that Langston's water supply is contaminated with lead and that the beautiful Adirondacks are in danger of...

Chapter 17

Michael left the Washington Marriott Hotel before eight. It was only a fifteen-mile drive to the US Geological Survey headquarters in Reston, Virginia. On an impulse he decided to drive past the EPA headquarters first.

Everything about the headquarters was in sharp contrast to the EPA regional offices, most of them located in sleek, high rise federal buildings in major cities. The headquarters building was run-down and crowded, a rat's maze of hallways, cubicles and temporary walls dividing and subdividing rooms laid out in a seemingly random pattern. Some branch chiefs even had to share an office, and hardly anyone had access to a window. He wondered how such poor planning could happen in Washington, a city that prided itself on having been so carefully planned by the French architect, L'Enfant.

He drove past the EPA headquarters, Harry's Liquor store and the Safeway, and crossed the 14th street bridge to Virginia. Traffic was heavy in the oncoming lanes as commuters from Northern Virginia drove to work in DC Crossing the beltway Michael took the new toll road to Reston. Traffic was light on his side of the divided highway, although it was still stop and go in the opposing lanes, backing up a half-mile at the main toll booth. Approaching Reston he noticed large areas of undeveloped land and other features unexpected in a community so close to a major city.

Michael reached the US Geological Survey building a little after nine, picking up a visitor's pass from the guardhouse at the gate. In contrast to EPA headquarters, the USGS building was white and modern, with rows of windows on each level looking out over the surrounding woods. He stood for a moment studying the sprawling building, trying to find the correct entrance. He tried the glass door nearest him which opened into a lobby, with elevators and hallways leading to different parts of the building. He decided to go first to the map room. Following signs directing him there, he paused to look at a mineral exhibit, displaying a large ore specimen with shiny specks throughout.

He went through an electronically controlled glass door into the map sales area, to a row of metal drawers alphabetized by states. Checking the large index map for New York State he located Langston in the Santanoni Quadrangle, and purchased a topographic map of that area. Next, he looked at a map referencing geological studies from that quadrangle. He found that there were two reports on the Langston area, one a groundwater study, the other a geological survey that had been done when the mine was in operation. A stern looking lady behind the high metal counter informed him that these reports could be found in the library upstairs.

The elevator took him directly to the entrance of the library. After finding the groundwater report among musty volumes of obscure books in the stacks, he settled down at a table to read. He copied down the references at the end of the report, intending to look them up later. He made two Xerox copies, hoping that they would be useful to Nate. But when he tried to locate the geological survey, his luck ran out. It had been checked out, but the librarian assured him that it was due back the next day. Michael frowned, annoyed at being delayed an extra day.

It was nearly noon, and he was hungry. After asking directions, he drove to a nearby shopping center and bought a sandwich and soda at a delicatessen. He walked to a dock on Lake Thoreau to eat his lunch and watched a sailboat drift by lazily in the slight breeze. Two men were fishing near the edge. A row of townhouses was being built along the shore, the sounds of construction equipment disturbing the placid scene. He lay back on the grass and watched the nearly cloudless sky for a while, listening to the whirring of unseen insects around him.

He was reminded of the afternoon on Mt. Marcy when he and Maggie made love amid the lulling insect sounds and pungent earth smells that stayed with them long afterwards. He savored the memory, indulged himself, allowed himself to re-experience the sensuousness of that afternoon. He saw her lying on the grass next to him, her wet hair curling, changing from dark to bronze as it dried. She had tasted like wild strawberries and smelled vaguely like the river, her warm skin bathed in sunshine and camomile.

A shudder ran over him and he rolled onto his stomach to ease the physical longing. Her body had felt firm and muscular but yielding, wanting, needing him. It frightened him how much he missed her, needed her. Impulsively, he thought of calling her right then, to reassure himself. He wanted to do something for Maggie, to reinforce their old friendship and new love. He reached into his pocket absently and touched the tiger eye. He took it out and looked at it thoughtfully. Smiling to himself, he wrapped the stone in a tissue and replaced it in his pocket.

He walked back to the shopping center, and entered the shop of a Vietnamese jeweler whose sign he had noticed earlier. Maggie was not one to wear lockets or pins, and Michael rejected the samples shown him. Then he noticed a silver cuff bracelet in the back of the display case, and knew he must have it. It was the perfect thing for Maggie, and he imagined the wide band encircling her narrow wrist. It would be a striking combination, the tiger-eye gleaming warm and golden against the cool, silver background. The jeweler was willing to set the stone for tomorrow--for a premium price.

He returned to the USGS library and highlighted the relevant information in the references that he had copied earlier. He decided that the library was a convenient place to begin evaluating cleanup options and estimating their construction and operating costs. He took out the sketches of the mine his father had lent him and, using an engineer's scale, calculated the volume of the old mine. With this he was able to approximate the volume of waste that could have been buried there. This would be used to estimate the costs of removal and hauling to a safe landfill, one potential cleanup alternative.

He knew that groundwater treatment would be required as part of the cleanup, and to block further movement of contamination. He decided that addition of lime for pH neutralization and metals precipitation would be most effective, since metals and acidity were the major contaminants in the groundwater. He drew a sketch of the treatment system, including major units. Using the groundwater study, he found the range of yields from wells in the Langston area. He sized the treatment units for this range of flows and prepared a detailed equipment list. Then he made a list of vendors to call to get cost estimates for the major pieces of equipment. He was engrossed in his work when the librarian flashed the lights on and off, signaling closing time.

After checking into a motel and having dinner at a Chinese restaurant, he felt at loose ends. The last few days had been so busy, his mind constantly occupied with problems. Now, for a few hours he had nothing to do but wait. Tomorrow he would make a copy of the Langston geological survey, pick up the finished present for Maggie, and head back to New York. But tonight he would call Maggie, talk to her, tell her what he had been doing. He needed to let Maggie know how much he loved her, how he missed her presence. She would be glad to hear about the progress he had made, and that he had good people helping them, helping Langston. But most of all, he just wanted to talk to her, to share the burden that hung over their lives, the way they had shared things before he married Becky.

There was no answer when he rang, and Michael hung up disappointed. For a moment he thought of calling Becky but rejected the idea. He couldn't very well ask his wife to track down Maggie. Not in good conscience. It wasn't likely that Becky would know where she was, anyway. Besides, Maggie was probably with Jake, and Jake didn't have a phone.

He sat by the window in the darkening motel room looking out at lengthening shadows on the grass below. He turned on the reading light. He wanted Maggie, more than anything right now. But the fact remained: he was married to Becky. And at one time, he had wanted her just as much.

The next morning Michael copied the report that had been checked out the previous day, then waited impatiently for the jewelry shop to open. The jeweler polished the bracelet carefully, checking his craftsmanship critically through his jeweler's lens before presenting the finished piece. Michael turned the gleaming cuff around in his hand with satisfaction, enjoying the contrast between the cool, polished silver and the deep, warm lights of the satiny tiger eye. It would be perfect for Maggie. She never wore delicate jewelry like other girls; small pendants or dangling earrings would look out of place on her. But this piece would make a statement, just like Maggie herself. And each time she wore it, she'd be reminded of the significance the tiger eye held for each of them. The stone was coming full circle. He wrapped it up carefully, filled with a sense of pleasure and anticipation.

Michael arrived back at Mount Kisco late Thursday afternoon, too late to go into the City. He called Nate at his office and arranged to meet him first thing the next morning. He spent the rest of the afternoon calling vendors and completing his calculations. When Ben arrived home, Michael asked him to review and check them for accuracy. It was after midnight before he had his notes in order for the meeting with Nate. Getting ready for bed, he took the tiger's eye bracelet out for a look and went to sleep thinking of Maggie.

In his dream that night Becky and Maggie were mud wrestling at the Tally-Ho bar and grill. Tom and Carolyn Lang were in the audience, cheering their daughter on. Jake was in Maggie's corner as her handler, and Michael was the referee. Becky was cheating, and he called her on it. He awoke before it was over, wondering if Maggie was going to win.

Nate was well prepared for their meeting, as usual. He had drawings and notes spread out on his work table, when Michael walked in.

"Michael! Any luck at the USGS?" Nate Maguire greeted Michael, offering him a cup of coffee.

Michael pulled a stack of papers and notes out of his briefcase and laid them on the desk before Nate. "I think I found what we need." He took the coffee and sat down across from Nate. "As you can see, I've highlighted what I thought was important for you to look over. If I read the groundwater report correctly, the yields from wells in the area range from 3 to 6 gallons per minute, certainly less than 10."

Nate studied the groundwater and geology reports for a few minutes. "You're right, but I think we can get it a little closer than that, combining the information from these two reports. I'd estimate that the total groundwater production from this area would be on the order of 30 to 60 gallons per minute," he said, pointing to the area surrounding the mine on the map.

"That would make groundwater treatment costs about $900,000 to construct a treatment plant and .... $100,000 per year for operations and maintenance," Michael said, after glancing at his notes and adjusting his figures to account for the new flows. "But groundwater treatment is only part of the solution. Did you learn anything from the materials I left with you?"

"I think I know why the contamination occurred," Nate replied, picking up copies of Michael's great-grandfather's diaries. "There is a lot of evidence here that a lineation runs straight through the mine and on to the contaminated well. It could be due to a major fracture system. These diaries show that for a couple of weeks mining was easy, and that extra shoring was required to support the walls. Then flooding occurred from an upstream channel and work stopped for a couple of days until they could install additional pumps. I found this channel in the sketches of the mine. This geology report you brought me confirms that there are fracture zones in the rock in the area."

"So the metals could have reached Jake's well without having to pass through soil," Michael said, looking to Nate for confirmation.

"That's what I think. It sure would explain it. If the water had to pass through soil, the clays and silts would have

223

adsorbed any lead, part of the natural cleanup process for groundwater. Of course you'd need to do some borings and perhaps a seismic survey to confirm the presence and extent of the fractured rock zone. A resistivity survey and placement of about 10 sampling wells would confirm the extent of groundwater contamination."

"How much would a typical survey like that cost?"

Nate thought for a moment, hesitant to quote a price. "You're beginning to sound like a client." They both broke out laughing.

"You know I won't be holding you to it. I know as much as you do about clients who wanted to pin us to earlier quotes and then tried to stretch our scope of work without increasing our fee. I'll use your numbers judiciously."

"OK. We've been running about $100,000 for similar investigations for private clients. I make that distinction from our EPA work, because, as you know, in those studies the information we gather can be used in court, and must be collected under strict rules of evidence."

"Well," Michael said, taking stock. "We have an initial assessment of how the groundwater contamination occurred, figured out what studies are needed to confirm our understanding, and made an estimate of the cost of pumping and treating groundwater. Now lets see if we can come up with a more permanent remedy."

"OK! You go first," Nate said, only half-jokingly. "Our first option would be to excavate the waste and rebury it in a secure landfill. I made some calculations on the volume of the mine from these old drawings and the ore ledgers. From that I figured that the volume of waste stored in the mine is about 15,000 cubic yards. What are the current costs for a similar excavation and disposal?"

"Lately, we've been using $10 per yard for excavation, 30 cents per ton-mile for shipping by truck, and $200 per ton for disposal at the secure landfill in Niagara Falls."

Michael punched a few numbers into his calculator. "Assuming the waste is about a ton per yard, that comes to a cost of $300 per yard or ...," he paused to punch in some more numbers,"...approximately $4.5 million for that phase of the cleanup. That's pretty high. Let's consider that the base option and see if we can improve on it with containment in place."

"I've been thinking about that. That may be the most feasible option for the site. You can't count on a single barrier to prevent all movement of contamination. First, I'd probably grout the upstream fractured rock to prevent any more groundwater from entering the mine."

Michael nodded. "How much grout would that take?"

"I'd estimate it to be about 200 cubic yards. As I was saying, after grouting I would plug up the entrance to the mine and put a clay cap on it to prevent rainwater from getting in. I'd also grout the exit channel and inject limestone into the fractured rock zone to neutralize any acid and precipitate any lead that got past the grout. Of course, this containment program would greatly reduce the volume of groundwater requiring treatment in later years."

"How much would this cost?" Michael looked at him, almost apologizing for the unavoidable question.

Nate smiled, knowing how critical this was to Michael. He opened a drawer and pulled out ten pages of carefully detailed calculations written on graph paper. "I figured you'd ask. I estimate about $600,000. You might want to check these numbers."

"That's what I needed to know. So, the total cost comes to $100,000 for the initial investigation, $1.2 million for construction of the groundwater treatment plant, and $600,000 for containment. That comes to $1.9 million plus $100,000 per year for operation of the treatment plant." Michael closed his notebook and collected his papers from Nate's desk. "Thanks for all your help, Nate. How can I repay the debt?" he said, shaking the geologist's hand.

"Take me out for some good fly fishing next time I'm in your area."

The door opened behind Michael and Carl Garrison hurried in, waving that morning's New York Times. "I was hoping I'd find you here, Michael. What did you think of this?" he asked, pointing to an article on page three.

Michael took the paper and read the headline aloud: "Adirondack Paint Company Taints Hudson." As the words took shape, his heart began to beat faster.

It was reported yesterday in the Langston Gazette, local newspaper of that small Adirondack community, that lead contamination of the Opalescent River, a tributary to the Hudson, previously reported in this paper has been traced to a local industry. According to Maggie Hughes, reporter for the Gazette, the population of Langston, a town of 5,000, is threatened by water tainted with lead leaking from an abandoned mine.

The mine was operated by the Lang Company, best known for its popular product, Opalescent Paints. In the 1930's, the mine was shut down after depletion of its high grade ore. In later years the company disposed of the wastes from its paint manufacturing operation in the abandoned mineshaft. Until Congress banned the sale and manufacture of lead-based paint in the 1970's, lead was a major component in most paints, and the disposed wastes contain a significant amount of the metal.

Unusually high concentrations of lead were discovered in the Opalescent River by Michael Ryan, the chemistry teacher at Langston High School. Ryan, also an Environmental Engineer, was studying the effects of acid rain on toxic metal release from rocks in the Adirondacks. He was taking samples from different reaches of the Opalescent when he found increased concentrations of lead in the river below the mine site. Investigating further, he took samples of a well located between the mine and the river. Analysis showed that the well was contaminated with concentrations of lead that were 1000 times the drinking water standard. The owner of the well was subsequently hospitalized with lead poisoning.

Recently, lead has been recognized as an insidious health threat to an estimated 42 million Americans, contaminating backyard dirt, food, dust, imported ceramic dishes and tap water. According to an EPA report, every year excess lead in the drinking water causes lower IQ scores in 240,000 children and hypertension in 130,000 middle-aged males while increasing the risk of miscarriages, lower birth heights and weights, premature birth and stillbirths in 680,000 pregnant women. The report claimed that unsafe levels of lead in the public water system come from corrosion of lead pipes and lead solder in residential plumbing systems.

Langston takes its drinking water from the Opalescent about 2 miles downstream from the mine-site. This water is treated by a sand filter and chlorine is added to control bacteria. Ryan said that these treatment processes are not designed to remove lead. He has sampled the water supply and found that it presently meets drinking water standards. However, he is convinced that so far only the leading edge of the lead pollution has reached the river, and that it is merely a matter of time before significant contamination of the river occurs.

According to the American Academy of Pediatrics, children are particularly vulnerable to the effects of lead, even at low absorption rates. Lead can cause certain low-level effects, often without obvious symptoms, known as the "silent epidemic." These effects include partial loss of hearing and IQ, growth retardation, inhibited metabolism of Vitamin D and disturbances in blood formation. If lead absorption increases beyond the threshold level of 25 micrograms of lead per deciliter of blood in children, lead poisoning occurs, and the child faces increased risk of acute diseases of the kidney, blood and gastrointestinal and central nervous systems, according to the Centers for Disease Control.

Until recent years the problem of lead contamination was thought to be confined to lead factories and ghetto tenements of chipping lead paint. Now, it seems that industrial pollution is not restricted just to the urban regions of the state....

Michael put down the paper and looked up, "Holy shit! She wasn't going to write anything until we had a chance to convince the Company to clean up on its own."

"Looks like you've got your hands full," Carl said soberly. "Did you finish your work here?"

"We were just finishing when you walked in," Nate answered.

"What are you going to do?" Carl asked.

"I'd better get home and see what I can salvage. Thanks for all your help. I'll keep you posted," Michael said as he shook hands, and gathering up his papers headed for the door.

Chapter 18

Michael tried to come to terms with Maggie's behavior during the six hour drive home. It just didn't make sense, breaking her promise to wait, to give him a chance to deal with things before revealing the problem publicly. She was well aware of the complications this would cause for all of them, not just for the Company but for the whole town. Writing that article was like lighting a match to a string of firecrackers. Once lit, they behave as if they had a will of their own and often find a lot of unintended victims. Had she become so nearsighted as to consider only Jake's predicament, to be interested only in a narrow and petty revenge?

Michael shook his head but his mind wouldn't clear, his thoughts remained confused. It was all so ironic, that while he was away working out a solution to their problem, she had been here quietly working against him. And just when he felt that he was getting close to an answer, she had blown the situation sky high. It hurt to think that revenge meant more to her than trust, even more than the love he thought they shared. Perhaps she had changed more than he realized in the years since childhood. Maybe he was only acting out old fantasies on Mt. Marcy, not really seeing her as she was now, but as she had been in a time long past.

Only it had seemed so real, so much a continuation of the friendship they shared before they grew apart, chose different paths. With her he felt renewed, relieved of so many unnecessary complications that had cluttered the past few years. He was beginning to think that they could return to that junction, rejoin the path they had abandoned so long ago. She had taken him by surprise, revealing feelings that had been inside him, unrecognized. Perhaps he had been slow to commit to her totally. Perhaps she had sensed his ambivalence and turned away from him in anger.

His confusion turned to anger at her betrayal of his trust. Maybe she was just out to get a story, getting information from him by whatever means, then proceeding to use it. Unlikely. She was more spontaneous, straightforward than that. But why didn't she wait for him to return rather than acting on her own? He had left the message for her with Becky, that he was working on the problem in New York, and asking her to wait for his return. Why did she ignore it? Obviously, she did not believe in him. Perhaps she had changed more than he had realized.

His thoughts were bitter as he pulled to a stop in the driveway and turned off the ignition. Rusty was barking inside the house, warning away the unseen intruder as he always did when he sensed someone invading his territory. The porch light was on, casting a bright circle around itself, throwing the trees beyond into even deeper darkness. He walked up the steps reluctantly, a dull ache at the back of his head. He felt curiously lacking in energy. He didn't want a scene with Becky, just wanted to give his tired mind a rest. It was close to eleven; she may already have gone to bed.

When Becky heard him fumbling with the lock, she ran down the stairs, hesitating at the bottom uncertainly. "Michael? I'm glad you're back."

He glanced at her, ignoring the longing in her eyes, and petted the dog that greeted him eagerly. "I've been driving since five and I'm beat. I have a lot to do. I'm going into the den." He turned to go, but her question stopped him.

"What are you going to do?"

"I don't know, Becky. I thought I did until a few hours ago when I saw the newspaper article. I can't understand what Maggie could have been thinking. You gave her my message, didn't you?"

Becky shifted her gaze to the spot on the rust colored carpet that she had been rubbing with the toe of her slipper. "I told her that you were in New York," she said evasively.

"So she knew what I was doing, and didn't wait," he said more to himself than to Becky. He failed to notice the smile that crossed her face as he called Rusty to his side and walked to the den, closing the door.

He made a small fire in the cold stove and sank into his comforting easy chair. The back of his neck ached from tension and he pressed it against the worn headrest. Rusty came and lay his head on Michael's leg, pushing eagerly against his hand. He scratched the dog's silky ears, smiling in spite of himself at the wet nose that nudged his hand for more. He poured himself an Irish whiskey, admiring the honey-gold liquid in the firelight. Sipping it slowly, he allowed it to warm and relax him, to penetrate and dissolve the knots of tension in his muscles. He reached for the picture of himself and Maggie at twelve displaying their catch of fish. The whiskey was beginning to work on his tired mind, and he looked at the photograph through a misty haze. He stared at it for a long time, allowing his mind to play tricks. The faces in the photo blurred, changing from the fresh, eager faces of youth to older, disillusioned ones. He laid it face down and closed his eyes.

He must have slept for nearly an hour for the clock read 12:30 when he opened his eyes. His mind was fuzzy and it took him a moment to orient himself. The fire had died down, leaving the room nearly dark. Only a few coals glowed in the stove. Before the stove knelt an indistinct shape, trying to breathe life back into the coals. He felt cold, and he watched her clumsy movements groggily. Becky had never been good at making fires or any of the other skills of camping, leaving those chores to him. It had always made him feel strong and competent to be taking care of her, to have her depending on him. Now, he only felt annoyed with her incompetence. He rose to take the poker from her, trying to control his annoyance.

"I thought you might be cold," she said, smiling up at him tentatively.

He smiled back at her as she rose to pour him another Irish whiskey. They sat on the rug before the fire, he shivering involuntarily, she pulling his old robe around her against the nightly chill. She saw a chill run down his back and knelt behind him to rub his shoulders. He leaned back gratefully, allowing the whiskey and her small, deft hands to relax his tensed muscles. After a while her hands stopped at the nape of his neck, teasing the small hairs with delicate strokes. Eyes closed, he lay back on the rug, slightly dizzy. He gulped the last of the whiskey, making him limp, detached. She lay next to him and kissed him lightly, her tongue tracing his lips. She smelled sweet and light, of that violet cologne she favored lately.

Her thigh gleamed cool and white where the robe slid open. He was mesmerized, waiting, wanting more. She saw his look, smiled a secret, satisfied smile, and moved away from him slightly. As if in a dream he reached for her, wanting only to touch her. He pushed the robe off her shoulders and covered her with kisses.

His reactions were slowed, yet he couldn't wait, grasping for her with frustrating urgency. She laughed, teasing him, moved just out of his reach, tormenting him. The bathrobe was still tied at her waist, and he fumbled with the knot ineffectively. With a sudden curse he tore it open, pulling her down on him.

She smiled, enjoying his obvious desire. She was in control. Her small, mocking smile burned into his brain, irritated him, even as a greater force drove him onward. His mind was reeling but he couldn't stop; waves of anger alternated with desire, and he found himself groaning desperately. But she only slowed down and pulled back, taking her pleasure as he watched. He felt himself losing control, pinning her under his weight before she stopped her moans. He took her then, mindlessly, selfishly, ignoring all but his immediate need.

The morning sunlight, filtering through leaves of an old maple outside the window, awoke Michael. He was stiff from sleeping on the floor, his mouth dry and bitter, his head fuzzy. He pulled the afghan closer around his shoulders. He surfaced from sleep with that vague, unpleasant feeling that sometimes remains after a bad dream, where the dream is forgotten, yet perversely the feelings are retained. He sat up on the rug and stared into the cold ashes of the stove, trying to clear his mind, waiting for his dreams and memories to separate themselves. He was startled by a noise behind him. He turned and saw

233

Becky curled up on the couch, shivering under an old quilt. He had no desire to go to her, to lend her his warmth. Then the memory of last night's fatigue returned, along with the effects of the whiskey, Becky's aggressive love making, all intertwined with bizarre dream pictures that left him floating, uncertain.

He felt distaste as he looked at her. The feeling alarmed him until he realized that it was directed more at himself than at her. Despite the intense sex, the situation had been wrong. Throughout, he was maddened by her expression, by the mocking, cold smile that never left her lips as she drove him beyond control. It was so unlike the Becky he had once loved. She had been soft and yielding, like a wild duckling he had found once, abandoned. He had always felt tender and protective towards her.

Suddenly he realized what was wrong, knew that their union had been without love. He had needed release from his tensions, needed to forget, if only for a short time. She offered him that, but she was also seeking something for herself, something not yet clear to him. There was that maddening, satisfied smile. What was it that she said when he arrived home? Something about the message for Maggie. She said that she had told Maggie about his going to New York, but something about her manner was devious, not right.

She opened her eyes and saw him watching her, muttered sleepily: "I'm cold, Michael."

"Wake up, Becky. We need to talk," he said, ignoring her discomfort.

She opened her eyes, stretched, allowed the quilt to slip to the floor.

"We get along much better when we don't talk."

"This is serious," he said, sitting down opposite her. "Exactly what did you tell Maggie when she came by?"

She looked down at her nails before answering him. "I told you. I said you had gone to New York for a couple of days."

"Did you tell her why?"

"She didn't ask."

"Was she upset when you saw her? Did she tell you that she was planning to write that article?"

"Oh, you know Maggie. She gets worked up pretty easily. But she didn't say anything about an article," she added hastily.

"Do you know why she was upset? Before I left, Maggie and I agreed that I would talk with Tom first, try to convince him to clean up the mine on his own, and that she wouldn't print anything yet."

Becky avoided his eyes and said nothing. He studied her intently, then, with sudden insight, changed the focus of his questions.

"There's more to this than you're telling me, Becky. What's been going on while I was gone?"

"Oh, I suppose you'll find out anyway," she said, looking up at him defiantly. "Maggie was upset at Daddy for taking Jake to the hospital, filling in his well, and boarding up the cabin."

"What?" He stared at her, shocked.

"He was making sure that no one else would drink from the well," she shrugged.

"Tom promised to take care of things, but if I had known that was what he meant, I wouldn't have left. No wonder Maggie was upset. But why didn't she talk to me rather than acting on her own?"

"You weren't here."

"So what did you tell her?"

"That you and Daddy were working together."

"You let her think that I had a part in closing down Jake's well and kicking him off his property?"

"Didn't you?"

He stood up, towering above her, clenching his fists, fighting for control. He wanted to shake her, to make her realize how she had compounded their problems with her half-truths. Instead he said, "You know I would never harm Jake or Maggie. Maggie should have known that, too. What were you hoping to gain by this?" he cried, exasperated.

"You, Michael! I want you back. I want us to be the way we were. Now you're always off in the mountains or with Jake Hughes. Why don't you take that job with the Company that Daddy offered?" She stood up and faced him, tears

blurring her vision.

He shook his head and walked quickly from the room as she cried after him: "Where are you going?"

"Out to Jake's place, then to find Maggie," he answered without stopping.

Chapter 19

He was waiting impatiently when Maggie arrived at the newspaper office in the morning. She looked him over before unlocking the door, this shaggy young man with an eager light in his eyes. He held a sheaf of papers under one arm that threatened to spill at any moment, and a dilapidated portfolio with Friends of the Wild printed on one side. He introduced himself as Eric Rhodes, shaking her hand awkwardly as he tried to keep from dropping his papers.

There was a message for her on the answering machine. Charlie Rattinger, the reporter from the Times, would be coming to talk with her that morning, probably before 9:30. Maggie nodded to herself, taking grim satisfaction in the interest she had created. She offered Rhodes coffee but he refused, leafing through his papers with intense concentration. He was anxious to get down to business, annoyed by her social niceties. She watched him unobtrusively while she stirred her coffee. Something about him made her uneasy. She glanced at her watch, reluctant to begin without Rattinger.

Just then, the reporter walked through the door, exuding energy and enthusiasm. Charlie Rattinger was a columnist for the Times and had a reputation for having an impartial, inquiring mind. He looked Eric Rhodes over curiously, uncertain about his involvement, until he noticed the logo on Rhodes' portfolio. He recognized the name, but didn't indicate his opinion of the group by any outward sign.

"You must be Mr. Rattinger from the Times," Maggie said, extending her hand.

"Please call me Charlie," he said, shaking her hand. "I was glad when you called me, Miss Hughes, or may I call you Maggie?"

Maggie nodded as he went on: "I was afraid you'd leave me without a follow-up on that acid rain story, but that feature on the lead mine really overshadows acid rain. Hazardous waste is hot news these days."

Rhodes looked up from his papers. "What does acid rain have to do with it? We are talking about a greedy company's abandoned hazardous waste dump that's now polluting the Hudson."

"It all started with acid rain," Maggie explained. "Michael Ryan, the chemistry teacher at our high school, and one of his students were studying the effects of acid rain on the Opalescent River. They found high concentrations of lead in the river near our abandoned lead mine."

Rattinger interrupted, "And I was doing a feature on acid rain when I picked up Maggie's article and asked her for a follow up."

"My first article attributed the high lead concentrations in the river to the effects of acid rain on the local soils. It was written prematurely."

She paused and looked down for a moment, collecting her thoughts before continuing. "Mind you, I'm not discounting the threat of acid rain to the Adirondacks, but follow up studies by Michael Ryan showed that the lead in the Opalescent came from the old mine. Until my last article, Charlie didn't realize that what we thought was caused by acid rain was actually caused by the company's waste disposal."

"Maybe it's not as different as you think, Maggie. They're both forms of industrial pollution, only the source of this lead contamination is closer to home and more tangible."

"That's to our advantage," Rhodes spoke up. "Because the lead can be traced, we'll be able to identify and stick it to the polluters more easily."

"Yes," Maggie agreed. "But our main concern is to clean up our water, or rather, to make the Company clean it up." She sat back and thought for a moment.

"Just what are Ryan's qualifications for doing this study?" Rattinger asked, taking out his notebook.

"He has a master's degree in environmental engineering. He worked for an engineering firm managing toxic waste cleanup studies before coming home to teach. So you see, he's eminently qualified," Maggie said with pride in her voice.

"And Opalescent Paints is responsible for dumping the waste at the mine-site," Rattinger said, more to himself than the others. Then, looking at Maggie, "That's the largest company in the Adirondacks, isn't it?"

Rhodes answered him: "Actually, it's the only major industrial activity remaining inside the Adirondack Park. Other manufacturers are located near the fringes, by Lake Champlain or at Rouses Point. The mining and the paper mill in Au Sable shut down years ago, for economic reasons. The only other local industry is tourism, one that's appropriate for the Adirondacks. We at Friends of the Wild have been watching Opalescent Paints for a long time, waiting for an opportunity to push them out of the Adirondacks. And I think we're finally getting our chance," he added excitedly.

Ignoring Rhodes, Rattinger turned to Maggie. "Just what kind of danger are the local people facing from the lead contamination?"

"It's uncertain, but the water supply should be protected as soon as possible. As I said in the article, a well near the river has already been closed because of high concentrations of lead."

Rattinger caught the bitterness in her words, discarded the question he had been formulating and followed her lead. "Who used that well?" he asked.

She searched his face before answering. "My father. The company poisoned my father's well. He is in the hospital, very ill," she said, staring out the window as she tried to control her voice.

240

Rattinger put down his pen and studied her pale profile before continuing. Rhodes hung on her words with satisfaction, nodding his head.

"Who's in charge of the company? Is he aware of what's happened? Is he going to do anything about it?" Rattinger asked in quick succession.

"Tom Lang is the president of Opalescent Paints. His family owns the Company. We asked him to move on it quickly."

"And?"

"He `solved' the problem by throwing my father off his land and filling in his well."

"Does he plan to do anything else?"

"No. He believes that there's no immediate threat to the town."

"No threat!" Rhodes burst out, dropping a pile of papers on the floor. "Is he blind? Hasn't he done enough harm?"

Rattinger and Maggie stared at him as the papers fluttered to the floor and slid under the desk. There was a moment of strained silence before Rattinger asked:

"What do you plan to do, Maggie?"

She hesitated for a moment, but when she spoke, her voice was firm. "I'm reporting the leaking mine to the EPA."

Eric Rhodes' features became animated. "We'll make an example of the Company, put it out of business!" he cried.

Maggie looked down. "I figured they're responsible," she said uneasily.

Rhodes stood up and walked to the window. He turned and faced them, his long, bony hands moving nervously as he talked. "The EPA's been very active in regulating lead. They recently recommended reducing the drinking water limit for lead by 60 percent and banning the sale of leaded gasoline. Other government agencies are also taking action. The FDA is pressing for further reductions of lead solder in cans. And HUD is studying the problem of lead paint in federal housing built before 1973." He stopped, out of breath.

Rhodes ran his long fingers through his hair and licked his lips, then noticed that they were staring at him. He took a deep breath, exhaled with a cough, and sat down stiffly. Rattinger was studying the other man with detachment.

Rattinger turned to Rhodes with exaggerated politeness, "Have you worked with the EPA before?"

"We've been pushing the EPA to clean up several sites over the past few years," Rhodes said more calmly.

"And have you been successful?"

"We will be. You have to understand that it usually takes years to complete a cleanup. But long before that happens, the company will be bankrupt. The factory grounds will be returned to nature. It's our chance to push industry out of the Adirondacks!"

"Yet bringing in the EPA isn't necessarily a cure-all. There can be unanticipated impacts," Rattinger said.

"Impacts? What impacts could possibly compare to what they've done to the Adirondacks?" Rhodes asked heatedly.

It seemed to Maggie that Rattinger was perversely leading him on. "Yet the lead industry considers the sudden concerns about lead unrealistic. They argue that natural occurrences have released far more lead into the environment than man, and that no conclusive evidence points to harmful effects from exposure to low levels of this metal," he said.

242

"They're just twisting the evidence to suit themselves," he said, looking at Rattinger with hostility.

Maggie watched the interaction between the two men, alternately admiring and resenting Rattinger's equanimity; feeling increasingly ill-at-ease with Rhodes' outbursts. It was natural for her to be emotional; after all her father and her home were threatened. At first she had welcomed Rhodes' interest, but now he seemed overly zealous. She felt uncomfortable, wishing the interview over.

"Are you familiar with the EPA's Superfund program, Maggie?" Rattinger asked, withdrawing from his discussion with Rhodes.

She shrugged, "Only vaguely."

"It's based on the Comprehensive Environmental Response, Compensation, and Liability Act, CERCLA, that was passed by Congress a few years ago, I can't remember exactly when."

"In 1980," Rhodes interrupted, taking over. CERCLA created a tax on the chemical and petroleum industries, and this tax money goes to a trust fund, or Superfund, to clean up abandoned or uncontrolled hazardous waste sites. The EPA uses the fund to pay for the cleanup of hazardous waste sites when the responsible parties can't or won't. The EPA can also force the responsible parties to clean up, or reimburse the fund for the cost of cleanup."

"But many steps are involved that can take years," Rattinger continued. "Once a site is identified, EPA or state officials review available information on the site, and perform what is called a preliminary assessment, to determine if further action is necessary. If they decide that a problem exists, a site inspection is conducted. Samples of wastes, soil, well water, river water, and air are collected to determine what hazardous substances are on the site. Based on the extent of contamination, the site is rated using the Hazard Ranking

System. Sites with high scores are considered for placement on EPA's National Priorities List. Only NPL sites are eligible for cleanup using Superfund money."

"Each NPL site undergoes a remedial investigation and a feasibility study, during which conditions at the site are studied, the problems are defined, and alternative methods of cleaning up the site are evaluated. The RI/FS process can take up to two years to complete. Then comes the remedial design for the recommended cleanup. The design phase can take up to one year."

Maggie looked at him, incredulous. "And while all this is taking place, is anything being done to clean up the site?"

"On those sites where the public is in immediate danger, the EPA can remove leaking drums or other wastes without delay and perform additional studies later," Rhodes said encouragingly.

"Yes. But that doesn't apply here. The danger is not immediate and the cleanup cost is probably higher than what's allowed for a Removal Action," Rattinger said. "It will probably be five or six years before cleanup starts."

"Why does it take so long?"

"The EPA is required to recover any money spent from the individuals responsible for the contamination. Each step in the process must be performed carefully so that any decision made can be defended in court."

"Oh. So how do they typically clean up a hazardous waste site?"

Rhodes answered her: "Contaminated materials can be removed to a hazardous waste facility for treatment, containment, or destruction. Or the waste can be contained, treated or destroyed on-site, by incineration or other methods. Either would remove the source of groundwater contamination and halt its further spread. Another possibility would be to move

244

people away from the site or provide an alternate source of drinking water for the area's residents. But, the method chosen must be cost effective."

Maggie looked at the men, dumbfounded. "I had no idea it was this complicated. But we haven't got five years to wait before cleaning up the site. In that length of time our drinking water could be contaminated and Langston turned into a ghost town."

Maggie looked helplessly from one man to the other. "What can I do, though? Lang won't act, so I must report him to the EPA!"

"Of course you must," Rhodes urged. "You really have no other choice. And we'll stand behind you all the way. We plan to sue the Company, to make an example of them."

Maggie watched him with antipathy. "My goal really wasn't to shut down the company. Most of the people in town depend on it. I just wanted to force them to clean up the mine-site. I don't want to put Opalescent Paints out of business."

"I'm afraid it's too late for second thoughts," Rhodes said, gathering up his papers. "Now that we know what's going on, we at the Friends of the Wild are going to move on this whether you do or not."

Without another word Rhodes walked out of the newspaper office, leaving Maggie and Rattinger listening to his footsteps on the stairs. She frowned as she turned to Rattinger: "What are your plans? Do you have what you need for your column?"

He shook his head. "Not yet. I'll stick around for a week or so, to watch the developments. I'm taking some vacation time and thought I'd do some fly fishing." Then he became serious and leaned forward, towards Maggie, in his chair. "If I read this right, you're going to have some trouble on your hands, Maggie. Although it may not seem like it, I am on your side."

Things are not working out exactly as I had envisioned, Maggie thought as she said good-bye to Charlie Rattinger.

Chapter 20

ADIRONDACKS

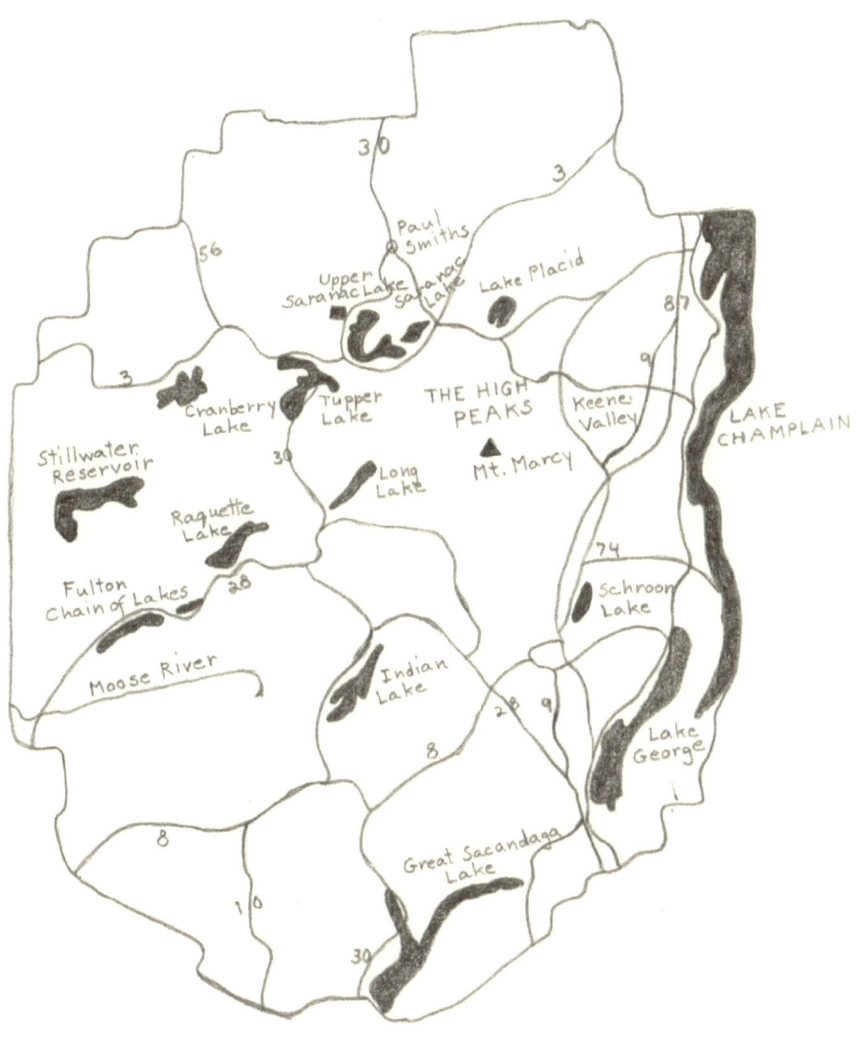

Michael sped toward town in his Jeep Cherokee, oblivious to the clear summer morning. Normally, on a day like this the mountains beckoned him, made him restless. But today he didn't notice their dark green outlines against the layers of blue; he ignored the wisps of clouds that floated like smoke above their peaks. He clutched the steering wheel tightly and squinted against the wind whipping through the open window. The Jeep's wheels spun in the gravel as he turned too quickly onto the road leading to the factory gate. A stranger in a red convertible was ahead of him. The guard was taking longer than usual to check the man's I.D.

While waiting, Michael stared beyond the guard house at the looming Opalescent Paint Billboard. It was the same design that John Ryan had conceived for the paint company when he and Richard Lang returned from the war. The sign needs painting, he thought. Ironic for a paint company. It had become weathered, the colors no longer capturing the bright, crisp hues of the Adirondacks. The autumn leaves, once brilliant oranges and reds, had faded to a dull brown, and the river had lost its greenish-blue fire. The company's characteristic paint can spilled over the timeless Adirondack scene, masking the colors of nature with tainted pigments. The paints had taken their hues from the Adirondack earth, sky and water, returning them now faded, soiled. Just like the company and the old lead mine, Michael thought.

Michael suddenly noticed that the guard had finished with the red convertible. They had been classmates in high school. Just about all of his classmates ended up working for the Company. He greeted Michael, and stopped him for a minute at the gate. "Sorry, it took so long, but the boss wants me to check everyone. What with that story and all. The guys are wondering what's going on? Have you been messing with your chemistry set again?"

"You might say so. Its nothing that can't be solved, though. Gotta run!"

He pulled quickly into a visitors parking space and hurried up the flagstone walk past the carefully shaped bushes to the Company's main office. He was angry as he brushed past the secretary, ignored her greeting, and threw open the heavy oak door without knocking. Tom Lang looked up from the phone, annoyed. Michael stood before Lang's desk, his face dark with anger, impatiently tapping on the smooth surface of the desk. Tom saw the turmoil in his son-in-law's face and ended the telephone conversation hastily. When he turned back to Michael, it was with the accustomed heartiness, all trace of annoyance gone.

"Michael! Becky said you'd gone to New York. How are things in the City?"

"Why did you do it?" he said, brushing Tom's question aside. "We had a deal!"

"What do you mean, `had a deal?'"

"I just came from Jake's place."

"Then you saw that I took care of things."

"You call forcing an old man off his land and plugging his well `taking care of things?'"

"Sit down, Michael," Tom said, putting his arm around Michael's shoulder and directing him to one of the easy chairs.

"No. I want an explanation," Michael demanded, pulling away. "What were you thinking of?"

"I don't have to explain anything to you, but I will. I tried to reach you, Michael, but you were off vacationing in New York. So I handled the situation myself."

"My trip to New York was hardly a vacation. I was getting advice from a geologist at my old company, looking for some way to clean up the old mine. I'll tell you about it, but first, what about Jake?"

"Jake needed medical care. I'm getting him the best treatment possible, and it won't cost him anything."

"You can't keep him in the hospital forever. What's he going to do after he's well?"

"Well, he can't go back to the cabin. You told me his well was poisoning him, so I plugged it. Now no one will be hurt by it again. To make sure, I posted the land. Jake can stay in a Company apartment in town."

"That won't work. Jake is like a wild animal; he needs his freedom. He needs open spaces. Besides, what about the agreement? The Hugheses lived on that land long before the Langs arrived. They were to live there, and be caretakers of the wilderness. The Langs keep breaking their side of the bargain."

Tom rose, moved to the window and beckoned Michael to join him. Michael followed reluctantly. For a few moments neither spoke. The two looked out over the paint factory and through the gate at the town beyond, thinking of all the people that depended on their decisions.

"I'm responsible for many more people than just the Hugheses. All these people depend on the Company," he said, sweeping his hand over the town. "The Company's changed with the times, doing what was necessary to provide for these people. We've had to adapt."

"I'm thinking of these people, too. You owe the people of this town more than just jobs. Filling in the Hughes' well and posting their land isn't going to contain the lead contamination, Tom." Michael forced himself to be calm, reasonable. "All you're gaining at most, is a few months time. Jake's well is a half mile from the mine-site. It is heavily contaminated. The Opalescent is only a few hundred yards downhill from the well, and there is already measurable lead in the river. It's only a matter of time before Langston's water supply is contaminated. The contamination must be contained before it spreads any further."

"And how do you suggest I do that?"

"First put in some sampling wells, then treat the contaminated groundwater. Install underground barriers to contain the waste and put a clay cap or rubber liner over the site to prevent water from getting in and dissolving more of the waste."

"That sounds complicated. How much would it cost?"

"That's what I came to talk about," Michael said, taking out his notes. On top was a summary sheet listing the estimated costs for cleaning up the site. "As you can see, the construction costs for containment and groundwater treatment would be approximately $1.9 million, and annual operating costs would run $100,000."

"Is there an easier way?"

"There is a simpler way, but it probably would cost more. You could dig up the waste and ship it to a state permitted hazardous waste landfill. The nearest one is in Niagara Falls. When you include excavation and shipping, the cost would be about $300 per ton. I've been looking at the old mine records, and the old shaft was about 15,000 cubic yards, putting the cost at about $4.5 million, minimum. It could be a lot more, if a lot of the surrounding soil has been contaminated and needs to be removed. And you would also need to provide groundwater treatment for the water that is already contaminated. That would be another $1.2 million plus $100,000 per year."

Tom shook his head. "Now you understand why I'm so hesitant to do anything more. These costs would be a major drain on the Company's profits. If the Company failed, Langston would be finished."

"Well, you've got to do something. The cost can only go up. The contamination is spreading, which will mean a larger area to contain or clean up. Besides, the news is getting out. If you wait until the contamination threatens the health of the townspeople, it may be too late. You won't be making the decisions then. The EPA will clean it up under Superfund, and bill you when it's over."

"Yes, Maggie's already threatened me with that," Tom said dryly.

"Maggie was here?" Michael asked, surprised. "What did she say?"

"Oh, she said something about calling the Friends of the Wild. How could some New York City group know more about what we need here than we do? We've weathered some rough times here, but we've always taken care of our own problems."

"They are a little extreme, but they've been effective in alerting the EPA to some problem sites. You can't ignore them; it's better to preempt them."

Tom looked at his watch and stood up. "I'm afraid I have to run, Michael. I appreciate your help, and I know you mean well, but I'm going to have to take some time to think about this and weigh my options."

"Time is running short, Tom. You're going to need to act sooner than you expect. I'm going to talk to Maggie, but I'll be in touch."

Tom put his arm around Michael's shoulder as he ushered him out the door. "We haven't seen nearly enough of you and Becky lately. Why don't the two of you come up to the house for dinner on Sunday?"

"I'll have Becky call you. I can't make any commitments right now."

Michael got into his Jeep and drove to the gate. The guard's attention was fixed on a crowd gathered on the other side of the fence. He checked his watch; it was nearly ten. The first shift should have started hours before, but some of the men who worked that shift were standing in a group at the gate.

Several women, some with babies and small children, were clustered in another group.

Michael pulled over to the shoulder of the road, got out and walked toward the group. As he approached them he became aware of a tension, an expectation that something was about to happen. He searched for someone he knew, and found Harry Flanders.

"What's going on, Harry? Why aren't you men working this morning?"

"The wives asked us to come with them. They're having a little demonstration," he answered, shifting his weight from foot to foot nervously.

"Is that what's happening? A demonstration?"

Harry spat in the dust behind him and shrugged. "I guess so." He acted distinctly uncomfortable, looking behind him frequently.

"Why?" Michael pressed.

"We've read the story about the Company poisoning our water, and the women are real upset about it. Frankly, some of the men at the factory are too."

Michael turned his attention to the women. They were beginning to form a line, holding signs and leading reluctant children, or pushing baby carriages. Slowly the line began to move, forming a continuous circle in front of the gate. The women turned towards him in their defiant march, and he could read the signs they were carrying. They had been printed in bold, red letters, shouting their messages: "Stop the Company before it stops you!" "Opalescent Paints is poisoning our water!" "Don't let the Company kill our children!"

Their faces were tense and determined. There was anger in their eyes, and fear. He recognized several--Harry's wife and Ann Callahan who had graduated in his class and was raising four young children, and Mary Readler, his mother's friend. He nodded to Ann but she was distracted and didn't respond. She continued scolding two of her children who were hitting each other with sticks, and delivered a sound slap to the two year old who refused to get up from the dirt. Michael paused for a moment to take in the scene. Ann was always so easygoing, relaxed. It was unlike her to be harsh with the kids; she was rarely upset with them for any reason.

Harry's wife, June, walked over to Ann and offered to take the baby. Michael was somewhat surprised to see her here. She and Harry had always been conservative, strong supporters of the Company. Harry and June had deep roots in Langston and knew they owed these to the Company. Their families were among the first to settle in the area, to make a home in the wilderness. They had come to work at the old sawmill and the logging camp, and stayed to help build the town of Langston. These early immigrants exchanged the poverty and unemployment of their native Ireland for the security of a steady job with the Company. At the same time, the Company also owed its existence to these immigrant families. June's face was set, her mouth pulled into a hard line. She held her sign stiffly in front of her, and took small, jerky steps as she urged the toddler along.

Michael greeted Mary and fell into step beside her. He had always liked her warmth, her direct attitude toward life. She was not one to be intimidated, and had supported more than one cause over the years. Her children were grown, one daughter married, with a baby.

"Well, Michael, have you come out to watch our little demonstration?" Mary shielded her eyes from the sun as she looked up at him.

"Not exactly. I had no idea you were going to have one."

"I always said, if you live long enough, you'll see everything. I'll bet this is the first demonstration Langston's ever seen." She stopped suddenly, causing the person behind to

254

bump into her. "How come you didn't know about it? I thought your mother would've told you."

"I've been in New York. Just got back last night."

They made one circle walking side by side silently. The guard stood at the entrance watching them, his cap pushed back to his crown, scratching his head, perplexed.

"Is my mother going to join you, Mary?" Michael asked.

Mary shook her head. "No. I tried to talk her into coming, but she said she couldn't."

"Didn't she go along with the idea?"

"I don't think it was that. It's got more to do with your father's position."

"She's not worried that he might lose his job as foreman, is she?"

"Oh, no, no. Your father just felt that he shouldn't take an open stand against the Company."

Michael nodded. "I think I understand. As foreman he's always been sort of a link between the men and the Company. They rely on him to smooth out any problems and to keep things going."

"And this looks like a bigger problem than they've ever had on their hands. Your father's just being cautious, diplomatic," she smiled wryly.

"What about you, Mary? What do you think this demonstration will accomplish?"

She remained silent for a moment before replying. "For one thing, it'll tell Tom Lang that we know something's going on. We insist on knowing the facts. We're not just going to sit back and let him do whatever he wants with us. We've had a good life here, Martin and me. We raised our kids here, and we want to

255

make sure that they have a chance to raise their kids in a good, clean place, too." Mary punctuated her sentences with short, quick nods of her head.

"I wish you good luck," he said as he broke off from the circle of demonstrators.

He walked over to his Jeep, but before getting in he turned back to watch the women for a moment. Their earnest faces stayed with him after he drove off, increasing his determination. These were hard-working people bent on one thing: to protect their families, their own. He wondered if they understood that they might have to choose between their health and their jobs. If he could help it, they wouldn't have to make that choice.

Things were moving faster than he had expected. Maggie had started the ball rolling, and it looked like it might be getting away from them.

Michael drove into town absent-mindedly, trying to collect his thoughts before seeing Maggie. He looked up just as he passed the familiar red and white pole in front of the barbershop. If there was one place in town to find out the latest gossip, it was at Ed's. Of course the men didn't call it gossip, they considered it the latest news. He pulled into a free parking place in front of the Rexall Drugstore and walked back to Ed's.

Ed had been Langston's only barber for as long as Michael could remember. He bought his high-necked white smocks wholesale from a dental supplier and wielded his instruments intimidatingly. A stiff brush-cut topped his humorous, pudgy face. His regulars always came away with his signature cut, a mirror image of his own. Michael had learned that to keep his hair and his pride intact he had to drive over to Long Lake for a haircut, but he often came in to hear the latest news. Ed took his work seriously. Besides barbering, he felt a responsibility for keeping his customers informed about the town news. He had a front row view of Langston and often stopped in the middle of a haircut and walked to the large window whenever something interesting seemed to be happening outside. Ed loved to talk, but what was more important, he was a great listener and rarely forgot what he heard.

The shop was unusually active for the time of day. Three men sat in vinyl covered chairs against the wall near the front window, facing the barber's chair and the large mirror behind it. A fourth man sat in the antiquated leather barber's chair while Ed worked on his hair. A low table, strewn with old Field and Streams and spotted with coffee stains, separated the waiting men's chairs from two empty ones. A trophy buck, chest deep in a woodland stream, stared up at the men from the cover of one of the magazines as they smoked or drank coffee, waiting their turns. In the back of the shop stood a card table with an electric coffee pot, packets of sugar and cream in a bowl, Styrofoam cups, and an empty coffee can with some change at the bottom. Ed's rates were posted above the mirror that faced the barber's chair, and Michael noted the recent increase.

The men looked up as he entered and exchanged greetings with him, then resumed their talk. John Ormsby, who worked in the factory on the late shift sat between the window and Bill Morely who had recently retired from the post office. Doc Mallory, Langston's general practitioner, sat next to the magazine table smoking his large briar pipe. Doc was trusted by all who knew him, and effectively treated most of their physical complaints.

Cal Collins, in the barber's chair, was the owner of Opalescent Mineral Waters. His grandfather had started the business, catering to those interested in "taking the waters." At the turn of the century, the baths were popular with wealthy socialites who spent several weeks every year summering at the spa. The spa was favored by high society in those days, with its elegant dining room, its comfortable guest rooms, and its spacious, landscaped grounds whose many paths encouraged guests to walk and enjoy the clean air of the mountains. Over the years, the clientele changed, and the baths were no longer as popular with the rich. Cal successfully adapted to the changing times by replacing the grand hotel with compact tourist cabins, bottling the sparkling waters and marketing it to the health conscious. People no longer had the leisure or the means to spend weeks in the mountains pampering their health, but they still drank the mineral water. And many did, to the benefit of Langston and Cal Collins. Now, people visited the Adirondacks more to fish or hunt, and Cal's family had done much to promote tourism in Langston over the years.

The men were talking about the slow pitch softball tournament when Michael came in. He walked past the three men and sat in the chair on the other side of the magazine strewn table. He picked up a dog-eared magazine, started to read an article on elk hunting.

"How's the ankle, John? You gonna be ready to play tonight?" Ed asked, his scissors keeping time to his words. Grayish piles of hair accumulated in small mounds around his feet and were rearranged in new patterns as he moved around his customer.

"I'd better be," John answered, taking a pack of cigarettes from the pocket of his tee shirt. "The Company team's counting on me. Mr. Lang offered to send us to Binghamton for the state tournament if we win."

Bill Morely suddenly interrupted. "Seems like Lang should be worrying about our poisoned water," he said, holding up the Langston Gazette. "What's really going on up at the paint factory, John?"

Michael looked up from the magazine.

"You can't believe everything you read in the paper. If you ask me, those Hugheses are just trying to stir up trouble. They've always had a grudge against the Company," John answered.

"You'd defend Tom Lang and the Company. You're just worried about your job," Bill said. "What about your family's health?"

258

"What about it? I've been working there, drinking this water for thirty-seven years, and I've never felt better," John said, slurping his coffee noisily to make his point.

"I hear all kinds of rumors, but nobody really seems to know what's happening," Ed interrupted. He turned to the waist-high, wooden cabinets behind him and removed a comb from the jar of green disinfectant. Carefully he wiped it on a towel before turning to Doc. "What do you think about this lead poisoning, Doc?"

"Well, I saw Jake Hughes at the hospital and he's pretty sick. His blood lead level was a hundred times what's safe. I think we've got something to worry about," Doc said, pulling on his pipe.

"If there's something wrong with the water, I want to know about it," Cal said from the barber's chair. "I have my water tested every month and I've never had a problem. But my distributor in New York read that damned news story and canceled his standing order. What makes them think it's from the water, anyway?"

Ed paused with the comb poised over Cal's head. "That article said the lead came from Jake's well. His well is right near the river where we get our drinking water." He reached for the straight razor and began whetting it on the strap that hung from the barber's chair. Then he looked at Michael closely for the first time. "You were the first to find lead in the water, Michael. What's really going on?"

Michael reluctantly laid the magazine down on the table and shifted in the chair as the other men turned towards him. He weighed his words carefully, not wanting to make light of the matter, or to inflame the men. He still hoped to find a cleanup plan agreeable to Tom Lang.

The door opened as he deliberated, and a thin, shaggy haired man in his late twenties walked in. Michael let out his breath as attention shifted to the stranger. Talk ceased while the men looked him over. He didn't seem like the type to want one of Ed's famous brush-cuts.

Doc rose and walked to the table in the corner that held the coffee and tossed a quarter into the empty coffee can that served as a cash register. He never took his eyes off the stranger as he refilled his Styrofoam cup and added two packets of sugar. He walked back to his chair, slowly stirring the steaming coffee, carefully balancing the brimming cup.

The young man stopped for a moment, confused, then walked to the magazine table. Picking up the magazine Michael had abandoned, he sat in the empty chair in the corner. As he stretched out his long legs, Michael saw that he was wearing new leather hiking boots. His brownish hair hung below the collar of his faded tan safari jacket. The stranger looked around at the men in the barbershop, noticed that everyone but Michael had the same, severe brush-cut, and ran his hand through his hair nervously. He uncrossed his legs and made a move to get up, then sank back down resignedly.

It wasn't that unusual to see strangers in town, but this man was obviously not a tourist. He was too grim, too nervous.

"Sure are a lot of tourists this time of year," Doc said, looking pointedly at the stranger.

The young man looked up, startled. For a moment he had the impression that an impenetrable wall of faces formed a barrier between himself and the street outside. Their faces were lined and weathered, revealing not so much a curiosity about him as a cautiousness, a certain wariness of strangers. "Oh, I'm not a tourist, actually. I'm here on business." He returned his eyes to the page before him.

Doc nodded, cleaning his pipe with a match. "I'm Doc Mallory. What business brings you to Langston, son?"

"I represent the Friends of the Wild. We're studying a problem in the area."

Michael sat up and looked at the stranger more closely. "I'm Michael Ryan," he said, offering his hand.

"Eric Rhodes." He stopped, did a double take. "Did you say Ryan? Then you're the one who discovered the problem with the water!" he cried excitedly.

"What problem are you talking about?" Bill Morely asked, eyeing Rhodes suspiciously.

"One that should concern you all, the poisoning of the Opalescent River."

The men looked at each other, and their expressions revealed nothing to Eric Rhodes. They had not worked out for themselves what the problem was or how to respond to it, but they seemed to be in silent agreement now that they were confronted by an outsider.

Ed's razor stopped in the air behind Cal's head. "Poisoning! Aren't you jumping to conclusions a bit?"

"No, sir! Aren't you people aware of what's going on in your own back yard? If you don't believe me, maybe you'll listen to one of your own. Ryan's the one who found the lead in the water."

The men looked back and forth between Michael and the pompous Rhodes. What was the link between these two? Had Michael, who had been so well liked, been contaminated by his years in New York?

Then Bill said to Rhodes, "What's it to you?"

"The Friends of the Wild are protectors of the Adirondack Park. Anything that threatens the Park is our concern. Besides, the Opalescent empties into the Hudson River, which is an important resource for millions of us in New York."

"That's all we need, some city slicker who doesn't know two and looks like he needs one of Ed's haircuts, to tell us our

261

business," John said, turning to his friends. "Next he'll be wanting us to put diapers on the fish before they swim in his damned river."

The men roared with laughter at Eric Rhodes expense. The young man flushed. "Laugh if you want, but before it's over, Opalescent Paints will be a memory. The cost of cleaning up their mess is going to shut down the Company."

There was a moment's silence while the men stared at him. Their faces reflected disbelief, then anger.

"What about them that work for the Company? What'll happen to them?" Bill asked.

John positioned himself in front of Rhodes, his large frame outlined against the window. "You've got one helluva nerve telling us what's going to happen to the Company! Most everybody here in Langston is dependent on the Company in some way or other. Most of us wouldn't be making a living without it. What's it to you, what the Company's done, if anything? We don't need no outsiders to solve our problems for us, we never have and we never will!" John shouted. His words echoed the resentment of the others.

Cal Collins, who was still sitting in the barber's chair even though Ed had stopped working on him minutes before, spoke: "If this thing gets on the news, it'll create havoc for the tourist trade. Nobody's going to come here to vacation or buy Sparkling Mineral Water if they think they're going to be poisoned."

"It'll be on the news, allright. In fact, we're going to see to it that there's plenty of coverage. People have a right to know what's happening. We want to make Opalescent Paints an example for those who think they can pollute the environment!" Rhodes said with single-minded fanaticism.

Michael looked at the faces of the men around him, concerned, worried, even afraid for themselves and their town, their very futures. For a moment he was afraid too, afraid of the young man with the burning eyes. Michael realized that he needed to speak, needed to explain his position. He needed to distance himself from Rhodes if he was ever to gain the townspeople's confidence.

"No one loves the Adirondacks more than I do, Rhodes, or than the people of Langston do. The last thing we would want is to see the mountains spoiled. And I'm going to do everything I can to see that they're not. There's more than one way to go about this thing. And your way isn't the best for Langston; in fact, it would be devastating. We have our own ways of solving problems here. We're the first to drink the water, and we're the last to want to see the river polluted," Michael said coldly.

Things were not going the way Rhodes had wanted, although he had not expected the townspeople to welcome him with open arms. After all, the town would probably have to be destroyed in order to save the wilderness. Nevertheless he continued, "I forgot, your father is the foreman at Opalescent Paints. I see now. You're just trying to protect his job. But thanks to your help, we'll be able to put an end to Opalescent Paints and return this place to the wilderness where it belongs." He began to pace the room before the angry men.

Michael wanted to shut Rhodes up, to punch him in the mouth. Instead he stepped between the men and put up his hand in an effort to calm them. "Leave this to us, and I promise you we'll take care of it."

Rhodes walked to the door, then turned back for a moment. "No way. This thing is too big. It's out of your hands now." The door slammed shut, leaving the men staring at it, staring after the man who brought distrust and turmoil into their lives.

Michael moved to the window and gazed out at Main Street for a moment to collect his thoughts, then faced the seething men. He wanted to present the problem to them

263

clearly and logically so they could understand their predicament. Then perhaps they would support him in cleaning up the mine.

"You know that something's been going on; you've all read the article in the paper. You deserve to know the facts. What it boils down to is this. The Company's been dumping its wastes in the old mine. Apparently, acid rain seeping into the mine has combined with waste acids disposed there to dissolve some of the lead wastes. The dissolved lead has been seeping into the groundwater."

"Is that how Jake's well was poisoned?" Doc asked.

Michael nodded. "Yes. The contaminated groundwater has been moving beyond Jake's well toward the Opalescent, the source of our drinking water. Already, the river is showing an increased concentration of lead."

"You mean, the river is poisoned?" Cal interrupted.

"The water is still safe to drink, although it's bound to get worse if nothing's done to stop it."

"What can be done?" Bill asked.

"A number of things, none of which are going to be easy. I'm trying to convince Tom Lang that if he's going to save the Company, he'll have to take charge of a cleanup and pay for it."

"Will it really bankrupt the Company?" John asked, concerned for his job.

"It's going to be expensive, but not nearly as expensive as a cleanup that's forced on us by outsiders would be. There are a lot of Rhodes in the world who'll see this as an opportunity to fight industry."

As the other men talked over what they had found out about the crisis, Doc Mallory took Michael aside. "What is Lang going to do? Have you convinced him to do the right thing?" Doc asked.

"I wish I knew. Somehow, I think he needs a little more convincing, and right now, I don't know how to do that," Michael said, walking to the door. "I'll probably be needing your help. The townspeople look up to you. They need to realize that the problem is serious, but that there is no need to panic." He stepped outside, with Doc behind him.

"I'll do all I can to help, Michael. Just let me know how. What are your plans?"

"I'm going to find Maggie. Rumors are flying, and that isn't good. I had wanted to keep the matter contained as much as possible, wanted to work with Tom Lang to solve it quietly, efficiently. Maggie needs to use the newspaper to convince Tom Lang, not to inflame the public."

"Let me know how I can help," Doc repeated as Michael started off toward the newspaper office.

"Thanks Doc."

"Good Luck!" Doc called after him. He took his pocketknife out and cleaned his pipe, absentmindedly dropping the spent ashes on the curb as Michael hurried away. Once he was out of earshot, he added under his breath, "I'm sure

You'll need it."

Chapter 21

Michael was disturbed by what had happened in the barbershop. He wasn't sure how much power the Friends of the Wild actually had or how much harm they could do before he could get Tom Lang to act. He must find Maggie and heal the rift between them. Somehow the trust they shared had been lost through a terrible misunderstanding. They must put all that behind them now and work together to put things right.

He wasn't sure how the misunderstanding had started, but it had escalated so quickly. He and Maggie parted reluctantly, with so much love and understanding. Together they felt they could work things out, but once they were separated things became so confused. What had happened in those few days to drive them apart? In his mind he reviewed the last few days: the trip to New York and DC; the shock of seeing Maggie's article in the paper; his anger and pain when he learned what Tom Lang had done to Jake; guilt from his evening with Becky. He shook himself, as if to shake off the feelings he had when she looked at him with that cold, contemptuous smile. Then he thought of Maggie, of the things she had gone through during the past few days. She found her family's home confiscated, her father taken away, and herself left alone to cope with it all. She must have thought that he had betrayed her, had turned his back on Jake and her. He shook his head slowly. She should have known him better. She should have had more faith.

He ran up the stairs to the newspaper office just as Emmett Wilkins was locking the door. Michael noted that he looked pale and ill.

"Emmett! I have to find Maggie. Do you know where she is?"

Emmett shook his head and leaned against the door for a moment. "I'd like to find her myself. I'm not feeling too well and need her to take over at the paper."

Michael looked at him with fleeting concern. "Did she say where she might be going?"

268

"Only that she needed time to think, to sort things out. If you find her, tell her I need her back here."

"I will. Take care of yourself."

He was back on the street when he heard Emmett call after him: "There's trouble brewing, more than this town's used to. I hope you and Maggie are on the same side."

It didn't take Michael long to realize the most likely place to find Maggie, and he was soon driving along the road toward the Hughes cabin. It was her home, her refuge. She and Jake had lived independent lives there, away from the town and its people. He noticed clouds moving in from the west, darkening the once brilliant morning. His thoughts were chasing each other in his head, urging him to speed down the uneven road.

He parked some distance from the cabin and walked the rest of the way over the deep ruts where heavy equipment had torn up the ground. Maggie's Jeep was parked by the woodpile, and she was sitting on the porch steps, her head resting against a weathered post. She was watching the bird feeder that they had hung in a tree opposite the cabin when they were kids. A pair of cardinals were feeding on sunflower seeds; a blue jay flew down from a nearby pine and started to bully the cardinals with its loud, harsh voice. The cardinals scattered as the jay settled on the narrow ledge of the feeder, its crested head bobbing among the sunflower seeds. The black and blue feathers on his tail shone like the panes of a stained glass window as he moved about, his bright, intelligent eyes alert for any returning birds.

He watched her for a moment, not moving, not wanting to disturb her. Something blue in her hand echoed the blue of the jay's nervously bobbing tail, and in a moment he recognized his kerchief as it moved in the slight breeze. He walked past the useless well quietly, approaching her from behind. She turned when he was a few steps away, startled. Her face was drawn, and circles under her eyes made her look older. He stopped a few steps away from her, suddenly unsure. She looked up at him, seemed to study his face carefully, feature by feature, but said nothing. He wondered what she read in his face, wondered how much of his turmoil was written there. Her own face was composed of sharp planes and shadows, accented by her paleness and fatigue.

"Maggie, I've missed you." It was all he could say, and he felt dumb, inarticulate.

She struggled with her feelings before responding. "Where have you been?"

"In New York, talking with some of the engineers at my old firm. I've been trying to work out a solution for the mine."

"Why didn't you tell me before you left?", she asked, hurt. "I waited up for you in my room."

"I tried to reach you, but I had to leave suddenly. I left a message with Becky. Didn't she tell you?"

Maggie shrugged. "She said you were in New York, but she didn't tell me why."

"What did you think? That I was running away from you again?"

"I wondered. I thought maybe the Langs were too strong for you." Her voice was barely audible as she answered him.

He moved up the steps and sat down next to her. "You should have more faith in me than that, Maggie."

"I suppose so. But what could I think, Michael, when I saw that they had taken Jake away and closed down the well?" She looked up, and he felt a stab of pain at the look in her eyes. "The last thing you said to me was that you'd take care of things. And Becky assured me that you had done just that."

"She said that?"

"She implied it. But it wasn't just that. I went to see Tom Lang with Emmett. We tried to reason with him. It was no good. And I came away with the impression that you had agreed to this," she said, sweeping her hand over the boarded up cabin and well. "Can you imagine how I felt?"

He touched her hand that was twisting the blue kerchief into a wrinkled rag. "I'm so sorry, Maggie. I had no idea what would happen here while I was away. You should have known I couldn't be part of anything like this."

Suddenly she was ashamed. "No, you couldn't. And I'm sorry, too. But sometimes I can't help thinking about your being married to Becky. And Tom Lang is your father-in-law. He's pretty powerful, and so is she, in her own way. I could never compete with her. You left me for her a long time ago, and I was afraid you might do so again."

"I could never leave you, Maggie; you've always been a part of me. I just didn't realize how much until the last few days."

She didn't answer him right away, but he could hear the rhythm of her breathing change.

Maggie broke the silence reluctantly. "I did something you won't like, Michael. I wrote an article about the Company and the mine."

Michael nodded. "I saw it in New York. That's why I rushed back."

"I also called the Friends of the Wild. I really thought I was doing the right thing, but I'm not sure anymore."

"What changed your mind?"

"The things that Eric Rhodes said. Or maybe it was the way he said them. He's the man from the Friends of the Wild."

"I know. I've met him."

271

Maggie looked at him, surprised. "You have? What do you think of him?"

"He worries me. I don't like his attitude. He's extreme, single-minded, a zealot. He is intent on closing down the Company, at the expense of everything else."

She nodded in quick agreement, concern on her face. "I regretted calling him as soon as he started talking. But I didn't know what else to do."

"Our only hope is convincing Tom Lang to take charge. He's stubborn and exasperating, but I haven't given up yet."

"I want to help you, if I can," she said, moving back under the protection of the porch. A sudden shower had started, splattering fat raindrops on the steps, turning the weathered wood a darker gray.

She stood up and brushed herself off. "I want to get inside. There are a few things I'd like to take with me in case they decide to raze the cabin without telling us."

Michael quickly removed the boards that had been nailed across the door. They stepped inside, into the eerie stillness that deserted houses possess. Everywhere traces of Jake remained, as if in a still life. A large brown spider had spun her neat, concentric web in the corner of the pantry. Already a fly had been caught in it, buzzing loudly in its fruitless struggle to escape. Ashes of the last fire lay cold in the stove, and a few unwashed pots, abandoned in the sink, had sprouted a growth of mold. A piece of cheese and a loaf of bread lay on the table, gnawed by the sharp teeth of some mouse that lived in the woodwork. Flypaper, dotted with the bodies of several flies, moved lazily in the draft from the open door. They went into the storage area to collect Jake's guns and traps, and carried them into the front room. Maggie stopped to listen for a moment. Only the chirping of a cricket somewhere under the floorboards broke the silence.

"It's so quiet and sad. It scares me. It's like a tomb." Maggie shivered, and Michael put his arm around her for a moment.

She picked up the pair of snowshoes that Jake had been mending and the Indian blanket that covered the couch, and placed them with the traps and guns by the door. Jake's favorite pipe lay on the arm of the easy chair. She knocked its ashes into the fireplace and slipped it into her pocket, then emptied the kindling from the old, woven basket.

"This basket was made by my mother, and I can't bear to part with it. I don't have much that was hers; I was only seven when she died," Maggie explained.

She moved to the window to draw the curtains, disturbing a large moth hidden in its folds. The moth flew into the window, its beating wings making a dull, thumping noise against the glass, in its effort to escape. She opened the window and brushed it out with the hem of her skirt.

From the bookshelves in the corner she removed two heavy volumes. Michael saw that one was the old photo album and the other a large Bible. He looked at her curiously. She had never been very religious, and no one had ever seen Jake attend church. Maggie went to Sunday school for a few months while her mother was still alive, but after she died Jake didn't make her go, and she soon stopped on her own.

She smiled and opened the Bible. Its leather cover was badly frayed and the binding was in danger of falling apart.

"Haven't you ever seen this, Michael? It's a record of our family, from the time that the first Jacob Hughes settled in the Adirondacks. Perhaps it's the only record of his marriage. He and his Indian bride were married in her village, following Indian customs, rather than in a Christian church. Jacob had brought this Bible from Ireland, and he taught his children to enter family marriages, births and deaths in it. It's a pretty complete record of the Hugheses in America, and I don't want to lose it. Especially since the line may well end with me," she added.

He felt the sadness in her voice and took her hand in his. "I hope not, Maggie. It would be a great loss."

They sat down on the braided rug in the center of the room and opened the photo album. It was only sparsely filled; bits and pieces of their lives captured in irregular installments, at ragged intervals. Jake wasn't interested in photography. He didn't believe that pictures could do justice to the events they tried to immortalize. Most of the pictures had been taken by Maggie, a few by Michael. The first showed her mother, holding Maggie as a baby, laughing, reaching for some object in the distance. Then there was Maggie at age four with both her parents, looking serious and stiff in a starched white dress. It was strange to see Jake so young, before Michael knew him, and Mrs. Hughes, whom he only vaguely remember. Her hair was a darker shade of red than Maggie's, but he recognized Maggie's gray eyes in her face. Jake had aged considerably since then. His skin had become weathered and lined, but his essence had remained unchanged. His eyes in the picture were the familiar clear blue, and his stance fearless and independent.

On the next page was a picture of Jake and Maggie in the guideboat with a dog. Michael looked at it closely.

"Is that Old Calamity?"

"Don't you remember? You took the picture."

"Of course! That was the trip we took to watch the loons, when Old Calamity tipped us into the water!"

Old memories came flooding back, and with them fleeting sensations and feelings. The scent of pine and campfire smoke, the sounds of night wind over the water and bullfrogs singing. The comfort of Jake's pipe glowing red in the night as the children were falling asleep, exhausted from a day's hike. Knowing that the other was in a sleeping bag just inches away, ready to talk if lonely or scared in the night. Michael brushed past these feelings, barely touching them, barely aware of their presence. But they left him with a sadness that was reflected now as they stripped the old, familiar room. It was still the Hughes cabin, holding generations of memories within its walls, but it was losing its personality as they removed Jake's belongings. Michael wanted to stop the change, return to the happy times he remembered.

"Old Calamity died just before I graduated from college," Maggie said. "I hadn't seen him for months and was really looking forward to coming home. I cried all night when I heard that he died."

"He was a great dog. I got Rusty partly because of him."

"I've been thinking of getting Jake a dog, but the only dog he's shown an interest in is Rusty. It's hard to replace an old friend."

They closed the album and went into Jake's room to get his fishing rods and tackle. He had been making lures from the tail of the deer he killed last fall, and a number of partially finished lures were spread out on the floor. They gathered them up carefully, making sure not to tangle the hooks.

"I want to get my sleeping bag before we go. It's up in the attic," Maggie said.

They called it the attic, but it was really just an unfinished storage area under the roof, only four and a half feet tall at its peak. They stored things there that wouldn't fit downstairs. When they were children it had been their secret hideout. They opened the trap door and climbed up the ladder, ducking their heads under the low roof. Maggie opened the tiny window that looked toward the river, welcoming the fresh air.

"Oh, Michael, look what I found," she said, pulling a heavy can from behind her. "It's our rock collection."

She opened the tin and took out rocks that hadn't been disturbed in many years. She lined them up in rows, granites, quartzes, shiny pieces of mica, bits of fool's gold, and sandstone embedded with tiny shells. They had worked hard on their rock collection, painstakingly labeling them with bits of tape. Sometimes in the evening they would climb up to their secret place and examine their rock collection by candlelight. Michael's hand fell on the stub of an old, dusty candle set in a cracked dish.

"I wonder, did we use this candle the last time we climbed up here?"

Maggie smiled. "I doubt it. I think I've been up here a few times since then."

He unrolled her sleeping bag and sat down on it, motioning her to join him. They picked up the rocks one at a time, passing them back and forth as they shared the memories tied to each.

"Do you remember the trip we took to Lake Champlain with my parents when we found this one with all the shells in it?", Michael asked.

"We thought that someone had brought it from the sea and left it there. Then your father explained that the Adirondacks used to be under an ocean. I didn't believe him then, although I was too polite to say so," Maggie laughed.

"Remember when we went fishing in Dudley Brook and found this fool's gold? We panned the brook for weeks, searching for the mother lode, before Jake told us that the rock was worthless. That was the first big disappointment of my life."

"It didn't bother me as much. Maybe because I had such a good time prospecting." She looked at Michael and smiled. Her face was relaxed and happy now in the dim light of the narrow attic.

He felt his earlier tension leave him, sitting next to her in their old hideaway, as forgotten memories crowded around them with unexpected clarity.

"I never told you this, but I used to come up here and play with the rocks by myself when you weren't here. I used to make up wonderful adventure stories about them," Maggie said shyly.

"Like what?"

"Well, my favorite one was that we were on a treasure hunt, and these rocks were the treasure that we found. Oh, we had to go through all kinds of adventures before finding them, but I knew that together we would succeed. When I was little I thought we'd always be together."

"So did I, Maggie."

"What happened to us, then?"

"I took a wrong turn somewhere."

They sat side by side looking out the small window, through the filtering branches of pine, at the oaks and maples beyond. Michael took Maggie's hand and played with her fingers for a moment. She left her hand in his passively, lost in her own thoughts. The rain fell steadily outside, and the changing breeze drove a light spray into their faces.

"Have you been unhappy, Michael?"

"Until the last few days I was neither happy nor unhappy. I was excited to be back in the mountains, and that should have made me happy. But I guess I've known for years that I made a mistake marrying Becky, only I didn't want to admit it. Our relationship wasn't so bad that I couldn't live with her, so I tried to make the best of it. I suppose I was deluding myself, but I had made a commitment that was hard for me to break."

She searched his face, saw a shadow of pain cross his features. Slowly, she withdrew her hand from his.

"So you're committed to staying with Becky." He was staring out the window and didn't answer. She watched him for a long moment. The pain of sitting next to him in their secret place and knowing that they could never be that close again, was almost too much. But if he decided to stay with Becky, he couldn't have her, too. She couldn't stand having to say good-bye to him over and over again. Slowly she picked up the rocks and started to put them back into the can.

He felt the sudden distance between them and returned from his reverie. "I said I was committed to her, but I can't let that mistake ruin the rest of my life."

She said nothing but continued to place the rocks in the can slowly, methodically. He touched her shoulder and tried to turn her face to look at him. His arm brushed her breast and made her shiver in spite of herself.

"Please don't turn your back on me, Maggie! You know I want you more than anything!"

He paused when he saw her hesitation, her uncertainty. Desperately, Michael tried to think of a way to convince her, make her see that he loved only her. Absently he reached into the pocket of his jacket and felt something hard, wrapped in a handkerchief. Of course! The bracelet. He had forgotten about it in the confusion of the past two days. But now it reappeared just when he needed it.

He unwrapped it, rubbed the silver with the cloth before holding it out to her. She looked up quizzically.

"I had this made for you, Maggie. I wanted to give you something special, something to symbolize our love. I hope it will remind you of me whenever you look at it. It has a special meaning that only you and I understand."

She took the bracelet in her hand tenderly, remembering how she had parted with the stone. The silver gleamed as she turned it in the dim light, the stripes of the tiger eye blinking capriciously. Lightly, she ran her finger over the stone and the curve of the cuff, appreciating their smoothness. Then she slipped it around her slim wrist and pushed it up her arm, until it felt secure.

He watched her anxiously, hoping that his gift would convey what words had been unable to. He saw how well the bracelet suited her, just as he knew it would. And then he saw her smile, a slow, quiet smile that lit up her face. Slowly, he felt the knots of tension loosening in him. She said nothing, just turned her face up toward him, but her message was as clear as the bracelet's had been.

He reached for her, pulling her down onto the sleeping bag, and kissed her long and hard. Her face felt hot and her mouth was salty as she locked her arms behind his neck and returned his kisses. They were lying under the eaves, the sloping roof just a few inches from their heads. The fresh smell of rain from the open window mingled with the smell of wood and dust around them. Her rapid heartbeat was matched by the sudden pulsing of blood in his temples as he reached under her shirt and covered her breast with his hand. Small tremors ran through her body. She opened to him, urging him on. Her light cotton skirt was pushed up as he lay on top of her, their closeness maddening through the layers of clothes. She opened her shirt to offer him her breast and locked her legs around him. He struggled with their clothes, not wanting to leave her, not wanting to break the intensity of their contact. Her breath was coming fast and she made little gasping noises as he took her. Her spasms triggered his own release, then he lay drained and breathless on top of her.

He almost said it out loud, but contained the thought: this was so different from making love to Becky. This felt right, and surprisingly, he felt no guilt.

Slowly, she became aware of the room around her once more. Michael was breathing deeply, and she wondered if he was asleep. She didn't want to disturb him, didn't want him to move away. She reached out her hand and traced a knot in the wood of the beam above them. The rain had slowed down and the attic was slightly brighter; the clouds were breaking up. A small puddle of rain had collected on the windowsill, its surface shaken by an occasional raindrop. The scurrying of small feet sounded somewhere nearby, and she smiled. Michael moved, caught her smile and returned it. He wove his fingers into the stubborn waves of her dark red hair pulled her face to his and kissed her softly, more gently than he ever had before. As they made love again she couldn't stop thinking that they would always have their secret place, even if the cabin no longer existed and they were old.

The sun broke through the clouds and shone brightly for a while, then began its descent in the west. The trees outside the small window cast long shadows when they finally climbed down from the attic. They laughed as Maggie tried to smooth her wrinkled clothes and wild hair. Michael had a smudge on his cheek, and his shirt was ripped where it had caught on a nail in the low eaves. She rubbed at the smudge playfully, then without thinking, threw her arms around his neck and pressed her face against his. He held her close, acutely aware of the warmth of her body against his.

"I wish we didn't have to leave here, Maggie," he said, burrowing his face into her hair.

"We don't, at least not tonight," she answered hopefully.

He pulled back to look at her, and suddenly saw in her eager face the child he remembered, Maggie the tomboy, who was always ready for an adventure. That image made him smile and relax.

"You're right. We don't have to leave tonight. The world can get along without us 'til tomorrow. Let them wait."

Her smile was joyful as she took his hand and led him into the kitchen. "It's going to be a cold night. Let's camp by the fire, like we used to."

He nodded, and without a word walked out to the woodpile. As Maggie worked in the kitchen, she heard him chopping wood, splitting kindling.

Maggie was waiting for him in the front room when he returned with his pile of wood. She had laid out two sleeping bags on the hearth rug and was sitting on the edge of one, lighting a kerosene lantern. He could barely make out the objects scattered around her in the gathering dusk. As the lamp suddenly threw its yellow light around the room, Michael saw that she had prepared a picnic for them. He smiled with pleasure as he arranged kindling inside the grating and held a match to the freshly split wood. How many picnics like that had they shared? Each time it had been different, Maggie serving whatever fantastic combination of edibles the pantry happened to have at the moment. Only dessert had

been the same each time, and now he looked at her questioningly.

Solemnly she held up a bag of marshmallows, a large Hershey bar, and a package of graham crackers, one corner of which had been nibbled open.

"S'mores. You didn't think I'd forgotten?"

"Never," he said happily.

"Only I've added something new," she said, pouring two large tumblers of red wine. They lay on the sleeping bags in front of the fire, nibbling at an eclectic feast of sardines, pickles, canned meat, slightly stale bread and cheese.

"It's so good to be with you again, Maggie. I can't tell you how good."

"I know. You have no idea how I've missed you." "I've spent my happiest moments in this cabin, with you and Jake."

"Will it ever be like that again?", she asked, suddenly serious.

"I promise you, it will. I just don't know if it'll happen here. I'm sure going to miss this old cabin."

281

She set down her wine and looked up at him. "What's going to happen, Michael?"

"We must take care of the lead problem first, then we'll see about Jake. After that, I'll deal with Becky."

"What are we going to do?"

"We can only hope that Tom Lang comes to his senses before the EPA takes over. I've tried just about everything to convince him."

She thought for a moment. "Maybe not everything. There's a town meeting this coming Thursday. It looks like this will be one of the main items on the agenda. Maybe if enough pressure is put on Tom Lang by a lot of different people, he'll come around. I'll feel out the townspeople, see who we can count on for support."

"Good," he said, handing her a burnt marshmallow. "I remembered that you liked them well done."

They tried to wash the sweetness of the s'mores away with more wine, but it only tasted sour, puckering their mouths uncomfortably. Michael put another log on the fire, spilling some of the wine on his shirt.

"I think you've had enough," Maggie laughed.

He looked at her in the firelight and pulled her closer. "No, I haven't." He kissed her, and her mouth was sticky and sweet with marshmallow. He thought he could never have enough of her.

Chapter 22

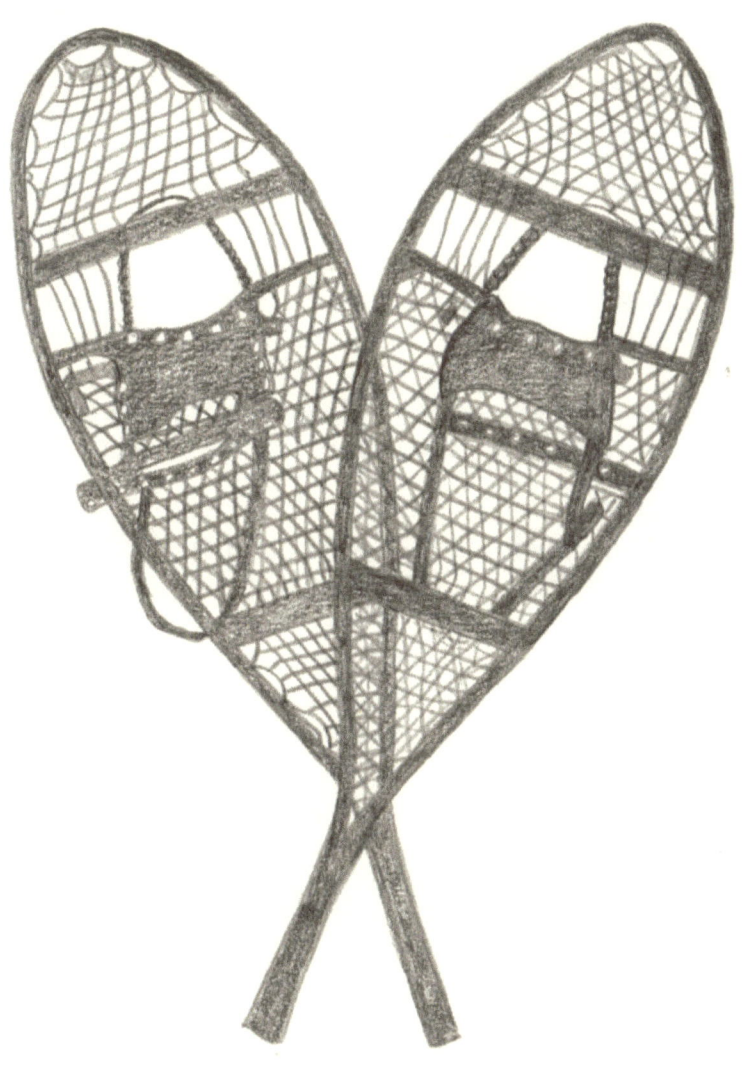

It was past five when Michael turned onto Yellow Birch Trail. He had left the Hughes cabin late in the morning, and followed Maggie to the newspaper office where they spent the afternoon working on an editorial for the next issue of The Langston Gazette. Shaping the words to convey the right meaning had been difficult, and he came away with a new respect for Maggie's journalistic abilities. They had to be careful to make the readers understand the situation and the danger without panicking them. They needed the townspeople's support if Michael was to succeed in convincing Tom Lang to clean up the mine quickly and willingly. They needed to present the problem clearly and lead the readers to the conclusion that cleaning up the mine was the only real alternative that would lead to both protection of their health and survival of the Company. They weighed each word carefully, keenly aware of their responsibility. It hadn't been easy, and he was tired when he pulled into his driveway.

Rusty's welcoming bark greeted him from the porch as he walked up to the house. Rusty jumped up to lick his master's face in excitement, his tail thumping against Michael's leg. Michael looked forward to spending the evening in front of a fire with his dog and a glass of brandy. Maybe Becky was out visiting her parents or a friend, he thought hopefully. But then the screen door opened and Becky stepped out, wearing a light pink dress with little roses on it. She continued brushing her hair as she confronted him.

"I was afraid that you wouldn't get home in time. Hurry up, or we'll be late!" she said testily.

"Late for what?"

"We're going to my parents' for dinner. I've been trying to get hold of you all day to tell you, but nobody knew where you were." He could hear the resentment in her voice.

"I've been all over. First with your father and some people at the factory, at Ed's, and with Maggie."

"With Maggie? Where? I tried to call the newspaper this morning but nobody answered," she said, blocking his way into the house.

"We didn't get there until this afternoon. We were out at the cabin," he answered, annoyed.

"All night?"

"Yes."

She waited for an explanation. Michael didn't offer one, and she started to say something, then changed her mind. Instead, she said, "I thought the cabin was boarded up. What were you doing there?"

"I went to find Maggie, to clear up our misunderstanding. A misunderstanding you helped to create."

"You're blaming me? After that article she wrote?"

"If you and your father hadn't misled her, she wouldn't have written that article."

She stepped very close to him and he noticed two bright patches burning in her cheeks. "Why is it that you're always siding with Maggie and Jake rather than with me and Daddy?"

He brushed past her and pulled the door open angrily. "We don't have time for this, Becky, not if we're going to dinner. It's about the last thing I feel like doing, but I can't afford to refuse. I don't want to antagonize your father right now."

"What about me? Don't you care about antagonizing me?" she shouted after him as he disappeared into the house, leaving the door open. She waited for an answer, and when he didn't respond she slammed the screen door shut, making it vibrate in its frame.

They made the ten minute drive to the Lang's in silence. Becky sat stiffly next to Michael, her face turned away from him. For the first time he fully realized the delicate nature of his situation. He must be careful not to alienate Tom any further, and make sure his relationship with Becky didn't deteriorate too rapidly. He often had the feeling that Tom only tolerated his views because of Becky. He hated to think what Tom's reaction would be if he found out that Michael was planning to leave his little girl. Without that complication, and with the help of the townspeople, he and Maggie might still convince Tom to take action. But not if he learned that Michael was in love with Maggie and was cheating on his daughter. If he knew, Tom might do something to hurt them all, out of rage and spite. Michael gripped the steering wheel tensely. He didn't like riding the fence, didn't like personal dishonesty, but right now he didn't seem to have a choice.

Tom and Carolyn were on the back patio sipping gin and tonics when Michael and Becky arrived. Tom was grilling steaks over charcoal. He laid down the tongs as they walked in and scooped Becky into his arms.

"How is my little girl? Still getting more beautiful every time I see her!"

Michael kissed Carolyn on the cheek and shook Tom's hand carefully. Becky's mother was a small, fussy woman with Becky's coloring, only faded. She tried to look younger by dyeing her hair and using too much makeup, but her efforts only served to remind everyone of what she had lost. Her main interests were growing flowers and directing their housekeeper to keep the house looking the way the home of Langston's leading citizens should look.

"I'm glad you're finally here. I was worried that the steaks would get done before you arrived, and that would've ruined our meal. You barely have time for a drink before dinner," Carolyn said, handing them gin and tonics.

Michael accepted his drink reluctantly, thinking that the Langs never asked him what he wanted to drink. They just assumed that he would want whatever they did. Becky always did.

"Michael didn't get home until after five," Becky said pointedly.

"I didn't know we were having dinner tonight. We had talked about Sunday." Michael wasn't sure why, but he felt the need to explain.

"Tom said you went to see him yesterday," Carolyn interrupted, turning to Michael. "I'm glad you're taking an interest in the family business."

"I wish he were!" Tom's voice boomed in. "Maybe then he'd understand that we can't be making impulsive decisions."

Michael looked into his glass, forcing a smile. Becky glanced at the two men, noting the tension between them. Less perceptive, her mother continued.

"Oh, I'm sure Michael understands. What did the two of you talk about?" she asked, fussing with the salad.

"Michael tried to convince me to spend the Company's money on a beautification project for the old mine-site," Tom said.

Michael walked to the edge of the patio, then slowly turned to Tom.

"I wish you wouldn't misunderstand me on purpose, Tom. If you would only believe that I want to help. If we work together, we can clean up the lead contamination."

"Bankrupting the Company isn't the kind of help I need," Tom said sarcastically.

Becky's eyes were wide as she looked at her father in alarm. "Bankrupting the Company? Could it mean that?"

"Oh, dear. Are we in some kind of trouble?" Carolyn asked.

"Nothing for my girls to worry about. Michael was just saying that cleaning up the mine-site could cost millions of dollars. And I was telling him that we weren't prepared to spend that much."

"Millions of dollars! What's going to happen to us if the Company goes bankrupt?" Carolyn was twisting her handkerchief nervously. She looked about ready to cry.

Becky turned to Michael, furious. "Now look at what you've done! Are you trying to destroy my family's business?"

"Now, Becky. I'm sure Michael means well. He just doesn't understand everything that's involved in running a business. He could still change that if he wanted to," Tom said in a demanding tone.

Michael ignored Tom's remark. "I'm trying to make you all aware of the facts," he said, looking at each of them in turn. "I'm sure once Tom understands how serious the problem is and how dangerous the alternatives are, he'll make the right decisions."

"Right for whom? For my family or the Hughes's?" Becky asked with hostility.

"Let's not argue and spoil the evening. Why don't we sit down and have our salad?" Carolyn stood by the table holding the salad bowl in one hand and a bottle of dressing in the other, vainly attempting to change the course of the conversation.

"I'm trying to tell you, Becky, that cleaning up the site quickly is the best for everybody. It's not a case of one side versus the other," Michael said, exasperated.

"Isn't it?" she said, her eyes narrowing. "Maggie wrote that article just to hurt Daddy. She's the one who's calling in the EPA and the Friends of the Wild. And now you're working with her, helping her!" Becky burst into angry tears.

"Would anyone like another drink?" Carolyn asked.

Tom went to Becky and stroked her hair. "Your face is hot, darling. Are you sure you're feeling allright?" Bursts of flame shot up from the grill, but no one paid attention.

Becky nodded, wiping her eyes. "I probably got too much sun." She sat down in a lawn chair, her back to Michael.

"Is it true, Michael? Are you working with Maggie?"

Michael set down his empty glass and faced Tom squarely. He hadn't wanted a confrontation in front of Becky and Carolyn, but now he couldn't back off.

"Yes. We're working together to correct the mistakes she made in the last article and to encourage you to clean up the mine-site properly."

"How can you trust her after that article?" Tom asked.

"I trust Maggie and Jake more than any two people in this world," he said without thinking. Becky and her parents looked at him in frigid silence. He hastened to correct his mistake. "I mean, she had reasons for writing that article. We cleared up our misunderstandings, and now we're working together."

Flames shot high above the grill, causing the fat from the steaks to sizzle and sputter. Quickly, Tom rescued them with the tongs, flipping them onto a wooden platter. "I hope nobody wanted his rare," he said.

Reluctantly, they gathered around the table. It seemed to Michael that he was isolated at one end, with the others clustered at the other. He played with a salt shaker shaped like a rooster while Carolyn served the salad and brought out corn-on-the-cob. He was determined not to say any more that could damage his relationship with Tom. But Carolyn, in her vague, unfocused way, persisted. "Maggie was such a nice girl. I can't imagine that she would write something to hurt us."

"She was just trying to make the people aware of the danger they're facing," Michael said.

"Oh, I don't believe for a minute that's all she wanted to do. She has a personal vendetta against Daddy because she blames him for Jake getting sick. She just wants to stir up trouble, trying to make the townspeople believe that they're in danger," Becky said.

"Are we really in danger, Tom?" Carolyn asked, turning to her husband.

"Don't you worry," he said, patting his wife's hand. "I won't let anything happen to you or to the townspeople." The reassuring smile left his face as he looked at Becky. The color had drained from her face, and she was staring at her steak. "Is the steak too well done for you, Becky?"

"No, no, it's fine. I'm just not very hungry."

"Do try to eat, dear. Your father made it especially for you."

Becky nodded, placing a small piece in her mouth and chewing half-heartedly.

"Well, that article sure caused me a heap of trouble. It got the town all riled up, and started a lot of rumors. They think they're being poisoned!"

"I know. I saw some women demonstrating in front of the factory this morning. They're really worried, for themselves and their children," Michael said.

"Ridiculous!" Tom exploded. "This business with Jake's been blown way out of proportion. He was poisoned by his well, and I've taken care of that."

"But I keep telling you, it's only a matter of time before the lead reaches Langston's drinking water, too," Michael said.

"I'll need more proof to convince me of that."

Michael stared at the row of strawberries that decorated the tablecloth. What more would Tom need to convince him?

Would more people need to suffer from lead poisoning before he'd be willing to do something?

"Could you get me a couple of aspirin, Mother?" Becky said. "I've got a headache." She rested her head on the back of her chair and closed her eyes. Except for the bite of steak, her dinner remained uneaten on her plate.

Tom looked at his daughter with concern as Carolyn disappeared into the house for aspirin. His words were aimed at Michael. "You kids don't seem to be very happy these days, and that's not right. You're young; you should be making plans for a family. I'll deal with the lead problem, you just work at making my little girl happy."

Michael didn't answer. He was filled with resentment toward Tom and Becky, at their arrogance and selfishness. And he was sick of playing the part expected of him, keeping Becky happy at all cost. They hadn't been happy with each other for a long time, but they had kept up the appearance of a good marriage. He looked at her sitting back in the chair, her smooth, golden skin framed by honey-gold hair, eyelashes highlighting the rounded curve of her cheek. Her headache made tiny lines of tension at the corners of her mouth and between her eyebrows, but she still looked as beautiful as she had in high school and college. She has matured very little with the years, he thought. Her features are smooth and regular, and blank, like the beauty of the porcelain doll she keeps on her bureau. We've been married seven years now, and what do we really know about each other? We know some of the things we should have paid attention to before we married. It's a good thing she didn't want children. She didn't want to be bothered, didn't want to be tied down. But lately she's been talking about a baby, how much it would please her father and bring us together again. I must talk to her soon. It isn't fair to lead her on, he said to himself, laying down his napkin.

Carolyn returned with the aspirin. "I can't believe that cleaning up that dreary old mine would cost millions of dollars,

291

Michael. Are you sure about that? Do we have that much extra money, dear?" she asked her husband.

"Not without deferring a lot of improvements in the factory for a long time, and risking the long-term health of the Company."

Michael pushed his chair away from the table and angled it to face Tom. "I worked with the EPA when I was with my old company in New York. Are you familiar with the Superfund program, Tom?"

"Not really."

Michael leaned forward. "If the EPA determines that you're responsible for creating the hazardous waste site, it can force you to pay for the clean up, but under their terms. The investigation and clean up are expensive and can take years to complete."

"Years? That just gives us more time," Tom said.

"But the longer it takes, the more it will cost."

"Why? I'd think the cost would be spread out over time."

"There are many steps involved. If the site is placed on the EPA's National Priorities List, more investigations are performed. Conditions at the site are studied and alternative clean up methods are evaluated. This takes about two years."

"Two years? Sounds complicated," Tom said thoughtfully.

"It is, sometimes unnecessarily so. But, because the EPA may need to take the responsible parties to court, all of these studies need to be done very carefully."

"I still don't see why it would cost so much more this way. Seems like we'd just be gaining time."

"Time costs money. The EPA's studies are more expensive than those that are performed directly for an industrial client. Any recommendations need to be defensible in court. And you'll eventually end up paying for them. As of yet, no one has successfully defended himself against these studies.

"Besides, while the site is being studied and evaluated, nothing is being done to clean up the pollutants. By the time the cleanup is begun, the contamination will have spread to a far greater area than it is now. Believe me, the costs go up tremendously with time."

"Doesn't the EPA assume any of the cost?"

"Superfund only pays for the cost of cleanup if the responsible parties can't be found or identified. The mine clean up could cost tens of millions before it's all finished. Not to speak of what the publicity could do to the reputation of the Company and the town."

"What do you mean?"

"It's a stigma to be identified by the EPA as being responsible for a hazardous waste site. You'll be crucified in the press as a company that doesn't care for the environment. The Friends of the Wild will have a field day. On the other hand, if you undertake cleanup voluntarily, you'll create a far more positive image." Michael watched Tom's face for a moment, then leaned back in his chair. For the first time, he was satisfied with the way their conversation was going.

Tom poked at the steak bone on his plate with his knife. He looked questioningly at Michael. "What did you mean about this affecting the town?"

"There are two industries in town--Opalescent Paints and tourism. With the river tainted, tourism is bound to suffer. Who will want to vacation or fish for trout in a river that's polluted, or drink mineral water that might contain lead? Not to speak of the health threat to Langston's population in postponing the cleanup. You've always prided yourself on taking care of the

293

people here, Tom. Think what it would do to their faith in you if you let them down," Michael said in a final appeal.

Tom remained silent for a while, absorbed in his private thoughts. Carolyn made futile attempts at conversation but the others remained unresponsive. The sun was setting in a cloudless sky, promising hours of twilight. Becky, still suffering from her headache, was quiet for the rest of the evening. The air stayed warm, yet she pulled her cardigan tightly around her. Michael glanced at his watch, trying to hurry the minutes along until it would be acceptable to leave without rudeness. At last, Becky made a motion to leave, and pushed away from the table. As she stood up, the color drained from her face and she swayed. She reached for the chair to steady herself, missed, and collapsed onto the flagstone patio as both Michael and Tom jumped to catch her.

"Doc! It's about time you got here!" Tom answered the door himself, practically pulling Doc Mallory into the house. Tom was obviously upset but tried to cover it up by his overbearing manner.

"I'm sorry it took me so long, but I had a couple of other calls to make first. Now, what seems to be the matter with Becky?"

"She fainted when she got up from dinner. Turned white as a sheet. Come with me, she's right in here," Tom said, urging Doc toward the downstairs bedroom. "I had a feeling something was wrong earlier. She had an awful headache, her forehead felt like she was running a fever, and she hardly touched her food."

Becky lay under a satin comforter, with an icepack on her head. Her eyes were bright with fever and two red spots colored her cheeks. Doc set his bag down at the foot of the bed and placed his glasses on the end of his nose. "How're you feeling, young lady?" he asked, taking her pulse with a practiced hand. Looking over the top of his glasses, he noted her unhealthy coloring.

"I've got an awful headache, and chills. A little while ago, I started having stomach cramps. They come and go," Becky said faintly.

Tom sat on a chair next to the bed, holding Becky's hand. Carolyn bustled about the room, arranging her pillows or bringing endless glasses of water and ice. Michael sat in a chair by the window, feeling like an intruder. Doc wrote out a prescription, tore off the sheet from its pad, and looked first at Tom and then at Michael. "Who's taking care of the patient?"

Michael rose to take the prescription, but Tom was closer and claimed it first. "She'll stay here while she's sick, Doc. I'll make sure that she gets whatever she needs."

Doc took off his glasses and put them in his pocket, then stood at the foot of the bed, looking at Becky. "You just take your medicine, and you'll be better in no time. And be sure to get lots of rest. I'll come back and check on you tomorrow."

Becky tried to smile, then closed her eyes as a sharp pain stabbed at her insides. Tom followed Doc and Michael out of the room, carefully closing the door behind him. He motioned the men away from the door. "Well, what is it, Doc, what's wrong with her?" he asked anxiously.

Doc was never one to be hurried, and he relished the sense of anticipation he could create before revealing his diagnosis. He only prolonged the drama when the situation wasn't serious or dangerous, allowing him an extra moment of indulgence. But this time he didn't seem to enjoy the obvious tension around him.

"Well, it could be the flu, or it could be something else. I can't be sure."

"What `something else'?" Michael asked.

"I don't want to say, not until I have more to go on."

"Look Doc, don't play games with me. Don't you think I'm upset enough as it is?" Tom stormed.

Doc nodded and set his bag down on a chair. "Becky's the third case like this that I've had since yesterday. Emmett Wilkins took sick yesterday morning, and Mrs. Simmons called me out to look at her boys. It's pretty puzzling, and I don't like it," he said, shaking his head.

"What are you getting at?"

"Well, the symptoms are an awful lot like Jake's."

"What are you saying? That Becky has lead poisoning?" Tom asked, appalled.

"I don't know, Tom. I'm only saying that the symptoms point to that. Headache, weakness, stomach cramps, intestinal upsets. It's something to consider under the circumstances."

"Well, how are you going to find out?"

"The only way to be sure is by doing blood tests. But I can't do much before Monday. Today is Saturday, and the lab is closed over the weekend."

"Should she be in the hospital?"

"No need for that. They can't do much more for her than what you're already doing until we know what it is we're treating. And we won't know that until we get the test results. Just try to keep her comfortable, and I'll check back tomorrow." He nodded to the men as Michael saw him to the door.

Tom was standing by the window when Michael returned, his hands thrust deep into his pockets. He looked dejected, his broad shoulders slumped forward, his whole body expressing his fear. Michael felt a stab of pity for his father-in-law, but the feeling was instantly replaced by something more complicated. He stifled his excitement at the thought, allowing only a faint flicker of hope. Becky probably had the flu. It was unlikely that she could be suffering from lead poisoning this soon, but there was no harm in letting Tom think so. Perhaps this was just what was needed to convince him.

Chapter 23

Jake was sitting on the sun porch when Michael and Maggie arrived. Tall potted palms and rubber plants separated the porch into small nooks, affording privacy for the patients and their guests. The red of his chamois robe lent color to his face, which had lost much of its tan during his hospital confinement. He didn't see them approach but continued leafing through an L.L. Bean catalogue. Maggie and Michael exchanged a quick smile as they paused behind him and saw that he was poring over the pages of sporting equipment--rifles and knives and waterproof Old Maine hunting shoes. He was shaking his head over a North American Fly Set when Maggie leaned down to kiss his cheek and Michael placed his hand on Jake's shoulder.

Jake's face creased into a smile as he hugged them both. "Just look at this," he said with contempt, pointing to the page before him. "They want $23.50 for this set of fishing flies. Why, I made better myself from the tail of a deer."

Maggie laughed, delighted. "What are you doing with a sporting goods catalogue, Dad?"

"Just thinkin' about doing some trading. I'm gonna need a new pair of boots for hunting. Last time my feet got pretty wet down in the swale."

"Slow down, Dad. I don't think you're going anywhere just yet," she said, smiling affectionately.

"Maybe not tomorrow. But I can see even from here, the maples are starting to turn. And that means hunting season ain't too far away."

How are you feeling, Jake?" Michael asked, leaning close to the older man. Jake looked better than the last time he had seen him, and Michael was relieved.

"Better, but still weak. Don't think I'm ready to climb Marcy, but by deer season I aim to be out there with my gun, the way I always been, every year since I was twelve." He accented his words with little nods of his head, and a firm, tightening of his jaw that meant argument was useless.

"And I plan to be out there hunting with you, if you'll let me," Michael said.

"You know you needn't ask; you're always welcome." A look of silent understanding passed between the two men.

Jake studied his daughter, saw that she had changed since the last time he had seen her. Where a few days before she had been angry and miserable, she was now filled with a quiet confidence. She sat close to Michael, and although they did not touch, there was an unmistakable bond between them. They glanced at each other frequently, and each seemed aware of the other's thoughts. Just like when they were kids, Jake thought, and that made him very happy.

"We came to tell you what's been happening in town, Dad."

"Good. Seems like I started something big by getting sick."

"You and me together, Dad. We started something big," Maggie said, slightly ashamed. "I caused things to get out of hand, and now I'm trying to put it right. Rather, Michael and I are."

Jake looked at them questioningly. "I hear the town's in an uproar, that folks are demonstrating against the paint company. What's really going on?"

"A lot. Maggie's article alerted people that waste from the mine is poisoning the groundwater, and people are worried about their drinking water. And rightly so; it is something to worry about," Michael said.

Maggie continued. "We've been trying to convince Tom Lang to clean up the mess before the contamination spreads any further, but he's stubborn. He says he doesn't believe there's an immediate danger. He probably just doesn't want to spend the money on it unless he's forced to."   "I've been telling him that if he waits until the EPA forces him to clean up,

301

it'll just cost him more," Michael interjected. "The Friends of the Wild, a nature group from New York, want to sue him. A law suit could take years. Tom would lose, the Company would go bankrupt, hundreds of people would be out of jobs, and the water would still be poisoned. It would be the end of Langston."

"And what did Tom say about all this?" Jake asked.

"He's hoping that he won't have to do anything."

Jake shook his head and brought his fist down on the arm of his chair. "He's gotta face up to what he done. Not to me, I ain't talking about that. But what his family's done to the land, first putting in that mine, then throwing their garbage down the old shaft. And what they've done to the river and the mountains, is what's makin' me see red."

"Oh, he's going to be held responsible one way or the other, Dad. We're just hoping that he'll come around before the EPA takes over. Tomorrow night is the town meeting, and maybe if we get enough support from the townspeople, he'll change his mind."

Jake nodded. "Who've you got behind you?"

"Well, I've talked to some of the women who were demonstrating at the paint factory the other day," Maggie said. "Some are really scared, especially the ones with young children. I think Doc is behind us, and Emmett and Mrs. Simpson, and the Fitzsimmons. A few people have come down sick, and they're worried it might be lead poisoning."

"Becky's sick, too, and I've never seen Tom so upset. We won't know if it's lead poisoning until later today."

"Becky's sick? Shouldn't you be home with her, Michael?" Jake asked, surprised.

Michael stiffened, then answered firmly. "No. She's at the Langs. That's where she wanted to be; they're taking care of her."

Maggie watched him relax again before she continued. "We're going to have trouble with some of the men from the factory. They're worried about losing their jobs. Their loyalty is to the Company and the Langs," she said.

"You'll be needin' all the help you can get," Jake said thoughtfully.

"We're hoping that this'll help some," Michael said, taking out a copy of next morning's paper. "Maggie and I wrote an editorial that should get plenty of people to the town meeting tomorrow night." He handed the paper to Jake.

Jake began to read, holding the paper at arm's length: "Langston is facing its greatest challenge. Your livelihood and your health are threatened. Exercise your right to be informed and make your opinion known. Attend the town meeting tonight."

Clearly and calmly, the editorial laid out the threat facing Langston, the origin of the lead wastes in the mineshaft, its movement in the groundwater, and the potential danger to the town if the lead were to reach their drinking water. It placed the responsibility for cleanup on the Company, as the source of the waste. Finally, it discussed alternative solutions, stressing the importance of quick, voluntary action on the part of Opalescent Paints, and compared it to the long, drawn-out and costly procedure that would be used if the government became involved.

Jake laid down the paper after reading it, and sat quietly for a moment. A nurse appeared from behind one of the palms, a tray of medication in her hand, rubber soled shoes muffling the sound of her quick, efficient steps on the smooth tile.

"Time for your medication, Mr. Hughes," she announced cheerfully.

When Jake didn't seem to hear her, she touched him lightly on the shoulder. "You seem to be in the middle of

303

something important. I hate to interrupt, but you must take your medicine if you want to get out of here soon."

Jake took the pills she offered, then sat resignedly while she placed a thermometer in his mouth. The nurse turned to leave, promising to return for the thermometer in a few minutes, then bent to pick up the paper that had fallen to the floor at Jake's feet. She stopped to scan the headlines and paused in the act of returning it to Jake.

She read the editorial, then handed the paper back to Jake.

"There really is a problem, isn't there?" The others nodded. "After what you've been through, Mr. Hughes, I would think Langston would be in a hurry to fix things."

"Not that many people know I been sick," Jake mumbled around the thermometer.

"Well, they should!" the nurse exclaimed. "You were very ill, and had us all worried for a time. You should've had treatment a long time ago. People should know how serious lead poisoning is!"

Jake nodded thoughtfully, removing the thermometer from his mouth. "Yeah. Maybe they should."

The nurse took the thermometer, read it and wrote in Jake's chart. "Dr. Mallory said he'll be stopping by to see you. He came in to drop off some blood samples yesterday. I heard him ask that they be analyzed for lead. Looks like you're not the only one in Langston with a lead problem." She picked up her tray and hurried down the hall.

"That nurse looked familiar, Dad," Maggie said as the nurse disappeared down the long hallway.

"Yup. She's Kate Mulligan. She grew up in Langston, and her folks still live there. She's been pretty good to me over the last coupla weeks."

304

"She seemed pretty sympathetic, not like the nurse I talked to when I first came to see you. That one seemed to think that the Langs could do no wrong."

"People ain't used to the Langs causing trouble. Tom Lang's always been helping out those in need, and people look up to him. They don't want to see that change."

Michael sat up as Jake's words took hold. "I think you've hit on something, Jake. That may just be the reason why Tom is so reluctant to assume responsibility. He doesn't want people to lose respect for the Langs."

Jake moved his wheelchair into a beam of sunlight and saw Doc Mallory approaching from the far end of the sun porch. Doc never hurried unless it was critical, and stopped to talk to a couple of patients sitting among the palms. He pulled up a chair next to Jake and sat down, placing his black bag on the floor.

"What brings you here, Doc? I know you don't like hospitals any better than I do," Jake said jokingly.

"That's true, but like them or not, hospitals can do some things that I can't. I brought in some blood and urine samples from a couple of my patients for the lab to analyze."

"They wouldn't be from the people who got sick the last few days with symptoms like Becky's, would they, Doc?" Michael asked.

Doc looked at him sharply, then nodded.

"You think they might have the same thing I got?" Jake asked.

"It's too soon to tell," Doc hedged. "But if they do, I want to make sure they don't wait as long as you did before getting treated." He turned to Michael, "How is Becky today? I haven't had a chance to see her yet."

Michael looked uncomfortable. "Neither have I. She's staying with her parents, and I came straight to see Jake this morning after picking up Maggie."

Doc looked questioningly at the two young people, opened his mouth to say something, then changed his mind.

"When I left the other night she was pretty weak from the stomach cramps. She had been throwing up a lot," Michael hastened to add.

Doc looked over the top of his glasses. "That's pretty much what I've been seeing with Emmett and the Simpson boys. Emmett's pretty sore, too, and he's dizzy when he tries to get out of bed."

"When will you know if it's lead poisoning?" Maggie asked.

"We'll know more by tonight. Becky's lab results should be back late today. By tomorrow we'll know what we're dealing with and can let people know at the town meeting."

Michael nodded. "I have a feeling this meeting will be well attended. We'll need someone to talk about the medical effects of lead poisoning. Can we count on you, Doc?"

"Certainly." Doc Mallory rose to go, then turned back. "Strictly between us, it wouldn't be such a bad thing if it did turn out to be lead poisoning. It could scare Tom into action, especially since his daughter is sick. And my patients aren't seriously ill yet; they haven't been exposed long enough."

Michael reluctantly pulled into the Lang's driveway that afternoon. He hadn't seen Becky since the dinner at her parents' Saturday night, and he had vague feelings of guilt. He sat in the Jeep for a moment looking up at the cloudless sky, thinking. Becky had been too sick on Sunday to want visitors, and when he stopped by on Monday, she had been sleeping. Carolyn didn't want to wake her, and Tom had discouraged his visit. "She needs rest now," he had said. "Don't you worry about her, Michael, we're taking good care of our little girl." Michael had felt relieved.

Mrs. Mattingly, the Lang's housekeeper opened the door and silently directed Michael toward the downstairs bedroom. He always felt like a guest in this house, he thought, irritated.

Becky lay in the large bed, the rose satin comforter pulled over her, despite the warm day. She looked pale, the hair around her face sticking to her damp forehead. Soothing music flowed from a clock radio, and a half-empty glass of lemonade perspired on the night table.

She didn't say anything as he opened the door, but her eyes searched his face. He stood in the doorway awkwardly for a moment, neither in nor out, then stepped quickly inside and shut the door.

"Hi."

"Hi."

Michael hesitated at the foot of the bed, then pulled up a chair facing Becky.

"How are you feeling?"

"Sick. Where have you been?" she asked petulantly.

"Working. Your parents said you didn't feel like visitors."

"You could have asked me, instead of them."

He nodded, not knowing what to say to this. Then, "I thought it best to stay away for a little while. Aren't you feeling any better?"

"I'm not throwing up anymore, if that's what you mean. But I feel weak, and the stomach cramps come and go." She turned on her side and pulled her knees into her stomach.

Michael studied the outline of her body under the satin comforter--the curve of her hip, legs folded up close to her chest, the line of her arm as she hugged herself protectively. Her head was bent forward on the pillow, and he could see the golden fuzz at the back of her neck where her nightgown pulled away. During the early years of their marriage, when they were still playful with each other, he used to kiss that fuzzy spot where her hair ended. She was ticklish and would laugh, pulling her neck into her shoulders.

She was watching him quietly from behind her long lashes. Michael avoided her gaze. His eyes roamed around the room, past the dresser with its intricately carved mirror frame, the porcelain shepherdess in her candy colored dress that reflected Carolyn's fussy taste, the muted still life hanging on the wall. He felt an urge to leave, to close the door on that part of his life forever. With an effort he focused on the drops of water sliding slowly down the glass on the night table.

"Does Doc know what's wrong with you, yet?"

Becky shook her head. "No." Then, "Why did you come?"

Startled, he looked at her. "What do you mean?"

She sat up, her face flushed. "I don't really want you here, Michael. Not after the way you talked to Daddy at dinner. I was ashamed of you for acting like that in their home." Awkwardly she reached for the lemonade, knocking over the glass.

He stared at her as the lemonade spread over the carpet. "You were ashamed of me?"

"Of course I was!" she cried as the door was swung open by Mrs. Mattingly. Becky's words hung in the air of the suddenly quiet room. Mrs. Mattingly looked at the estranged couple, noted Becky's tension and the growing stain on the carpet. Her rough features became more severe.

"You mustn't get so excited, Missy. The Mrs. told me to make sure you get plenty of rest and quiet," she said, pulling the comforter over Becky. "In fact, you shouldn't be having company," she said, eyeing Michael sternly.

"I'm hardly company, Mrs. Mattingly. If you don't mind, I'd like to talk to my wife alone," Michael said, returning her gaze.

The tall woman turned to Becky questioningly before leaving.

"It's all right, Mrs. Mattingly. Michael won't stay long."

He felt his anger rising, wanted to tell them both that he would leave when he was ready. Instead, he turned his back on Mrs. Mattingly as she picked up the empty glass and left the room. It was too late now. He should have said something years ago.

The distance between him and Becky was widening. It might have been bridged earlier, if he had started by reaching his arms out to her. But now the gap seemed infinite. He felt a sadness, a sense of failure, as well as the all too familiar emptiness. Absently he ran his hand over the satin comforter at the foot of his wife's bed. Her foot jerked away from his fingers.

He searched her face for some understanding of his own feelings, looking for a reflection of his own sadness. "I'm sorry you feel that way about me, Becky."

A shadow passed over her face but it was gone before he could recognize it. "What did you expect?" she asked, her voice sharp.

"I guess I expected a little understanding."

"I think it's a little late for that, Michael. Seems like we don't speak the same language anymore."

We're finally agreeing on something, he thought. We agree that we don't understand each other. But he said, "I don't know that we ever did, Becky."

"Didn't we? I thought we were heading in the same direction for quite a while. At least until this lead business made you forget your priorities."

He shook his head slowly. "No. We've always had different priorities. Only it took this crisis to make us admit it."

"Well, I'm beginning to admit some things, too. Like, maybe you aren't the man I thought you were."

"Meaning?"

She turned her head away and the corner of her mouth trembled uncertainly. "I can't live with you, Michael, unless you apologize to Daddy and agree to help him in the business." She caught her breath and faced him with an air of expectancy. Her eyes were large and luminous in her pale face, questioning him.

He felt his rage and frustration rise once more, then subside quickly. He nearly laughed as he realized what she was doing, how she was trying to manipulate him. But she only succeeded in trapping herself.

"I guess we just can't live together anymore, then," he said, relieved.

There was fear in her eyes, and anger. "You're not going to do what I want," she said in a low voice.

"You know I can't."

"No. I don't know that at all. If you wanted me enough, you could."

He said nothing. She sat perfectly still, her head turned from him. A large tear ran down her cheek to the corner of her mouth.

"I'll move out as soon as I find a place, Becky."

She shrugged. "There's no hurry. I'm going to stay here for a while." She pulled the ribbon from her hair and was twisting it around her finger. "It's not just me, is it?"

He opened his mouth then closed it again as she shook her head slowly. "I guess I've known for a while. But I never thought Maggie would be any competition for me."

Why not, he wanted to say. Because she isn't considered to be as beautiful and as desirable as you? But he only said, "It couldn't have been anyone else."

He knew she wouldn't understand. He didn't expect her to, but her pain was real nonetheless. He closed the door quietly behind himself and listened to her muffled sobbing as he stood for a moment outside before leaving.

Michael felt relieved of an immense burden as he walked down the long hallway. He was momentarily ashamed of his happiness as he remembered Becky's tears. He was also relieved that he would never need to come to this house again, where he was always treated like a stranger, someone who didn't really belong in the Lang's world. He would never need to accept another favor from Tom Lang, or put up with the patronizing attitude of his father-in-law. He would no longer need to sit through the interminable dinners, politely listening to Tom's suggestions on what he should do with his life, or swallow his anger as Becky mindlessly nodded in agreement.

He was no longer bothered by the thought that leaving Becky might make resolution of the conflict between himself and Tom Lang more difficult. After all, Becky had decided that she couldn't live with him anymore. Tom didn't need to know that Michael was planning to leave Becky. But at the moment none of that mattered. He just wanted to find Maggie and tell her that he was free.

He heard Tom's voice coming from the study off the main hallway. The door had been left open, and Tom beckoned to

311

Michael as he tried to hurry past. Michael stopped in the doorway, not wanting to offend Tom. He listened to one side of the phone conversation reluctantly.

"What do you mean cutting back?" Tom said. "After all these years?" Then a moment's silence as he listened to the response.

"If that's the way you feel, Don. But you'll regret this. The whole thing is a huge misunderstanding!" He listened for another moment, then slammed the phone down.

Tom Lang brought his fist down hard on the desk and stared at the phone, muttering to himself. His face was red, and his jaw tense. Suddenly remembering Michael, he beckoned him inside.

"That was Don Harrison, my distributor in New York. You met in my office a couple of weeks ago. He was calling to cancel that extra order of paint. Opalescent Paints has been his biggest seller for decades. Do you know the reason he gave?"

Michael shook his head, uncertain what to expect.

"Sales of Opalescent Paint have plummeted since that article was printed in the New York Times. He said that bad publicity is getting to the store owners!" Tom said incredulously. "They have been taking down our signs and moving our paints to less prominent shelf space!"

Michael couldn't imagine that. Ever since he could remember, Opalescent Paints had had a place of prominence in every paint and hardware store in New York State. He remembered how homesick he felt as a freshman in college, away from home for the first time. He had walked into a hardware store for a hammer and some nails, and came face to face with a pyramid of Opalescent Paint cans. The picture on the paint can was multiplied many times, increasing his longing for the mountain stream with the jumping rainbow trout, and the changing colors of fall. Now Opalescent Paints would be hidden on a center shelf, replaced by another, lesser brand.

"I'm sorry to hear that, Tom."

"I just hope Maggie is as sorry as you. Maybe she'll retract some of her ridiculous statements and put an end to all this nonsense," Tom fumed.

"Maggie and I've written an editorial for tomorrow's paper. We were very careful to present the problem calmly and logically. But we couldn't avoid mentioning the Company. We had to explain the role of Opalescent Paints in the lead contamination."

"Dammit, Michael! Don't you understand that the family business, our reputation are at stake?"

Michael nodded soberly. "Very much. That's why we hope you'll take the initiative and clean up the mess while your reputation can still be salvaged."

Frustrated, Tom pulled off his tie and tossed it on the desk. "Don't you understand? It would be admitting guilt. They don't expect that from me. The Langs have always been pillars of the community. Contributors to worthwhile causes. Someone to turn to when a donation was needed. They look up to us, and I can't let them down." With an exasperated sigh he walked to the window and looked out at the woods beyond. His damp shirt clung to his back, and Michael saw his shoulders rise and fall with each breath.

You mean, you don't want your image tarnished, Michael thought. "You'll be letting them down if you don't take care of the problem right away," he said.

Tom turned toward him, and Michael saw the indecision and worry in his eyes. Michael pressed his advantage. "If you act on your own, the townspeople will think even more highly of you. They'll know that you care enough about them to risk your reputation and the Company's profits. You could turn this potential disaster into a personal victory."

Michael saw Tom waver, could almost see him weigh the alternatives. But something was still bothering him. The phone rang unexpectedly, returning him to the present.

"Hello? Doc?" Tom was instantly on the alert.

A brief interchange followed, then Tom hung up.

"Does he have the test results?" Michael couldn't wait to ask his question.

"No," Tom shook his head. "The samples were messed up, and have to be repeated. "He's coming out now to get more blood and urine from Becky."

"Damn. Will he have the results by tomorrow?"

"No. Thursday at the earliest."

"After the town meeting."

The two men stared at each other, their thoughts on parallel tracks. Was Becky suffering from lead poisoning? Tom feared the worst, but had hoped to know by now. If her test results were positive, there would be no question as to what he must do. But now, well, he still wasn't certain.

Michael's feelings were ambiguous as he left. He had wanted to know, too, and was frustrated by the delay. But on second thought, uncertainty might make Tom Lang more receptive to change. Negative results might have reinforced his obstinacy.

Chapter 24

Except for graduation night and the annual fireworks display on the Fourth of July, evenings were generally quiet in Langston. Most people have their dinner between six and seven, then watch television until bedtime. Those on the day shift at the factory retire early, like most of the population. So it was unusual to see a crowd of people on Wednesday evening, milling around in front of the high school.

The spotlights outside Langston High had been turned on, and the sign advertising the next football game was brightly lit up. Beneath the sign, a homemade banner proclaimed in wobbly block letters that a town meeting would be held at eight o'clock on Wednesday night. As usual, everyone was invited to attend. Usually, very few did. But tonight people were standing around the front steps at seven-thirty, shuffling uncomfortably in the chilly night air, waiting for someone "official" to arrive and open the high school doors. Tension and anticipation filled the air.

Hugh Fitzsimmons, the Town Supervisor, was the first to arrive and unlocked the doors. Councilmen Cal Collins and Tim O'Leary came together and checked the seating on stage where A long table had been set up on the stage with five chairs. Three microphones were on the table. They were rarely needed, since it was unusual to see more than a single row of the auditorium filled for the town meetings. Ethan Polk, the Town Attorney, laid out his papers on the table in front of his seat and poured himself a glass of water. Audrey Brockman, the Town Clerk, was the last to arrive. As usual, she had forgotten her reading glasses and had to hurry home to get them. Finally, taking her place on the stage, she whispered to Hugh, "Looks like we're going to have a full house. You'd better make sure the mikes are working tonight."

When Michael arrived at the auditorium he paused to look over the sea of familiar faces. Some were friendly and nodded to him encouragingly, others wary, and a few were openly hostile. His parents sat towards the back, next to Mary Readler. He stopped to speak to them and tried to read his father's face, but it was noncommittal.   Michael looked for Maggie and found her in the front row, sitting up straight, watching the occupants of the stage. She was leaning forward in her seat and appeared ready to join the others on stage. He sat down next to her and touched her hand. She glanced at him, then smiled and relaxed slightly.

"Nervous?"

Maggie nodded. "Yes. So much depends on tonight."

Michael looked around him, nodding to Ed the barber, and Bill Morely seated two rows behind. Charley Rattinger walked down the isle casually and spoke to Maggie. She greeted him, then turned to Michael.

"Michael, this is Charlie Rattinger, the Times reporter I told you about. Charlie, this is Michael Ryan."

The two men sized each other up as they shook hands.

"The teacher who discovered the lead contamination and started all this," Charlie said, waving his hand over the crowd.

Michael nodded. "Maggie's told me about you. Hope you give us a fair shake in your column. We need you on our side."

"He will," Maggie assured him. Charlie sat down next to Maggie and took out his notebook.

Michael looked up to see Eric Rhodes staring at him from the other end of the row. He wore a faded corduroy sports jacket with suede patches on his elbows and a scowl on his face. Rhodes continued staring at them as Michael pointed him out to Maggie. They didn't like what they saw, and exchanged a meaningful look.

Hugh Fitzsimmons reached for the middle microphone and prepared to call the meeting to order when Tom Lang walked in. All heads turned to the back of the auditorium. Tom paused, hitched up his belt and scanned the faces before him. He nodded to some, as he walked down the aisle to the front of the room and took a seat in the center. Then he nodded to Hugh, as if granting him permission to start.

Hugh cleared his throat and continued. "The August meeting of the Langston Town Council will now come to order." He waited until the room quieted down and attention was directed at the stage. "I would like to welcome you all tonight. Didn't know there was this much interest in our order for the new snowplow," he smiled, looking at the audience over the top of his glasses. A few people laughed, but their laughter trailed off uneasily. Most remained quiet, expectant.

Cal Collins bent over and spoke into the microphone closest to him. "I think that we're all here to discuss the lead problem," he said bluntly. "Its something we need to talk about, so let's not pussyfoot around. Frankly, it's something I'm worried about, and I'm sure these good folks are, too." He swept his eyes over the audience, noting the nods and murmurs of agreement. "I move that we dispense with our scheduled agenda and discuss the problem that brought us here."

"Now hold your horses there, Cal," Hugh interrupted, turning to Ethan Polk. "What about it, Ethan? Can we do that?"

The attorney quickly looked through his sheaf of papers before replying. "It doesn't say you can't."

"Well, then. Is anyone going to second my motion?" Cal urged.

After a moment's silence, Tim O'Leary raised his hand. "I second."

"Good." Cal moved the microphone closer to himself. "Let me just tell you my feelings on this lead problem. Frankly, folks, I'm worried. And not just about the possible threat to our health, but because this problem is also threatening our businesses. Even if it isn't true, word is getting out that there's lead in our water. If my customers start believing those rumors, they're going to stop buying my Sparkling Mineral Water; they'll stop using the baths. In fact, they'll avoid Langston altogether."

"That's right," Tim O'Leary said, taking over. "It could really stop the tourists from visiting our area. Who wants to fish in a river that's polluted with lead? Who would want to eat a trout that's loaded with lead? And if the tourists stop coming, what happens to those of us who make our living off them? Like Cal, here, with his mineral water, and me with my sporting goods store. And I know it's not just us; a lot of you depend on the tourist trade, running motels and restaurants and stores."

Hugh leaned forward to his microphone. "Now wait a minute here, boys. Let's not get ahead of ourselves. We don't know anything for sure, yet. Let's not jump to conclusions until we know all the facts." He turned to Audrey Brockman, who was scratching away on a pad of yellow paper. "You getting all this down, Audrey?"

Audrey nodded, writing faster. Her glasses had slid to the end of her nose and looked ready to fall off.

Maggie leaned over and whispered to Michael. "Hope she's got her hearing aid turned up. At the last meeting she thought they were still discussing the sewer system after they had moved on to snow removal." Michael suppressed a smile and turned his attention back to the Town Supervisor.

"I think the best way to go about this," Hugh was saying, "is to open up the discussion to you folks in the audience. That way we can get a better idea of what we're facing here and how you all feel about it. Then maybe we can figure out what our options are. Who wants to be the first to take the floor?"

There was a general stir in the room and a low murmuring as people looked around, waiting for someone else to begin. The invitation had been so sudden, and no one seemed to be prepared to start. Michael hesitated. He could get up and speak first, but he didn't want to be rushed. He preferred to have someone else introduce and explain the topic and allow him to read the mood of the audience before speaking. However, if Tom spoke first, he might sway the audience by the force of his personality and influence, or by playing up the importance of the Company to Langston. He also worried that Eric Rhodes would start off with an inflammatory speech. That would only succeed in alienating the moderates in the audience, moving them to support Tom and the Company against the outsider, rather than toward the interests of the environment.

People turned to watch Tom Lang slowly begin to rise from his seat. Then Michael felt Maggie firmly squeeze his arm as she rose from her seat, and before Tom had a chance, she was moving to the aisle and standing in front of the microphone. She looked over the audience and her eyes lingered on Michael's before she began. Tom Lang sat back down and folded his arms over his chest.

"I hope you will forgive me for being the first to speak. I know there are others here who are more knowledgeable or better speakers than I am." Here Maggie looked at Tom Lang with an apologetic smile. "But I feel strongly about the problem that was discovered and that I've written about in the paper these last few weeks. Quite frankly, Langston is facing a crisis. As I said in my article, lead wastes were dumped into the abandoned mine some fifty years ago. Lead has leaked out of the mine and has contaminated the groundwater. The groundwater is moving toward the river and is threatening our drinking water." She stopped, looked down at the upturned faces watching her in tense silence.

"Opalescent Paints put their wastes in the mine and is responsible for this lead contamination. The Company needs to clean up the mine before our drinking water is poisoned. Not only will the environment be polluted, the waste also threatens the health of all of us who drink water from the Opalescent."

A man's deep voice came from Tom Lang's section of the auditorium. "How do you know all this? Seems like the water's

320

allright now. How can you be so sure it's going to be poisoned?" A few people around the man nodded in agreement.

Maggie felt a wave of hostility from that part of the room. She started to answer, then changed her mind.

"I'm going to ask Michael Ryan to answer that. He discovered the problem, and he knows more about the technical aspects of it than I do."

She looked at Michael gratefully as he took her place in front of the microphone.

"As most of you know, I am a registered professional environmental engineer," he began. After engineering school I worked in New York City cleaning up hazardous waste sites and designing groundwater treatment plants for cleanups. In other words, I worked with hazardous wastes such as lead, and know how to predict their movement in soil and water. I came back to Langston partly to get away from the contaminated sites in New Jersey and to return to a pristine environment.

"I was studying the effects of acid rain on our water when I found unusually high concentrations of lead in the river downstream from the old mine. The concentrations didn't exceed safe drinking water standards, but they were much higher than what I found higher up in the mountains where the effects of acid rain are the greatest. So I investigated further and traced the source of lead to the waste deposited by the paint company in the old mine . I do not say this lightly. For several generations my family has worked for the Company, often acting as a bridge between the needs of the Company and the well-being of the employees. I'm trying to live by my father's example.

"I know many of you are wondering how I can predict what is likely to happen to the river, to our drinking water. I base it on what has happened so far and what I know about lead movement in groundwater. At least one person in town is already suffering from lead poisoning. Jake Hughes' well is already heavily contaminated, and Jake is in the hospital, very ill."

An old man in the audience spoke up. "That waste was put down the mine when I was hardly more than a kid. I remember, because I worked on that job. It's been there for fifty years. Why would it start causing trouble now, after all this time?" There were murmurs of agreement from the people around him.

"It takes a long time for lead to travel through the soil," Michael answered. "But once the front of contamination reaches a certain point, the concentration can shoot up dramatically. In time the bulk of the lead will reach the river and contaminate our drinking water, making us all candidates for lead poisoning. The lead contamination must be stopped without delay. The longer Opalescent Paints waits, the more difficult and costly cleanup will be." Michael stopped, allowing his words to sink in. He looked over at Tom Lang, who had risen from his chair and was heading toward the aisle. Michael left the microphone and walked back to his seat.

Tom looked at the audience and smiled his broad, expansive smile before beginning. Michael couldn't help thinking that Tom looked at ease, in control of the situation. "It's good to see so many of you here tonight and to know that you're concerned about what happens to our town. The way my family's always been concerned," Tom began. Michael felt the crowd's sympathy swinging towards Tom.

"I'm concerned about what I've heard here tonight. What we do here tonight could affect our town, affect you and your families. And I'm concerned about your health, our health. But frankly, I'm not convinced that the wastes in the mine are a threat." He moved to the edge of the stage and looked directly at the faces before him, challenging them.

"After all, what do we know for sure? We know that the level of lead in the river is higher than normal, but that it isn't toxic. We know that the lead may be coming from the old mine, but that it has taken fifty years to come this far. We know that the lead may get into our drinking water, but we don't know when, or how much. Perhaps it'll take another fifty years to become a problem. We do know that Jake Hughes has lead poisoning, and that he got it from his well. His well is a good ways upstream from Langston." Tom paused, looked meaningfully into the faces of his audience. Some of the people shuffled and squirmed in their seats uncomfortably.

Tom continued. "Michael wants me to act quickly. He tells me any cleanup could cost millions. Our company has survived, in fact Langston itself has survived, because the Company has invested its funds judiciously. From the beginning we have always planned for the future welfare of the Company and the town. We have invested our excess capital in new ventures, ensuring a living for the people of Langston. Before logging and lumbering played out we started the lead mine. After the First World War, when demand for lead dropped, we expanded into paints.

"Again, we need to think in terms of `what's next'? What can we do to diversify the Company and keep the townspeople employed? Whatever our next venture turns out to be, we'll need capital to pursue it. Michael wants me to commit the Company's resources to a cleanup program for a potential problem we're not even sure exists. I'm sorry, but while I respect Michael's motivation and interest in our health, I just can't commit the Company's capital until I am convinced that there is a problem and that there is a less risky way of solving it."

The room was completely quiet. Then someone coughed and a chair creaked. Michael could feel the uncertainty around him. Tom left the microphone, and immediately Eric Rhodes took his place.

He ran his hand through his untidy hair and fidgeted nervously with the microphone before beginning. He was an outsider, and the crowd watched him curiously. He didn't belong in their town, and he was obviously ill at ease. It was unusual to have a stranger interested in the town's affairs.

"What we've just heard from Mr. Lang points out what his priorities are. He's only interested in the profits of his company. He's not interested in taking any risks, unless it is in his own interests. He wants you to risk your health, to save him some money. He's willing to risk the environment, if it can increase his profits."

Someone from the back of the room called out, "Who the hell are you, and what's your interest in this?" A ripple of laughter ran through the audience, relieving the tension.

Startled, Rhodes stopped. "I am Eric Rhodes, and I represent the Friends of the Wild."

"Friends of the what?" the voice asked.

"Friends of the Wild," Rhodes repeated, irritation in his voice. "For those of you who don't know, we're a group of concerned citizens interested in protecting the wilderness. We are concerned when companies like Opalescent Paints pollute the environment. Mr. Lang refuses to believe that his company is polluting the river, or to accept responsibility for it. He would like us all to believe that no problem exists, despite all the evidence to the contrary.

"It's been proven that lead from the mine has contaminated the water. Someone has already been poisoned. Lang wants to ignore the evidence, out of greed, so he might save some money. But he won't get away with it. I'm here to make sure of that."

"Just what are you here for?" a woman's voice asked. Michael turned around and recognized Mary Readler in the audience.

"I'm here to gather evidence against Opalescent Paints. The Friends of the Wild is going to sue the company and the Langs for all they're worth. When we get through with them,

324

there won't be a company left. We plan to accomplish two goals here. We want to make an example of the company, to discourage other companies from polluting. And we want to shut down the last major industrial activity in the Adirondack Park." Rhodes looked pleased with himself as he finished his speech.

There was a stir in the audience and a low muttering as people digested his words. Michael shifted uncomfortably in his seat and leaned over to whisper to Maggie: "This isn't going well. Rhodes is going to turn off the townspeople with his fanaticism." Maggie's face looked worried as she nodded in agreement.

"You're out to ruin the paint company?" Mary was asking indignantly. "Have you any idea what that would do to us?"

"It would return this area to nature. It would put an end to the lead pollution. It would be a major victory for the Friends of the Wild."

"It would put us out of our jobs!" Harry Flanders shouted from the audience. As if on cue, others took up the protest with cries from every corner of the room.

"You're trying to destroy this town!"

"How are we going to make a living if the Company goes under?"

"I have a family to feed!"

"Langston is my home, and I don't want to leave!"

"Go back to the City, where you belong, and let us solve our own problems!" Several applauded and cheered this remark.

"It's our environment. We can protect it without your butting in!"

Soon most of the audience was standing, shouting angrily, a few shaking their fists at Rhodes. Rhodes was also getting angry. He tried to continue, but his words were drowned out by the general confusion. Hugh Fitzsimmons tried to restore order, then looked at the other members of the town board helplessly. Audrey pushed her chair away from the table and stood up. She looked around for something, grabbed her umbrella and reached for the microphone. She rapped on the microphone with the handle of her umbrella, then tapped the other end sharply on the floor until the room quieted. Satisfied, she handed the microphone back to Hugh.

"Thank you, Audrey." Then, turning back to the room, "Let's try to keep it down, folks. You'll all have a chance to say your piece, if you'll just wait your turn."

John Ormsby stood up and began to speak. "I think I speak for all of us who work for the Company, when I say that we're not going to sit back and let some outsider take away our living. The Company has done pretty well by us, and by our fathers and grandfathers. It's given us the chance to earn a good living, and a town we can call home. The Langs have always treated us fairly. No one can say that they don't care about us. And I, for one, have trouble believing that Mr. Lang would do anything that would make us all sick." Murmurs of agreement followed his speech.

The room quieted as a well groomed older man, the chairman of the Hospital Board, stepped up to the microphone. "It would be ridiculous and ungrateful to say that Tom Lang is anything but deeply concerned about the welfare of the people of this town. It was because of his great generosity that we were able to complete the new wing of the hospital. He has always contributed his time and money to help with any health related or other charitable project that I have been involved with over the years."

Maggie and Michael exchanged a concerned look. Together they followed every speaker's words, their hopes rising and falling with each individual's point of view. The mood of the townspeople swung rapidly back and forth. Maggie turned and searched the rows of faces behind her. Where was Doc? They needed Doc's help to convince the people that the dangers of lead poisoning were real. They needed to believe that the threat was real if they were to help persuade Tom to clean up the mine.

Maggie turned her attention back to the front just in time to see Charlie Rattinger leave his seat next to her. He walked up to the microphone as the last speaker finished. The audience eyed him warily--another stranger in their midst.

"My name is Charlie Rattinger," he began. "I'm a columnist for the New York Times. I'm here to cover this story, but I'd also like to help you if I can."

"I know that I'm a stranger to you and an outsider in your town. But I come up to visit the Adirondacks whenever I can-- not often enough I'm afraid--to fish in the Opalescent and to hike in the high peaks region. Those of us who live and work in the city view the Adirondacks as a refuge, a place to get away from the problems caused by our industrial society. The Blue Line surrounding the Adirondack Park is thought of as a fence protecting this retreat. When that retreat is threatened, a great number of people outside of your town become interested." Charlie spoke easily and confidently. He singled out individuals in the audience and seemed to appeal directly to them. Before long, the last traces of hostility in the faces around him began to evaporate.

"You need to realize that the problem you're facing here, in Langston, is no longer just a local matter. Ms. Hughes' article was published in the Times, and the story attracted a widespread audience. Hazardous waste is a hot topic in the news these days. It concerns millions of people who are, at one time or another, affected by industrial pollution. And it attracts environmentalists, like Friends of the Wild, who are fighting to protect the environment.

"I know that the people in the Adirondacks, and especially in a self-made town like Langston, are proud and independent and close knit. I've heard throughout the evening how you don't want outside interference, how you prefer to solve your problems from within your community. I've always found that attitude to be admirable. But you must realize that this problem could be taken out of your hands. If you want to solve the problem yourselves, you need to act on it quickly, before the federal government becomes involved."

"What does the federal government have to do with it?" Bill Morely asked.

"Well, the EPA, or Environmental Protection Agency could take over the responsibility of cleaning up the site."

"How can it take over, just like that?"

"Quite easily. Once Langston is reported as a potential hazardous waste site, the EPA can take over and the matter is out of your hands. And I don't think you would want to see that happen."

Many shook their heads, and there was an air of uncertainty in the room. "What happens if the EPA takes over?" someone asked.

"Well, the EPA has a series of very complicated steps they have to follow. Believe me, the final costs will be much higher going through the EPA, than if cleanup is undertaken independently," Charlie said, looking at Tom Lang.

"Will the EPA get rid of the lead in the water?" a female voice asked.

"Eventually. But by the time they get around to it, cleanup will be much more difficult and the contamination more widespread."

There was silence in the room before the woman spoke again. "You mean we could get poisoned before they clean up the water?" Her voice rose hysterically.

"If the cleanup process takes long enough. But by that time your drinking water may have been declared unsafe, and the town may have to be evacuated if another source of water isn't found."

Once again, confused murmuring and protests rose from the crowd. Hugh Fitzsimmons tapped his microphone, trying to restore order. Suddenly the auditorium doors banged open, admitting a wave of cool night air. Michael and Maggie turned at the sound, then exchanged a surprised look. Doc Mallory walked down the center aisle, pushing Jake in a wheelchair. He parked Jake in front of the stage, in clear view of everybody.

"Hope we're not too late. I was asked to talk tonight about the health dangers posed by the lead wastes at the old mine. Jake Hughes wanted to be part of this meeting too, and I felt that he should be the one to tell you what it's like to be suffering from lead poisoning. If you look at him, you'll see what it could do to you."

Jake looked at the people in the first few rows, most of whom were staring at him, shocked. No one could recollect Jake ever being ill. He was their symbol of strength and independence, a man who relied on his own capabilities and resources. Some resented him because he didn't need the town, preferred to live his independent life-style. But nearly everyone held a grudging respect for him. Sitting there in a wheelchair, wearing a robe over his hospital gown, he looked weakened, diminished. The lines that crisscrossed his face seemed to have deepened, and his frame shrunk.

"I made up my mind to come here tonight so I can tell you what happened to me. Maybe I can convince you to do somethin' before it gets you, too. Because you won't know when it's happening 'til it's too late." Jake looked around him at the silent crowd, gathering strength to continue.

"I reckon I don't even know when I started getting sick, it snuck up on me so slow. First, I started feeling tired, like I had no energy to do things. Figured my age was finally catching up with me. Then I lost my appetite and started getting headaches. I never had them before in my whole life. Still, I didn't think that much about it. When I started upchucking and getting awful pains in my stomach, I figured I had a touch of the flu. Only it didn't go away; it kept getting worse. By the time they got me to the hospital, I was in a pretty bad way. Guess I was lucky, though. They gave me a lot of medicines, and Doc says I'm gonna be O.K. But my well ain't, and most likely I won't be able to live on my land again." Jake sat back in the wheelchair and took a deep breath.

"How come Maggie isn't sick?" someone asked. "She must have been drinking the same water you have."

Doc took the microphone. "Not exactly. Since she worked in New York she's been spending most of her time in town, so she's had a lot less exposure than Jake's had to the contaminated water. Also, she's a lot younger than Jake, so she hasn't drunk the water for anywhere near as long. But of course, she'll have to be tested for lead, too."

"Is it true that people in town are starting to get sick? Does that mean that our water is poisoned already?" a young woman asked.

"We don't know that for sure. We're doing some tests on the sick people, but the results aren't back yet."

Mrs. Simpson stood up in the middle of the auditorium, creating a stir. She was a large woman who wasn't shy about attracting attention. "Well, my boys are sure as hell sick," she announced. "And it sounds an awful lot like what he's got," she said, pointing to Jake.

Michael glanced over at Tom Lang, who was squirming in his seat uneasily. Michael made a quick decision and spoke up. "Becky is sick, too, with the same symptoms. I think we all

330

have very personal reasons for wanting to see the lead contamination stopped." He looked Tom in the eye, making the older man shift his gaze.

"Just how sick can lead make you, Doc?" Ed asked.

"Well, I've been doing some reading in my journals and medical books. And there seem to be plenty of things for us to worry about. Even small amounts of lead can hurt people, especially children. The EPA has found that excess lead in drinking water alone is responsible for hundreds of thousands of lower IQ scores in children, high blood pressure in middle aged men, and increased risk of miscarriages, lower birth heights and weights, premature birth and stillbirths in pregnant women.

"Low level lead poisoning is called the `silent epidemic', since it often causes no obvious symptoms. Some effects include partial loss of hearing or IQ, growth retardation, poor metabolism of Vitamin D, or disturbances in blood formation. In fact, lead is considered by the American Academy of Pediatrics to be the most serious toxicological danger to children.

"And there's even evidence that unborn children can be affected when their mothers are exposed to even small doses of lead. One study showed that children who absorbed the most lead before birth performed worst on physical and mental tests in their first years of life."

Doc paused as a young, very pregnant woman in the back row rose and moved to the aisle, followed by her husband. She looked white and shaken as she walked unsteadily to the door. In a few moments her husband returned. He didn't take a seat but remained standing, leaning against the door.

"How can I tell if I've got lead poisoning?" someone cried out.

"Well, there are certain signs to look for, although the early symptoms are a lot like the flu," Doc answered. "At first you'll feel tired and weak, lose your appetite and get constipated. You might start getting headaches, have a metallic

331

taste in your mouth, or get irritable. Later on you'll start vomiting and have pains in your joints and abdomen. You may also feel dizzy or have palpitations. With severe lead poisoning all of these symptoms are worse. Untreated, it can lead to convulsions, delirium, paralysis, or even a coma."

"How can we tell if it's lead poisoning or the flu?"

"The only way to be sure is by having blood and urine samples tested. There is often a lead line on the gums, which is a good indicator, and lead lines in the wrists and knees can show up on x-rays. I hope you can see that lead poisoning is serious."

Lewis Grant, the high school principal, stood up before Doc had finished. "I have to agree with Doc on that. Studies have traced the lowest IQ scores among children to those with the highest lead count; intellectual impairment has been traced to the lowest detectable blood lead levels. So I'll have to agree with those who say that no lead levels are the only acceptable lead levels. It's our mutual responsibility to make sure that our children aren't exposed to this danger."

Ann Callahan stood up and faced the room. Her youngest was asleep on her shoulder, cheeks rosy, mouth slightly open. "What I have to say is mostly for the men. I know that you're all concerned about your jobs and feeding your families. After all, most of you owe your living to the Company. My Joe does, too, and he'll defend the Company whenever there's a need. I understand that, and I respect him for it. But you've got to get your priorities straight, right here and now. I refuse to take chances with my children's health. No matter what it takes, I want you to make sure that they're not harmed by the lead. Even if it means speaking out against the Company, or forcing it to clean up the mess." She sat down to cheers from all corners of the auditorium. Her little girl opened her eyes momentarily, then snuggled back against her mother's shoulder.

The young man with the pregnant wife spoke up from the back of the room. He had to raise his voice to make himself heard. "My wife is going to have our first baby in a couple of weeks. She's real upset, hearing what was said here tonight about lead poisoning. She's upset because it's too late for her to protect our baby. For all we know, the baby might already be suffering from lead poisoning. But I say, maybe it's not too late. If the lead isn't in the water yet, we can still stop it before the baby is exposed. But we've got to have action now, not hear excuses!"

Shouts of agreement greeted his words. Several women jumped to their feet, speaking for their families, their children. The men, their passions slower to ignite, joined them more reluctantly. Maggie squeezed Michael's hand and spoke into his ear, "It's happening. Things will take care of themselves now."

"Tom has to listen to the people he says he cares about, even if he won't listen to us."

"How can we protect against the lead?" someone asked.

In two quick strides, Michael was in the aisle, speaking into the microphone again. "First of all, everyone's blood needs to be tested for lead levels. Secondly, the town needs to test for lead in our drinking water regularly until the mine is cleaned up. Finally, Opalescent Paints needs to investigate the extent of lead contamination and begin to clean up the site as soon as the best method is determined."

There were shouts of: "What about it, Mr. Lang?" "Do you really care about the people, or are you just interested in your profits?" and "We won't let our children be sacrificed!"

All eyes were on Tom Lang as he rose slowly and walked up to the microphone. The noise and confusion were replaced by total silence. Only a cough and Tom's footsteps interrupted the air of anticipation. Maggie felt the tension

333

around her as the people waited for Tom's words. Tom appeared hesitant, defeated, no longer totally in control.

"I've decided to go along with Michael's recommendations." Maggie heard the collective expulsion of held breaths as Tom continued speaking. "I am going to pay for a study to see if there is a lead problem." An excited murmuring passed through the crowd at these words, then died down as he explained.

"I was undecided as to what I should do when I came here tonight, although I may not have seemed that way to you. As you've heard, my daughter is sick. She has the same symptoms that Jake Hughes suffered. We were supposed to find out today if the symptoms were caused by lead poisoning, but the tests weren't completed in time. Then, when I saw how deeply concerned you all are for your children, it really hit me. My little girl might be suffering from an illness that my family might have unknowingly caused. And if I hesitated to do something about it now, your children might become ill, too. Seeing you and listening to your concerns and to Doc's advice convinced me that I couldn't take a chance with your health, not now that I understand the risks."

Someone at the back of the room began to clap, slowly, rhythmically. Michael saw his father stand and continue clapping as others joined him. Soon, nearly everyone was standing, clapping, shouting, stomping their feet. The tension in the auditorium was changing, transforming from one of confrontation to a mood of release and celebration. Tom tried to continue, but was drowned out. His features relaxed as he held up his hand. It was several minutes before the room quieted down sufficiently for him to be heard.

"Thank you. It's good to see that we are a community once more." He smiled, regaining control. "We'll have to establish some ground rules. The testing of the drinking water I'll leave to the town, and the testing of people to Doc. However, the Company will pick up the costs." Tom paused as another burst of applause followed.

334

"As I said, we're going to go ahead with the studies, on one condition. I want to keep the work as close to home as possible, to bring in as few outsiders as necessary. Like most of you, I believe we should solve our own problems. I trust the people I know, who have the same interest in our town as I have. So I want someone local to manage the study, and if necessary, the cleanup. I want Michael Ryan to take charge. He seems to know the most about the problem and how to solve it, and I know he wants what's best for Langston as much as the rest of us."

Attention turned to Michael. He sat in surprised silence, taken aback. Maggie squeezed his arm in encouragement. "Go. Don't hesitate," she whispered.

He walked up to Tom and shook his hand. A look of new respect passed between the two men. "Thanks for your vote of confidence, Tom. I appreciate it."

"We may not agree on everything, Michael, but I feel that you're the best man for the job. We'll talk about the details and the arrangements we need to make tomorrow in my office."

People stood talking in clusters after the meeting was adjourned, reluctant to end the evening's excitement. In Langston an event remained important long after it happened, for as long as people continued discussing it. And this evening would become one of the most discussed events in Langston's history.

Tom and Michael were sitting in the front row, making plans for the next few weeks when Maggie pushed Jake up in his wheelchair. Michael looked up in surprise at the empty auditorium. He hadn't noticed when the people had left, or when the lights had been dimmed. Audrey Brockman was gathering up the last of her papers from the table and straightening the chairs. She smiled at them as she walked past and nodded to Michael.

"You won't mind locking up, will you, Michael?" She handed him the keys, and bid them a brisk `good night'.

"There is something we need to discuss, Tom," Maggie began.

"I'm fixing to leave the hospital soon, and I need to know where I'll be going," Jake said. "Seems that the cabin's no good, because I won't have no water there. I'd be obliged if you'd let me know what your plans are, Tom."

"I'd be willing to let you use the Company apartment in town, Jake, but Michael assures me that you have no interest in staying in town."

Jake shook his head. "I have no interest in changing my ways. I been living in the wilderness all my life, and that's where I reckon I want to die."

"I guess I can understand that. I've given it some thought, Jake. I want to do right by you, to show you that the Langs' word is worth something. I can't give you back your cabin and that land, because I don't know how long it will take to make it safe. The best I can do is offer you a piece of land further away from the mine, and build you a cabin on it."

Maggie's eyes lit up as she looked at her father. Jake nodded at Tom, then chose his words carefully. "Where would this piece of land be?"

Tom took out a map from his pocket and spread it out before Jake. "I've marked out three locations where I can let you have a few acres in exchange for the land you've lost," he said, pointing out the areas.

Jake studied the map. "This one would be fine," he said, poking his finger at a spot north of Langston, stretching along the shores of a small lake. Then he looked up at Tom skeptically. "But how do I know you won't kick me off the land if something comes up? Maybe you'll want to turn it into a blueberry farm or something. What happens then, if I get in your way?"

Tom smiled wryly. "I guess I deserved that. We have no plans for developing that area, but I aim to make sure there won't be misunderstandings in the future. I'm going to give you this land legally. We'll draw up a deed in my office, so it'll belong to your family forever. Is it a deal?"

All three were watching Jake intently. He looked at their faces in turn: his daughter hopeful, Michael concerned, and Tom anxious to conclude the business. And then he thought of the land he had picked, off in the wilderness, by his own private lake. Suddenly he wanted to be free of the wheelchair, out in the mountains, exploring his land. He looked up at Tom, and his clear blue eyes met Tom's directly. "It's a deal," he said, offering his hand.

Chapter 25

Michael stopped to watch the V-shaped formation of Canada Geese fly overhead, their loud gaggling having alerted him to their flight. He lowered his axe, resting it against a tree stump on which he had been splitting firewood, and stood with his head tilted back, watching the birds cross the brilliant blue sky. Rusty sat on the ground nearby, ears perked, following the bird's movement with his gaze. An ancient instinct stirred in him, and his nostrils dilated rhythmically, trying to catch their scent.

As the geese flew past, their gaggling fading into the distance, Michael lingered a moment longer, looking after them. The trees on Sanford Hill were changing color; each day he saw more patches of yellow and orange and flaming scarlet mingled with the surrounding green. Tomorrow it would officially be fall, but here in the North Country the colors had been emerging for weeks. A chipmunk scurried up the pile of split wood, pausing at the top to study Rusty with its bright eyes before disappearing into an opening. Its cheeks were too full of acorns to allow it to chatter a taunt at the dog.

A breeze passed through the trees, sending the winglike seeds of silver maples, twirling, to the ground. Rusty jumped into the air to catch one in his mouth, lost his balance and landed clumsily on his rear. Michael laughed as he picked up his axe again. Rusty chased a rabbit into a thicket of Devil's-walkingstick, the heavy clusters of berries swaying as the branches closed behind him. He returned before Michael had a chance to split more wood, and sat staring at his master. Michael knew the look; it meant that Rusty was bored and wanted him to go for a walk. He sized up the pile of wood that remained to be split, then laid down his axe. It was hard to refuse a walk on a day like this.

They walked around to the front of the cabin, and Michael stopped to admire it. This was the first new home that the Hugheses had owned in a hundred and fifty years. Three steps led up to the porch that ran half way around the cabin. It was much more spacious than the old cabin had been, and far better insulated. There were three bedrooms, a living room, and a loft which Maggie and Michael were using until they could build their own cabin. A field stone fireplace dominated one end of the living room, and a large picture window looked out on the lake. The kitchen had modern appliances and the bath had running water. At first, Jake grumbled about "all the unnecessary fuss over something that I don't need," but he accepted it for their benefit more than anything else. Later he confessed to Maggie that he had grown to like taking hot baths in the hospital without having to heat the water first. And it was reassuring to know that there was central heating if needed, even though they all preferred a fire in the fireplace.

About two hundred yards directly west of the cabin lay Bittern Lake. It was a small lake, round and calm, marshy at the far end but clear and with a rocky shore on the other three sides. It was among a number of small Adirondack lakes that had never been officially named because of their size and remote location. Jake had always liked fishing there, perhaps because no one else frequented it. On one of his fishing trips, many years ago, he had spotted a bittern among the cattails. The bird stayed around most of the day, warily keeping an eye on Jake, but never leaving. After that, Jake called it Bittern Lake. Michael and Maggie had always thought of it as his lake, and now, legally, it was.

It hadn't taken long for Michael and Tom Lang to work out the details of their agreement. When Becky's blood test results finally came back, Tom learned that she didn't have lead poisoning. He was so relieved that he enthusiastically supported the cleanup study. Becky's illness had frightened him badly, and he didn't want to risk it happening for real.

Michael reached an agreement with the high school principal to teach just one course, chemistry, so he could devote most of his energies to directing the groundwater investigation and cleanup efforts. He had convinced Tom Lang to hire Garrison and Connely for the investigation and cleanup. The sampling wells had been completed before the first snow.

Sampling during the winter and spring confirmed that the groundwater contamination was confined to the narrow zone of fractured rocks mentioned in Michael's great-grandfather's journal. That simplified containment of the waste as well as groundwater treatment. The treatment plant was under construction and would be finished before winter, when limestone injection in the fractured rocks and capping of the mine with clay would be completed.

Unfortunately the first Jacob Hughes had built his cabin over that narrow band of fractured rocks and dug his well into the channel of water it provided in abundance. The old cabin had to be levelled to make room for the treatment plant.

The new homesite was not too near to town yet not too far either, so Maggie could commute to the newspaper office. The cabin and a roomy storage shed were built the next spring and summer. Jake spent most of his daylight hours in the shed, working on a project he kept secret. Michael and Maggie learned to leave him alone, and not to ask questions. Michael heard the tapping of a hammer as they came nearer the shed.

"Jake!" Michael called to him.

The tapping stopped, and Jake answered: "Be right out."

Jake emerged in a moment, brushing sawdust from his hands and trousers. He squinted at the bright sunlight as he faced Michael. He was the old Jake again, Michael thought. The Jake he had known ten years ago. His step was firm and quick, and his skin was brown and rough again from being out in the wind and the sun.

"Didn't know you were back already. Thought you'd stay in town longer," Jake said.

"I've been back for a while. Started chopping some wood, but couldn't keep at it. I wanted to come and tell you."

"Tell me what?" Jake looked at Michael sharply.

"I went into town to see my lawyer. I wasn't expecting it yet, but my divorce is final. Now Maggie and I can get married!" He nearly shouted the last words.

Jake broke into a grin, the hundred little creases around his eyes and mouth changing shape. He started to speak, choked, coughed, then started again.

"Finally! A few years ago, I thought I'd never see it happen." He put his arm around Michael's shoulder. "You two belong together. I knew it since you were kids. I never said nothin', but I was real disappointed when you went different ways. And I know Maggie was, too, though she hid it from everyone else."

The two men looked at each other with affection. Michael felt closer to Jake and thankful that the older man had remained his friend despite the wrong turn his life had taken. This was the first time Jake had ever expressed his feelings about his relationship and Maggie.

"I know, Jake." It seemed to Michael that he was answering Jake's thoughts as well as his words. "We do belong together, the three of us. I'm just glad it isn't too late."

Jake nodded soberly and the two remained quiet for a while. When Michael spoke again, the mood had lightened. "I shouldn't be telling you before Maggie, but I just couldn't wait. She's chasing a story somewhere, and I didn't know where to find her. But I wanted to be here when she got home."

"Since you did tell me, I'm gonna show you something that I've been keeping quiet, too." Jake led Michael towards the shed.

He threw open the door, and Michael saw resting on sawhorses in the middle of the room the half-finished form of an Adirondack guideboat. The frame was completed, and Jake had begun to attach the planks that would form the hull. A handful of gleaming brass screws lay amid a pile of sawdust, surrounded by tools and a stack of carefully bevelled planks.

343

Michael breathed in the pleasant aroma of freshly cut wood and pine resin. Jake stood back, allowing Michael to walk around the boat, to examine it from all sides. Michael ran his hand over the exposed ribs and felt the smooth texture of the partially completed hull. He nodded approvingly, admiring the fine handiwork, the care Jacob had taken with the fitting and the bevelling.

"So that's what you've been working on for these past few months!"

Jake nodded, smiling.

"It's beautiful, Jake. Really fine. But why another guide boat? Yours will certainly last another twenty years."

"I wasn't going to replace the old boat. This one's meant for you and Maggie. A wedding present." Jake beamed at Michael with boyish pleasure.

Michael started to speak, cleared his throat, then started again. "Thank you, Jake. I'm sure Maggie will love it. We'll both treasure it, always."

Jake nodded. "I didn't want to show it to you until I knew what you and Maggie were planning to do. Didn't want you to feel like I was being pushy." He paused, grinning. "But I guess I musta figured you'd be getting married sooner or later."

"As soon as we can get a license."

"Well, I'm gonna keep working on the boat. I wanna finish it before hunting season."

"Why?"

"Well, I been asked to guide three men on a hunting trip, and one boat ain't big enough to hold them all. I been hoping you and Maggie might wanna try out the new boat and come with me on the trip."

344

"You know we'd love to, Jake. It'll be like old times. If Maggie can get away from the paper and I can leave the cleanup and find someone to take over my chemistry classes for a week."

"At least you don't have to worry none about teaching full-time now," Jake said, picking up a screwdriver and moving to the guideboat.

"No. Lewis was more than glad to let me teach just chemistry for two years while I manage the clean up of the mine."

"Is that how long it's gonna take to clean up? Two years?" Jake finished driving in a screw and straightened up.

"Oh, no. We'll probably be treating groundwater for years. But most of the engineering and construction takes place in the first two years. We're trying to get the new treatment plant finished, and the construction crew is grouting under your old cabin and putting a clay cap over the mine. After the construction is done and the treatment plant is running smoothly, I can go back to teaching full time. It feels good to be working on an engineering project again. Looks like I'll be doing both for at least another year."

Jake paused before asking his next question. "Are you having any problems working with Tom Lang?" He waited for Michael's answer, concerned.

"Not really," Michael said slowly. "Of course, things between us have changed. He dropped his manner of hearty affection towards me and has become more businesslike. I rather prefer him this way; somehow he seems more honest. But he's shrewd; he stops to question everything we do, wants an explanation. It's very hard for him to let someone else be in charge, and he can be annoying.

"But Tom hasn't regretted his decision to clean up the mine. The article Charlie Rattinger wrote led to a lot of favorable publicity for the Company. Opalescent Paints are selling better than ever. Tom'll have to watch his costs for a few years, but it looks like the cleanup won't hurt the long term health of the Company."

"There ain't no hard feelings about Becky?"

Michael shrugged. "I suppose there must be. Or maybe he's relieved that she's home again. It helped that she moved out first."

Jake nodded and turned his attention back to his work. Michael watched in silence as the boat took shape slowly, board by board. He wanted to help, but knew that this was something Jake wanted to do by himself.

"I'd better go back and split some more wood while I wait for Maggie." He stood up reluctantly and walked out into the brilliant sunlight. Rusty ran to meet him, his feathery coat dripping water in his wake. He shook himself and Michael jumped reflexively. "Maybe we've made a mistake, living here on the lake with you, Rusty," he said, laughing.

Maggie drove up the gravel drive shortly after noon and parked near the woodpile. She jumped out of the Jeep and ran around to the front door, looking for Michael. She shouted his name, but there was no one inside. She stood on the porch looking toward the lake, when she noticed his blue shirt. He was sitting on a log, his back facing her.

"Michael!" she shouted, running toward him.

Michael turned, smiling as he recognized her, and waved. Maggie had changed during the past year. She had blossomed, filled out in some way he couldn't define. She was still tall and lean, but the angles of her face and figure had softened, becoming less severe. Perhaps it was her smile--a warm, lasting smile that started in her eyes and gradually engulfed her whole face. Or perhaps it was the new confidence with which she moved, calm and sure and contented. Michael loved to watch her moving about the cabin, intent on her chores, loved to see her perform the homey tasks that meant love and comfort and security. Often she would catch him looking at her and smiling, and she would stop what she was doing, put down the kitchen knife or the broom, and look at him questioningly, then laugh: "If you have nothing better to do than watch me, come and help!" He would go to her and they would embrace, the half-peeled vegetables or boiling soup quickly forgotten.

Maggie slid on a patch of fallen leaves as she reached him, and Michael caught her, laughing.

"What's the rush? Or maybe you just couldn't wait to see me," he teased.

"Both. But I have some news to tell you!"

"So do I, but you go first."

"I had a talk with Emmett today. He's thinking of retiring next year and he wants me to take over the paper."

"Does that mean I'll never see you again?" he joked. "Or just that I'll need to make an appointment first?"

"Don't be silly. Once I'm in charge, I can hire some bright, enthusiastic kid straight out of college and make her do all the work."

They laughed, and he hugged her. "That's wonderful, Maggie. I'm proud of you."

He waited as she savored her moment, her thoughts on the future. They sat on the log side by side and looked out over the lake. Maggie was planning how she would run the paper, use her education and Emmett's practical training to continue a newspaper he would be proud of. After a while she put her arm through Michael's and looked up at him.

"I almost forgot, you had something to tell me, too," she apologized.

"I hope this'll make you as happy as Emmett's offer did. My divorce became final today."

"Really?" She studied his face, searching out his intentions.

"Yes. You know what this means?"

"What?"

"That we can get married, that is, if you're still willing."

She tried to speak but her words came out jumbled, and she laughed, brushing the tears from her eyes. He ran his fingers through her hair playfully, pulling a strand.

"Does that mean `yes'?"

She nodded. "You know it does. It's been `yes' since we were twelve." She put her arms around his neck, and he felt the cold silver cuff with the tiger eye against his neck. Then she pushed him away so she could look at him.

"Was it difficult?"

He shook his head, "No. I didn't see her today, just her lawyer. Becky's keeping the house, of course. But she didn't ask for any money. She has plenty of her own."

Maggie nodded. "I couldn't have lived in that house anyway. It has nothing to do with us."

"No. We'll build our own here, by the lake."

"I insist on running water and indoor plumbing, though. Maybe even a washing machine. Otherwise no wedding."

"You've got it."

Then the smile left her face and Maggie became thoughtful. "I'm going to miss the old cabin, as ancient and rickety as it was. I'll miss lying there on stormy nights, listening to the rain on the roof."

"So will I. We had so many good times there. But all of that is really a part of us. We'll always have those memories."

"And now we can start over, on Bittern Lake. I love it here; it's so peaceful, seems so far away from town and the rest of the world. Like living in the wilderness."

"Yet it's close enough so that we can work. You with the paper and me with the school and the cleanup. It's the best of both worlds, Maggie."

"Where is Dad?" she said, jumping up. "Have you told him?" As Maggie turned to look for Jake, she saw him leave the cabin and walk towards them, carrying a small bottle and three glasses. She read her answer in his face. He sat down on a rock across from them and arranged the bottle and glasses in the grass. Maggie recognized the bottle. It had been stored at the back of a cupboard since she could remember; only a small amount was missing. Jake had said that he was saving the rest for a special occasion.

Jake said, "It's time. I been saving this bottle of brandy since Maggie was born." He dusted the bottle with his shirt sleeve, then removed the cork with difficulty. It squeaked as he forced it out of the bottle and came out with a pop. "Maggie's mother, my brother and me, we drank to Maggie's health when she was born. We saved the rest for when she would get married. I know it's a tad soon, but I just couldn't wait!" He filled the glasses and handed one each to Michael and Maggie.

They raised their glasses and drank in silence. The strong brandy felt hot as it went down Maggie's throat, bringing tears to her eyes. She shook her head and smiled at her father. He answered her smile, but she saw tears in the corners of his eyes. As Jake lifted the bottle to refill their glasses, Michael stopped him.

"Wait, Jake. Let's save some of that brandy. Who knows, maybe we'll have another occasion before too long to toast someone else's health.

THE END

www.ingramcontent.com/pod-product-compliance
Lightning Source LLC
Chambersburg PA
CBHW030418290526
45786CB00001B/31